# Spatial Dynamics in the Experience Economy

This book explores the dynamics of place, location and territories from the perspective of an experience-based economy. It offers a valuable contribution to this new approach and the planning and management challenges it faces.

This book emphasizes three key avenues to understanding the experience economy. First, the book reconsiders innovation processes and the relationship between the consumption and production of experience value. Second, it considers emerging forms of governance related to experience-based development in businesses and cities. Third, it examines the role of place as a value, resource and outcome of experiential innovation and planning.

This book will be of interest to researchers concerned with urban and regional development.

**Anne Lorentzen** is Associate Professor at University of South Denmark, Denmark.

**Karin Topsø Larsen** is a PhD student in the Department of Planning at Aalborg University, Denmark.

**Lise Schrøder** is Associate Professor in the Department of Planning at Aalborg University, Denmark.

# Routledge Advances in Regional Economics, Science and Policy

# Spatial Dynamics in the Experience Economy

**Edited by Anne Lorentzen, Karin Topsø Larsen and Lise Schrøder**

LONDON AND NEW YORK

First published 2015
by Routledge
2 Park Square, Milton Park, Abingdon, Oxfordshire OX14 4RN
52 Vanderbilt Avenue, New York, NY 10017

*Routledge is an imprint of the Taylor & Francis Group, an informa business*

First issued in paperback 2019

*British Library Cataloguing in Publication Data*
A catalogue record for this book is available from the British Library

*Library of Congress Cataloging in Publication Data*
A catalog record for this book has been requested

ISBN: 978-0-415-71034-3 (hbk)
ISBN: 978-0-367-86869-7 (pbk)

Typeset in Times New Roman
by Wearset Ltd, Boldon, Tyne and Wear

# Contents

# Figures

# Tables

# Contributors

**Lene Feldthus Andersen** is Director of the Centre for Regional and Tourism Research on Bornholm in Denmark. Her main interests are in the strategic development of local and regional knowledge institutions, the transfer of knowledge from research to practice and the strategic management and leadership in regional development, particularly in relation to tourism. Lene Feldthus Andersen has been part of many different regional development and applied research projects in many different ways – both as project manager, researcher, practitioner and decision maker.

**Shauna Brail** is a senior lecturer in the Urban Studies Program at the University of Toronto. Her research interests lie broadly in the area of economic geography with a focus on the social, cultural and economic changes associated with shifting industrial strengths of cities and with a particular focus on the cultural/creative economy.

**Taylor Brydges** is a doctoral student at the Department of Social and Economic Geography at Uppsala University in Sweden. Her research interests include labour and entrepreneurship in the fashion industry, with a focus on retail. The subject of her PhD dissertation is newly founded fashion brands in Canada and Sweden, with a focus on the emergence of the slow fashion industry.

**Olivier Crevoisier** is a professor in Territorial Economy at the Institute of Sociology and Director of the Research Group on Territorial Economy (GRET) at the University of Neuchâtel. He is also a member of the European Research Group on Innovative Milieux (GREMI). Research interests include innovative milieus, finance industry and cultural resources.

**Anne-Marie d'Hauteserre** is a tourism programme convenor in the Geography, Tourism and Environmental Programmes of the School of Social Sciences at the University of Waikato, Aotearoa, New Zealand. Her research investigates issues linked to or caused by tourism development from a critical social science perspective. Her main areas of interest are indigenous tourism development in the French Pacific; Foxwoods Casino Resort and the rapports of its American Indian owners with surrounding white residents; the Principality of Monaco; and the urbanization of the Eastern Paris Basin in France. She has numerous publications on these topics in both English and French scholarly journals and books.

**Jens Kaae Fisker** is a postdoctoral research fellow at the University of Southern Denmark, in the Danish Centre for Rural Research. He is a human geographer concerned mainly with the ways in which spatial dynamics under capitalism influence the everyday lives of people in challenged localities. In particular he is interested in the roles performed by planners and other place-makers, who occupy privileged positions in place governance. Asserting the right of citizens to creatively produce their place of inhabitance is a prime motive in his work.

**Lars Fuglsang** is a professor at Roskilde University. His main research interest is how institutional and organizational frameworks are created to deal with the impact of innovation, technology and other forms of change on business and society with a particular view to services and experiences. His current research is focusing on a practice-based understanding of the innovation process in services and experiences, i.e. innovation is seen as closely connected with practices and routines. Lars Fuglsang has participated in many national and international projects about service innovation, experience economy, cooperation between public and private companies, public innovation and trust and innovation.

**Delphine Guex** is a researcher at the University of Neuchâtel, at the Institute of Sociology, and a member of the Research Group on Territorial Economy (GRET). Her research interests include tourism, history, economic sociology of communication, cultural resources, presential economy.

**Szilvia Gyimóthy** is Associate Professor at the Department of Culture and Global Studies, Aalborg University. Her main field is tourism marketing communication, specializing in studies of narrative practices of commodification in the experience economy. Empirical contexts entail, among others, mid-market hotels, adventure destinations and niche festivals.

**Atle Hauge** is a senior researcher at the Lillehammer University College. He has a PhD from the Department of Social and Economic Geography at Uppsala University, and held a postdoctoral position at the University of Toronto from 2007 to 2008. He has worked on several projects on the cultural industries, and his PhD thesis was on the Swedish fashion industry. In particular, his thesis focused on the production of symbolic value and brand building. Other research interests are regional dynamics and industrial competitiveness. Recently, he is a part of the team that the Norwegian Ministry of Culture awarded a five year project as a Norwegian national centre for knowledge on the cultural industries.

**Brian J. Hracs** is a lecturer in Human Geography at the University of Southampton, UK. He is interested in how digital technologies and global competition are reshaping the marketplace for cultural products and the employment experiences of entrepreneurs in the creative economy. He has published articles on the contemporary music industry, the linkages between music and fashion and the commercial strategies independent producers use to 'stand out in the crowd'.

**Doreen Jakob** is an artist and scholar at UNC Chapel Hill, USA and at the University of Exeter, UK. She has held research positions at the Center for an Urban Future in New York City, at the Urban Research Program at Griffith University, Brisbane, Australia, at the Center for Metropolitan Studies in Berlin, for the German Research Foundation, for the Emmy Noether Program and, most recently, with the UK Arts and Humanities Research Council. Doreen received her PhD from Humboldt University, Berlin.

**Hugues Jeannerat** is a postdoctoral research fellow at the University of Neuchâtel, in the Research Group on Territorial Economy (GRET). Among his main research interests are economic geography and economic sociology of knowledge, innovation and markets. His main investigation fields relate to the watchmaking, media, tourism, med-tech and clean-tech industries.

**Karin Topsø Larsen** is a PhD student at the Department of Planning at Aalborg University, whilst on a daily basis associated with the Centre for Regional and Tourism Research. Her research interests revolve around regional development in peripheral areas. She is particularly interested in geographies of capitals, knowledge and education in relation to youth life choices, mobilities and place attachments.

**Deborah Leslie** is a professor of Geography and a Canada Research Chair in the Cultural Economy at the University of Toronto. She is the author of a number of recent articles on the links between cultural industries and urban economic development. Recently she has been exploring the role of historical and geographical path dependencies in the evolution of the Montreal circus. She has also conducted research on art, fashion and music.

**Anne Lorentzen** is an associate professor in Innovation and Regional Development at the department of Border Region Studies, University of South Denmark. She has done research on innovation, regional development and urban planning, experience economy and tourism. A main interest of hers is geographic inequality and globalization, in particular in relation to small cities and non-metropolitan areas. She has published extensively, also in acknowledged journals, and has been the main editor of many books.

**Ole Kjær Mansfeldt** is an industrial PhD researcher with The Royal Danish Academy of Fine Arts – School of Design, Roskilde University and Wonderful Copenhagen (the tourist organization of Copenhagen). He is working on a PhD thesis on what he terms as 'in-between experiences'.

**Lise Schrøder** is an associate professor at the Department of Planning at Aalborg University. Her main research interests are cultural heritage issues related to spatial planning and digital communication technologies. Furthermore, she has a specific interest in design methodology and methodological aspects related to collaboration and innovation processes in interdisciplinary communities of practice.

# Part I
# Introduction

# 1 Spatial dynamics in the experience economy

*Anne Lorentzen, Karin Topsø Larsen and Lise Schrøder*

This volume seeks to explore the dynamics of place, location and territories from the perspective of an experience-based economy (Pine and Gilmore 1998, 1999, 2011). Our use of the notion of the experience economy in this book is related to the crucial role of experiences understood as (positive) emotions, values and identities in value creation and how this is related to local and regional development, urban and spatial planning and business development, for example within tourism.

The book builds on the collaborative efforts of a Regional Studies Association (RSA) research network on the same topic. The research network was established in 2009 and focused on the spatial dimensions of production–consumption relations in transition. It understood the notion of the experience economy as a promising new research perspective with the potential to capture a change in production and consumption relations toward a much more co-productive process. The research network discussed questions about changed spatial and territorial configurations connected to new production and consumption relations. Debates about changed production and consumption relations as drivers of innovation processes also took place. Finally, the implications for governance and planning that arise from the new roles of place as intrinsically ingrained in the product were considered, and along with that ideas of planning as a co-production of space. These topics were also present in a special issue of European Urban and Regional Studies, edited by central figures in the RSA research network, Lorentzen and Jeannerat (2013). Thus, this volume builds on a number of research discussions, which have evolved since 2009 in the interdisciplinary meeting between different research traditions.

Three research perspectives unite the contributions in this volume traversing the four thematic sections. One is the perspective on innovation and innovation processes in businesses and planning, and the question of how experiences contribute innovatively to market value and citizens' identity with the place. The second perspective is that of the governance of innovation and planning processes related to experiential development. What values, and whose values, govern innovation and planning related to emotional satisfaction? The third and encompassing perspective is related to the role of place in creating experiential value and vice versa. Both economic and socio-psychological dimensions are at play here. Places are constructed in economic processes of location and specialization in experiential production. They are also socio-material constructs for actors who relate to localities through located social ties and daily practices. Together these three perspectives represent our perception of the spatial dynamics of the experience economy.

## What is the experience economy?

Originating in strategic marketing and consumer behaviour, the phrase 'the experience economy' invites images and inspires imagination among researchers from many disciplines, and it has triggered new ideas among entrepreneurs as well as among public planners. Probably the everyday use of the word 'experience' makes it so appealing. Most people are able to imagine experiences and even experiencing into their field of activity and work. The drawback is, however, that experience economy is taken to mean many different things as it is interpreted into different contexts (Sundbo and Sørensen 2013; Bille 2012; Lorentzen and Jeannerat 2013). The seemingly mutual understanding of the experience economy concept therefore appears to us to be more imagined than real. This does not mean that we, the editors, want to subscribe to specific definitions or concepts or to advocate particular theoretical perspectives. However, we take our point of departure in the role of experiences in value creation in different contexts of business development and planning. Moreover, we intend to go about the topic of the experience economy critically as well as scientifically. By this, we also indicate that we do not advocate the experience economy, we scrutinize it.

## The experience economy and innovation

Innovation is a constitutive and crucial dimension of the experience economy. The context of the discussion of Pine and Gilmore on the experience economy (Pine and Gilmore 1999) is how businesses enhance their competitiveness on the market in different phases of economic development. Today producers compete in a very crowded market for goods and services, and a strategy is to make their offerings still more differentiated. The challenge is not to lose the attention of the customers in the increasingly differentiated market (Callon *et al.* 2002). Therefore, non-functional values connected with the firm and its products become interesting as competitive assets. Mundane goods and services therefore become the object of experiential innovation. Not surprisingly, the journey does not end here, also because experience offerings face competition and need to be innovated in an endless circuit (rat race) of innovation.

Initially customers are anonymous and assess the value of the experience offering and the innovation by their decision of purchase. Innovation may thus be directed towards the creation of loyal customers, who identify with the product and choose it again and again. Customers may also be involved in innovation more directly, not only by their assessments, but by providing and applying their values, emotions and knowledge to the innovation process (Andersen 2015; Mansfeldt 2015). Producers need to learn from consumers (Hauge 2015) who on the other hand may need education or initiation to the more intangible features of products (Jeannerat 2013). Experiential innovation becomes valuable to customers when it resonates with their values and thus becomes meaningful to them (Hracs and Jakob 2015; Leslie *et al.* 2015). What drives them is not just expectation of economic maximization, but rather emotional satisfaction (Gyimóthy 2015). Shared values may become not only social but even gain economic importance, and (self-)organized consumer groups may play an important role in experiential innovation (Hauge and Power 2012). Within tourism and planning, innovation revolves around the strengthening of users' identity with the place of residence or of visit. If we add that the production side, as well as the consumption side, consists of various actors in different positions, the innovation process becomes complex and unpredictable. The experiential innovation system is therefore messy. This volume provides examples of how different it can be (Jeannerat 2015; Gyimóthy 2015; Hauge 2015; Guex and Crevoisier 2015; Lorentzen 2015; Fuglsang 2015).

## The experience economy and governance

Complexity as well as uncertainty is characteristic of innovation in the experience economy. This makes it important to consider governance in an experience economy context, both from the perspective of private producers or firms and from the perspective of policy and planning. The more or less intentional innovation of goods and places through experiential innovation is closely connected with governance and with the questions of who, what and why. In business economics, network governance among firms is suggested as an alternative to both (firm) hierarchy and market solutions (Jones *et al.* 1997). Network governance is a response to task complexity and demand uncertainty (Jones *et al.* 1997: 911). Equally in planning, governance means 'collective action' (Healey 2007: 17) as a contrast to hierarchic forms of public government. Dismantling hierarchies enables new constellations between actors and resources, conducive of experiential innovation.

More than in other types of innovation, in experiential innovation feelings are at stake. These are feelings about the city, about the tourist destination or about the purchasable identifiers of who you are, such as clothing. No wonder users as stakeholders often have deeply felt interests in the innovation of experience offerings and even involve themselves as co-creators. Stakeholder roles are thus often blurred in the experience economy, in a business context as well as in a planning context, and the governance processes that assemble and mingle interests and knowledge may be long and complicated.

Throughout the book, the contributors discuss the issues of stakeholders and governance, theoretically and illustratively by case studies. Who are the actors and stakeholders, what are they interested in, and why is the innovation process (or urban planning process) of importance to them? To the question of who, Pine and Gilmore (1999) allude to the employees of the individual business, Fuglsang

(2015) considers the horizontal cooperation among experience producers, and Jeannerat (2015) reflects on complete hierarchies of suppliers in the production system. Lorentzen (2015) and d'Hauteserre (2015) address the complicated stakeholder landscape and the relationships between stakeholders in urban planning. Relations of power and dominance become evident in Fisker's work, which points at planners as influenced by business interests (Fisker 2015). In essence, consumers are looking for meaning because they need emotional satisfaction, while producers look for loyal customers because they need economic gain. Multiple actors emerge on the producers' and the customers' side. Eventually they may meet in common endeavours. Inspired by the theatre metaphor used by Pine and Gilmore (1999), 'staging' or 'staging system' is suggested as a description of the process of combining interests and resources in experiential innovation processes.

## The experience economy, space and place

Spatial relationships and dynamics represent the encompassing perspective of this volume. In economic geography, it is acknowledged that any techno-economic paradigm or phase, whether agricultural, industrial, knowledge or whatever label is used, has specific spatial characteristics and locational dynamics of specialization (Hayter 1998). It has been suggested that the experience economy can be considered as a techno-economic paradigm in itself, however closely related to the global knowledge economy (Lorentzen 2009). Resources, economic actors, competencies and cultures are located and sometimes even place-bound. Spatial relationships have hitherto not been scrutinized by research, even if it can be argued that places, in terms of spatially embedded relationships, not only represent experience offerings, but also potential experiential resources (Jeannerat and Crevoisier 2010). These potentials are related to history, lifestyle and tradition as expressed in the built environment and social practices (Guex and Crevoisier 2015; Lorentzen 2009).

Place, as a category within the social sciences, is complicated. In brief, place results from lived practice and is formed by power or decisions related to its appearance and use (Massey 1993; Healey 2007; Harvey 2006). Place is constructed by endowing physical spaces with meanings, as argued by Healey (2010). Place qualities are therefore negotiable. Cities can, for example, be approached as industrial or cultural, water shores as functional transportation nodes or recreational areas, adding to quality of place and housing prices. Thus, the experiential quality of places is socially constructed (Schrøder 2015). Places are, more often than not, contested due to differing values and interests of different social groups. The complexity and messiness of innovation and governance within the experience economy is also related to the contested value setting of particular places by different users, i.e. what may be of value to one social group may be less valuable to others. The dominance of particular social groups, who are able to wield their perception of which qualities are valuable, may supersede the values of other social groups, thus estranging them from the place. The specific governance of innovation and planning decides whose values will dominate.

Place approached as a resource for product innovation, can be understood as the reference to particular places in experiential products and artefacts (Guex and Crevoisier 2015) which imbues products with value, because it provides them with a quality of authenticity (Gilmore and Pine 2007: 136). Authenticity is related to meaning, and authentic places are places that are meaningful to people. Referential products inherit some of this place-based authenticity. Place can also be understood directly as a particular meaningful and thus authentic location. Such places are able to attract residents, tourists and investors much better than places that are more anonymous.

In this book, the contributors show how producers, consumers and other stakeholders imbue places with meaning in processes of negotiation, and how this meaning, on the other hand triggers innovation and sales across space. From a systemic perspective, it can be suggested that the experience economy is produced in spatial staging systems related to particular localities, regions or cities, or to particular branches of industry. Place is not only related to production, but also to consumption. Experience consumption is often attendance based (Smidt-Jensen *et al.* 2009) or place bound (Lorentzen 2009), and attractive landscapes of consumption are created to enhance the experience of consumption and boost sales. Experiential staging takes place in distant as well as in proximate relationships. Regionally or locally embedded staging systems are in any case permeable, due to high mobility and globalization, as shown by, for example d'Hauteserre (2015), Mansfeldt (2015) and Gyimóthy (2015). And they are imbued with power (Fisker 2015).

Summing up, the three encompassing perspectives on innovation, governance, place and space in the experience economy are closely interlinked as a combined spatial dynamic rooted in actors' experiential intentions, innovative relationships and power. Experience value as an important perspective in innovation and planning is thus embedded in time and space.

The volume brings together theoretical as well as empirical work that share the intention of coming to grips with the spatial dynamics of the experience economy. The contributions are rooted in economic geography, tourism studies and planning. They include, as Part II, theoretical contributions, which challenge and develop the notion of experience economy and value. Part III focuses specifically on innovative relationships in the experience economy on the micro-level. Part IV deals with the regional perspective in the discussion of how stages and places are constructed in the experience economy. Finally, Part V takes up the issue of governance in planning and business networks in terms of motivation, discourse and power.

## Chapter organization

**Part II**, entitled *Theoretical developments and methodology challenges* brings together work on the emergence of the experience economy as a major discourse in economic geography and planning, and contextualizes it theoretically and historically.

**Hugues Jeannerat** conducts theoretical groundwork in Chapter 2, 'Towards a staging system approach to territorial innovation', by suggesting a way forward for research within territorial innovation systems based on some of the questions raised by theorizing from an experience economic approach. While territorial innovation systems research is characterized by productionist and technologist approaches to innovation, the experience economy approach stresses the socio-economically constructed use-value of experiential products.

Jeannerat suggests framing the research agenda for the experience economic approach within the concept of the Territorial Staging System (TSS). The TSS is not an innovation model, but an exploratory research approach, which presents and frames three avenues of research questions. These are: How are particular production resources turned into territorial stage settings? How are particular stage settings and consumption resources turned into territorial experiences? And: How is experiential engagement turned into territorial revenue?

In Chapter 3, 'Negotiating and producing symbolic value', **Atle Hauge** encapsulates and refines the understanding of symbolic value production. Symbolic value is co-constructed through a process of negotiation, which takes place in particular socio-economic contexts and in interaction with multiple social actors. According to Hauge, an important, but often overlooked, group in these negotiation processes is the consumers. The spatial dynamics of social actors' negotiation processes have at least two spatial features. First, symbolic value is context dependent and varies across time and space. Second, space and place are powerful resources in the production process of symbolic value, because they are unavoidably imbued with geographical associations. Hauge also stresses that symbolic value is constructed along the entire value chain. The experiential staging processes are purposefully set up to deliver products' symbolic value, and all have a certain spatiality with the aim to place the products in a shared system of meaning.

In Chapter 4, 'Municipalities as experiential stagers in the new economy: emerging practices in Frederikshavn, North Denmark', **Jens Kaae Fisker** takes a critical approach to the experience economy by stressing this new economy as yet another form of capitalist accumulation. This time it is the human experience of place, which has been commodified. Places thus compete on how well they are able to engage citizens in 24/7 human experiencing, i.e. to provide or frame the provision of work-based and leisure-time experience opportunities.

In this climate of place competition, municipal planners find themselves as key players, simultaneously in positions of power and exploitation. On the one hand, it is under their jurisdiction to plan the materiality of public space as well as to regulate activities within it. On the other hand, they may be influenced by business interests to frame or stage experiential offerings. Based on an empirical case study from Denmark, Fisker concludes that municipalities function as experiential stagers in three ways: as material stagers in the provision of infrastructure; as symbolic stagers, through place branding; and as institutional stagers, through initiating municipal policies and projects, the purpose of which is to enhance the quality of place on competitive place markets.

**Part III**, entitled *Relations in the experience economy*, substantiates theoretically and empirically the importance of relations on different scales in the experience economy. In particular, relations connected with the consumers and consumption can be seen as distinctive for the experience economy, but the consumer perspective may even cause experience providers to relate to each other in new ways.

In Chapter 5, 'Selling the stage: exploring the spatial and temporal dimensions of interactive cultural experiences', **Brian J. Hracs** and **Doreen Jakob** focus on how new relations between independent music producers and craft artists are forged in order to attract the attention of customers in an extremely crowded market. They manipulate four different aspects of their experience offerings and thus harness consumer desires for symbolic value, authenticity and creative expression. The first mechanism is exclusivity, which is the creation of value through offering unique and limited experiences. The second is to generate interactive experiences, which involves catering to consumers through immersive, participatory and interactive, rather than passive, experiences. The third effort involves enhancing experiences through the manipulation of physical and virtual space. Finally, the fourth type of relational forging is to enhance experiences through the manipulation of time, including limited temporality as well as the development of long-term relationships.

The next chapter (6), by **Deborah Leslie, Taylor Brydges** and **Shauna Brail** on 'Qualifying aesthetic values in the experience economy: the role of independent fashion boutiques in curating slow fashion' continues with an exploration of how value is created. This is done by exploring the role of small independent retail boutiques in qualifying slow fashion goods, and in carving out alternative relationships, experiences and spaces. Space is here perceived as both a site for staging experiences, but also as a site of networking and negotiating the assessment of quality. The mediating role played by independent retailers illustrates the increasingly close ties between retailers and consumers, and the complex interdependencies between the two. This relationship is forged and curated through the provision of customized service as well as deep supplier, labour and client relationships, often involving a reiterative teaching and learning process.

**Ole Kjær Mansfeldt** in Chapter 7 on 'The "Airbnb experience" and the experience economy: the spatial, relational and experiential in-betweenness of Airbnb' explores the concept of in-betweenness and the phenomenon of Airbnb as alternative accommodation form and indicator of a transition within tourism demand. Mansfeldt argues that there are spatial, relational and experiential implications for using Airbnb, which collectively can be grasped through the concept of in-betweenness. Experiential in-betweenness gives a perspective on the ambiguous ways of experiencing, with guests being tourists and locals at the same time. Relational in-betweenness offers a perspective on the ambiguous relations between hosts and guests. Spatial in-betweenness gives a concept for the places that are in-between the defined and designed tourist places: places that are not developed for tourism, but attract tourists looking for experiences.

**Part IV**, entitled *Construction of stages and places in the experience economy*, focuses theoretically and empirically on the spatial relations, which constitute experiential stage setting and place construction by activating resources and actors in experiential innovation processes.

In Chapter 8, 'A comprehensive socio-economic model of the experience economy: the territorial stage', **Delphine Guex** and **Olivier Crevoisier** examine the role of territorial transactions among embedded actors. Territorial transactions refer to the complex network of interactions involved in value creation and puts focus on the meaning of the territory for the consumer. This understanding is conceptualized into a socio-economic model, the Territorial Economic Transaction model (TET), which contributes to the understanding of how producers mobilize the symbolic aspects of the territory. Guex and Crevosier emphasize experience-based values as the central issue of postmodern economic transactions and they introduce the idea of a complementarity of presential and referential transactions. Presential transactions are related to real physical co-presence in a place, while referential transactions are related to goods enriched by symbolic territorial meanings.

In Chapter 9, entitled 'Val d'Europe: an experience economy landscape tamed by affect', **Anne-Marie d'Hauteserre** investigates the construction of Parisian suburb Val d'Europe, as an example of the construction of experience economy spaces. D'Hauteserre introduces affect theory as an analytical approach to the transformation of this space into a significant arena for economic and residential investment and development. The author emphasizes how this kind of transformation requires the recognition of the role of affect in order to understand whether people and activities will remain anchored in space and transform it into a place. D'Hauteserre demonstrates how the collaboration between the French state and the Walt Disney Company in Val d'Europe has balanced the conflicting interests of the welfare of the citizens versus economic development interests in contested places.

In Chapter 10, 'Bollywood-in-the-Alps: popular place-making in tourism', **Szilvia Gyimóthy** presents a study on popular cultural place-making for Indian tourists in Switzerland. The author focuses on the reconstruction of the Alps into Bollywood background scenery, thus redefining the area as a tourist destination. Gyimóthy shows how the demand for recreational space by pop-cultural consumers transforms the landscape of regional competitiveness, and how this has led to the emergence of new destinations and the repositioning of established ones. The author provides novel insights concerning place-making mechanisms, and puts focus on identity and place as contested due to conflicting stakeholder interests. The chapter introduces 'the pop-cultural place-making loop', which contributes to the understanding of how mediatized practices interlink consumption-related features with place-production processes.

In the final section of the part, Chapter 11, entitled 'The spatial and experiential dimensions of coastal zone tourism in Denmark', **Lene Feldthus Andersen** focuses on how coastal tourism in Denmark can be understood in spatial and experiential terms. Based on two accommodation-defined types of tourism – holiday home tourism and attraction tourism – Andersen analyses how value is created in the interaction between production, consumption and place. Andersen contributes with specific insights on tourism destination innovation in relation to the demands of tourists attracted by the two accommodation forms and the construction of experience spaces. Andersen also provides an understanding of the heterogeneity of tourist experiences in groups such as families, and the role of the common place of the holiday home as setting for different types of experiences.

The last part of the volume, **Part V**, entitled *Governance in the experience economy*, takes a closer look at the experience economy as a trigger for new ideas within the field of entrepreneurial practices related to spatial planning and governance. The chapter explores how place-bound experiential resources can function as a means for collaboration processes in municipal planning contexts as well as in local business networks.

In Chapter 12, 'Pursuing happiness in planning? The experience economy as planning approach', **Anne Lorentzen** focuses on the emotional aspects of the experience economy. The author translates Pine and Gilmore's classic concepts of the experience economy into the context of spatial planning and compares the role of the citizen to a customer, who can be mobilized in co-producing meaningful urban spaces. The chapter is based on Vancouver and is an empirically based analysis of the effects of innovative urban planning. A central contribution of the chapter is the general experiential perspective on planning as a theatre, where the city functions as a stage which facilitates experiential engagement and citizens' involvement as a means of creating new urban quality places, shared identities and trusting relationships.

In Chapter 13, 'Engagements in place: bricolage networking in tourism and the experience economy', **Lars Fuglsang** contributes to an understanding of how companies with limited resources and interest in cooperation can become engaged in the construction of place in an experience economy perspective. Inspired by Levi-Strauss's concept of bricolage, Fuglsang introduces the idea of experience networks as 'garbage cans' and sources for innovation based on available resources, including the familiar relations between actors in a given locality. Based on case studies in Denmark, the author explores how micro-companies in a rural area can become involved in networking based on a lifestyle, hobby and familiarized approach to place-bound resources. In particular, the chapter contributes to the understanding of how these kinds of tangible, low-cost, small-scale activities make it possible to create new innovative value constellations that contribute to the local economy and the construction of place.

In the final chapter, entitled 'Cultural heritage as an experiential resource in planning', **Lise Schrøder** takes a closer look at the qualities of cultural heritage in the built environment as a place-bound experiential resource in urban planning processes. The research is based on experiences from a cultural heritage project and the transformation of a former industrial harbour area in the municipality of Aalborg in Northern Denmark. Theoretically, the research draws on the concept of territorial staging systems as introduced by Jeannerat in Part II of this book, which is translated into the context of planning, based on conceptualizations of space as defined by Henri Lefebvre and Patsy Healey. The chapter provides a conceptual framework, which makes it possible to distinguish various aspects of the relations between stakeholders, who collaborate in urban planning processes.

## Conclusion and perspectives for further research

This volume explores the dynamics of place, location and territories related to the experience economy. The chapter contributions all revolve around the geographic assumption that changes in economic activity have spatial repercussions on and across different geographic scales, spanning from the individual and the business to the global scale. These repercussions materialize through the linkages and learning processes that characterize social production. Three overall perspectives permeate the contributions and parts of the book. The first is related to innovation and innovation processes in the experience economy. We not only consider business development in networks, but also the planning of urban spaces. The second is related to the governance of experiential innovation and development. What kind of cooperation emerges in experiential innovation processes, and how can it be enhanced? The third is the role of place in creating experiential value and vice versa. What are the spatial practices that strengthen the affiliation between people and places and interactively create experiential value?

In the following, we sum up and pose questions for future research within each of the three perspectives.

Concerning innovation, we acknowledge that experiential innovation is indeed much more than an add-on to mundane products and services, as it is deeply rooted in values and feelings. As such, the experience economy can be seen as a commodification of feelings. The consumption rather than the production of experience offerings is where value is generated, and in many respects, the customer and the consumption process are the keys to understanding value creation in the experience economy. Equally, experiential consumption as a spatial practice decisively forms places and territories, either as frames or as objects of consumption. The innovation process related to experiential values can be seen as a sequential negotiation process among consumers and producers reaching from design, to retail and consumption. Much value is created in the micro-relationships between providers and customers in creative branches of industry such as music and fashion, as well as in tourism services. The providers strive to enhance the experience connected to the purchase and use of goods and services by mechanisms such as exclusivity, interaction, time as well as space, and customers contribute as co-producers. Curation can be seen as a staging of experiences, in which small providers may capitalize on their smallness as uniqueness in a crowded market. The creation of customers through education and initiation is an important part of the relationship. Theoretically, innovation in the experience economy can – with some caution – be approached as part of a system, which is centred around the staging of experiences. The necessary cautiousness is related to the ambiguity of experiences, and the blurred roles of providers and consumers. Nevertheless, the idea of a staging system can be used as approach to detecting innovative relationships in the experience economy.

Methodologically, future research could take its point of departure in the staging system idea and frame research based on its elements, linkages and processes. A staging systems approach can be applied on different scales, reaching from the micro- or firm level to the global, inter-firm and institutional level. Innovative relationships, processes and outcomes in terms of experience offerings and engagement can be detected and analysed. We would expect interesting differences to be found in relation to big versus small providers, between different branches of industry, and between different levels of planning.

The focus on experiential staging should, however, not make us forget that mundane services and facilities contribute to the good experience, which in themselves may not be experientially engaging. What is the relationship between the core experiential production and consumption and the rest? To this question also belongs the consideration that low paid jobs constitute a considerable part of the cultural-cognitive economy (Scott 2007).

With respect to governance, the experience economy innovation is about relationships and values, and therefore governance is an important part of its development. Governance is about what values and whose values are to guide innovation. It is about who the participating actors are in the sequential innovation process and how they are selected. And, not least, it is about how they interact or work together. All contributions deal with the handling and development of experiential value by actors of different kinds. Actors may have conflicting values, for example in relation to the development of experiential qualities of places, where different types of stakeholders have very different views and interpretations of the place. Place qualities are contested. Actor relationships exist on different scales, from the micro-level of the small tourist firm to the global scale between international providers – and between customers and local communities and small businesses, and between multinational companies and regional governments. The stories in the volume cannot be reduced to yet another tale of commodification of new human fields such as experiencing, by global capital. On the contrary, we are told that democratic and local values may decisively form the experiential development of places.

Experiencing can also be a tool in the governance of networks, as narratives of the past may arouse interest and mobilize citizens as in urban design and area development. In addition, narratives of the place may unite small businesses in a common endeavour to create an interesting locality or region to visit. This understanding goes deeper than, for example, Landry's creative city making (Landry 2000), in which joint culture projects are seen to mobilize new citizen groups in neighbourhood development. Our understanding is related to people's engagement based on feelings, meanings and aspirations as they are related to place. This engagement eventually materializes as participatory experiential staging of cities and neighbourhoods. Another contribution of the book is the view that experiencing can be seen as a social phenomenon related to citizen groups and groups of customers, rather than as an entirely individual one as argued by Pine and Gilmore (1999). This makes experiencing a social force in innovation.

The governance of the experience economy in businesses and planning as discussed in this book opens a vast array of potential research questions. One is related to the values governing experiential relations between providers and customers. Will values such as social, economic and environmental sustainability be able to engage people experientially in other fields than fashion and tourism? Another question is related to the governance of values. More knowledge is thus needed about how values of consumers as well as of citizen groups can be mobilized and used to create socially and culturally sustainable consumption and consumption spaces. Issues of competing values, domination and power belong to the study of governance in the experience economy, and narratives of innovation in the experience economy need to include the issue of how conflicting values are mediated and resolved.

Finally, regarding the perspective of space and place, throughout the book the relationship between experiential production, consumption and innovation, on the one hand, and the development of places, on the other, is discussed. Economically, places serve as locations for experiential consumption, with considerable implications for the quality of place. They can be consumed as such by visitors, residents and companies. They may provide symbolic value related to history and culture and physical qualities that contribute to particular place narratives.

Together, embedded actors and their productive relationships in the co-production of experiences have been seen as territorial staging systems. When spatially embedded resources and actors are mobilized such as in tourism, we see a territorial staging system integrating various types of actors and resources in which experiential engagement eventually is turned into territorial revenue.

The book argues that the line between the two processes of production and consumption is blurred because the two processes are deeply integrated. Place is important not only for the production, but also for the consumption of experience offerings. The role of place in experiencing can be differentiated according to consumer groups as shown in relation to tourism. Place may be important for experiencing, or it may be just an anonymous platform for the consumption of spatially more neutral events. This also means that different types of places attract different kinds of people, such as tourists. As object of consumption, urban vibrancy has been much in focus, but rural cosiness and tranquillity actually corresponds with the values of many families. In the planning and innovation of experience offerings, it is thus of importance to see the roles of places as differentiated.

In terms of experiential offerings, places compete and specialize (Lorentzen 2012). The global economy has been interpreted as a mosaic of places with varied global linkages (Storper and Salais 1997), and this picture is probably also applicable to the qualitatively very differentiated territories of experience production and consumption. Place matters to people and industries (Florida 2002, 2008), but the book shows that the experiential qualities of places play more subtle and interactive roles than earlier research has been able to show.

Many questions are left to discuss in relation to the experience economy, space and place. The construction of places involves processes of inclusion and exclusion. What characterize negotiation processes about the value of places?

How do actors meet and how are interests and place-related values mediated or suppressed? In an economic stance, the notion of territorial staging systems and processes should be further explored. Apart from a few examples, we do not know much about how place can be seen as potential resource in innovation and local development. What is it about places (and their social construction) that makes them (differently) valued? How are actors, linkages and resources spatially embedded, and how do cross-regional and global linkages form qualities of place? Finally, revenue as outcome of experiential innovation needs further scrutinizing from a regional development perspective. Is experiential innovation able to contribute more substantially to the development and well-being of cities and regions? Moreover, is experiential innovation and development a general opportunity, or is it restricted to particular cities or regions with certain endowments?

## References

Andersen, L.F. (2015) 'The spatial and experiential dimensions of coastal zone tourism in Denmark', in A. Lorentzen, K.T. Larsen and L. Schrøder (eds) *Spatial Dynamics in the Experience Economy*, Abingdon: Routledge.

Bille, T. (2012) 'The Scandinavian approach to the experience economy – does it make sense?', *International Journal of Culture Policy*, 18(1): 93–110.

Callon, M., Méadel, C. and Rabehariosoa, V. (2002) 'The Economy of qualities', *Economy and Society*, 31(2): 194–217.

D'Hauteserre, A.-M. (2015) 'Val d'Europe: An experience economy landscape tamed by affect', in A. Lorentzen, K.T. Larsen and L. Schrøder (eds) *Spatial Dynamics in the Experience Economy*, Abingdon: Routledge.

Fisker, J.K. (2015) 'Municipalities as experiential stagers in the new economy: Emerging practices in Frederikshavn, North Denmark', in A. Lorentzen, K.T. Larsen and L. Schrøder (eds) *Spatial Dynamics in the Experience Economy*, Abingdon: Routledge.

Florida, R. (2002) *The creative class*, New York: Basic Books.

Florida, R. (2008) *Who's your city?*, New York: Basic Books.

Fuglsang, L. (2015) 'Engagements in place: Bricolage networking in tourism and the experience economy', in A. Lorentzen, K.T. Larsen and L. Schrøder (eds) *Spatial Dynamics in the Experience Economy*, Abingdon: Routledge.

Guex, D. and Crevoisier, O. (2015) 'A comprehensive socio-economic model of the experience economy: The territorial stage', in A. Lorentzen, K.T. Larsen and L. Schrøder (eds) *Spatial Dynamics in the Experience Economy*, Abingdon: Routledge.

Gilmore, J.H. and Pine, B.J. (2007) *Authenticity. What consumers really want*, 1st edn, Boston: Harvard Business School Press.

Gyimóthy, S. (2015) 'Bollywood-in-the-Alps: Popular culture place-making in tourism', in A. Lorentzen, K.T. Larsen and L. Schrøder (eds) *Spatial Dynamics in the Experience Economy*, Abingdon: Routledge.

Harvey, D. (2006) 'Space as a key word', in N. Castree and D. Gregory (eds) *David Harvey: A critical Reader*, Malden, MA.: Wiley Blackwell.

Hauge, A. (2015) 'Negotiating and producing symbolic value', in A. Lorentzen, K.T. Larsen and L. Schrøder (eds) *Spatial Dynamics in the Experience Economy*, Abingdon: Routledge.

Hauge, A. and Power, D. (2013) 'Quality, difference and regional advantage: The case of the winter sports industry', *European Urban and Regional Studies*, 20(4): 385–400.

Hayter, R. (1998) *The dynamics of industrial location: The factory, the firm and the production system*, Chichester: John Wiley & Sons Ltd.

Healey, P. (2007) *Urban complexity and spatial strategies: Towards a relational planning of our times*, The RTPI Library Series, Abingdon: Routledge.

Healey, P. (2010) *Making better places: The planning project in the twenty-first century*, Basingstoke: Palgrave Macmillan.

Hracs, B. J. and Jakob, D. (2015) 'Selling the stage: Exploring the spatial and temporal dimensions of interactive cultural experiences', in A. Lorentzen, K.T. Larsen and L. Schrøder (eds) *Spatial Dynamics in the Experience Economy*, Abingdon: Routledge.

Jeannerat, H. (2013) 'Staging experience, valuing authenticity: Towards a market perspective on territorial development', *European Urban and Regional Studies* 20(4): 370–84.

Jeannerat, H. (2015) 'Towards a staging system approach to territorial innovation', in A. Lorentzen, K.T. Larsen and L. Schrøder (eds) *Spatial Dynamics in the Experience Economy*, Abingdon: Routledge.

Jeannerat, H. and Crevoisier, O. (2010) 'Experiential turn and territorial staging system: What new research challenges?', paper presented at Regional Studies Association Workshop on the experience turn in local development and planning, Aalborg University, Aalborg, September 2010.

Jones, C., Hesterly, W.S. and Borgatti, S.P. (1997) 'A general theory of network governance: Exchange conditions and social mechanisms', *Academy of Management Review*, 22(4): 911–45.

Landry, C. (2000) *The creative city: A toolkit for urban innovators*, London: Earthscan.

Leslie, D., Brydges, T. and Brail, S. (2015) 'Qualifying aesthetic values in the experience economy: The role of independent fashion boutiques in curating slow fashion', in A. Lorentzen, K.T. Larsen and L. Schrøder (eds) *Spatial Dynamics in the Experience Economy*, Abingdon: Routledge.

Lorentzen, A. (2009) 'Cities in the experience economy', *European Planning Studies*, 17(6): 829–45.

Lorentzen, A. (2012) 'The development of the periphery in the experience economy', in M. Danson and P. de Souza (eds) *Peripherality, Marginality and Border issues in Northern Europe*, Abingdon: Routledge.

Lorentzen, A. (2015) 'Pursuing happiness in planning? The experience economy as planning approach', in A. Lorentzen, K.T. Larsen and L. Schrøder (eds) *Spatial Dynamics in the Experience Economy*, Abingdon: Routledge.

Lorentzen, A. and Jeannerat, H. (2013) 'Urban and regional studies in the experience economy: What kind of turn?', *European Urban and Regional Studies*, 20(4): 363–9.

Mansfeldt, O. (2015) 'The "Airbnb experience" and the experience economy: The spatial, relational and experiential in-betweenness of Airbnb', in A. Lorentzen, K.T. Larsen and L. Schrøder (eds) *Spatial Dynamics in the Experience Economy*, Abingdon: Routledge.

Massey, D. (1993) 'Questions of locality', *Geography*, 78(2): 142–9.

Pine, B.J. and Gilmore, J.H. (1998) 'Welcome to the experience economy', *Harvard Business Review*, 1998 (July–August): 97–103.

Pine, B.J. and Gilmore, J.H. (1999) *The experience economy: Work is theatre and every business a stage*, Boston: Harvard Business School Press.

Pine, B.J. and Gilmore, J.H. (2011) *The experience economy*, Boston: Harvard Business School Press.

Schrøder, L. (2015) 'Cultural heritage as an experiential resource in planning', in A. Lorentzen, K.T. Larsen and L. Schrøder (eds) *Spatial dynamics in the experience economy*, Abingdon: Routledge.

Scott, A.J. (2007) 'Capitalism and urbanism in a new key? The cognitive-cultural dimension', *Social Forces*, 85(4): 1465–82.

Smidt-Jensen, S., Skytt, C.B. and Winther, L. (2009) 'The geography of the experience economy in Denmark: Employment change and location dynamics in attendance-based experience industries', *European Planning Studies*, 17(6): 847–62.

Storper, M. and Salais, R. (1997) *Worlds of production*, London: Harvard University Press.

Sundbo, J. and Sørensen, F. (2013) *Handbook on the experience economy*, Cheltenham: Edward Elgar.

# Part II

# Theoretical developments and methodology challenges

# 2 Towards a staging system approach to territorial innovation

*Hugues Jeannerat*

This chapter provides a reflexive account on the fundamental issues raised by the experience economy for urban and regional studies in the last decade. Through the concept of 'territorial staging system' (TSS), a possible research agenda is proposed on the basis of current and ongoing debates in economic geography. Rather than a closed-ended understanding of regional development, the concept of TSS is proposed as an open and exploratory framework to build upon in order to address new critical research avenues.

Along with an initial definition of the TSS, three main research avenues are drawn out. The first draws particular attention to the way particular production resources are turned into territorial stage settings. The second emphasizes the way particular stage settings and consumption resources are turned into experiences. The third finally questions how experiential engagement is turned into territorial revenue.

## Why the experience economy in regional and urban studies?

Over the past years, mainstream models of territorial innovation and competitiveness have been largely challenged by various critical reviews and alternative theoretical propositions. The traditional models of industrial districts, innovative milieus, innovation clusters or regional innovation systems have become objects of debate upon which new concepts have been formulated. In a knowledge- and service-based economy perspective, more specific attention has been dedicated to cultural and creative activities. The concept of 'creative cities and regions' has become, for instance, a new headline to describe the fertile ground upon which competitive economic activities can be generated and global talents attracted. Policies of 'creativeness' have gained attention as alternative models of public intervention to conventional industrial cluster policies or as new incentives to regenerate regions in crisis (Cooke and Lazzeretti 2008a; Costa 2008; Miles and Paddison 2005; Pratt 2008; Scott 2006).

In the past decade, a more subdued but not less critical approach to traditional models of territorial competitiveness also started to convey alternative views on regional development around the notion of 'experience economy'. Parallel to the debates instigated by cultural economic geographers, this approach drew its inspiration from marketing and management studies (Lorentzen 2013a). Not presented as 'another' specific 'turn' (Grabher 2009), the experience economy critique of traditional territorial innovation was driven by three intentions.

The first intention was *theoretical*. While territorial innovation models (TIMs) were almost exclusively conceived and discussed from a production perspective, the experience economy approach adopted a reversed perspective: the economic value of regional activities is created out of consumers' memorable engagement (Pine and Gilmore 1999). Not merely did such an approach broaden existing models; it also implied a new interpretive lens on territorial competitiveness. While the geography of innovation was mainly built on an exchange value approach, asking how economic goods or services were innovated and produced differently from one place to another, the geography of experience economy primarily draws on a use-value approach, asking how these goods and services were consumed in specific places. The consumption of goods and services was no longer conceptualized as footloose (Malmberg and Power 2005) but bound to particular geographical places of experimentation, imagination and enrolment (Lorentzen 2009a).

The second fundamental intention was *pragmatic*. In line with Pine and Gilmore's (1999) thesis describing the rise of a new historical phase of business making, the concept of 'Experience Economy' was approached as a pragmatic analysis of the new economic challenges that firms and territories face in a postmodern and globalized economy (Harvey 1989). If it was not denied that 'economies of experience' had always existed, it was nevertheless advocated that value created through consumers' experience had become a new dominant techno-economic paradigm (Lorentzen 2009a) applicable to leisure activities as well as to conventional goods and services. Valuing consumer experience was not only considered as creating a new added value to economic activities, it was also regarded as a contemporary opportunity for firms and regions to distinguish themselves and draw competitive advantage in a global market. Besides the global race for talents and high-end technologies supporting the models of 'creative city' or 'technopole', the experience economy was perceived as an alternative approach to innovation in regions and cities.

The third intention was *policy based*. Usually mentioned but only addressed indirectly in most European 'cultural' or 'creative' economic policies, the experience economy approach received more specific attention in Nordic and Scandinavian countries (Freire-Gibb 2011; Lorentzen 2013b). Interpreted in various ways (Bille 2011) and implemented with variable degrees of success (Power 2009), this concept was explicitly acknowledged and promoted as part of a strategic knowledge or industrial policy of innovation. This specific policy attention boosted a common research agenda among Nordic scholars and contributed to the formation of a research community sharing a common aim: investigating territorial innovation in the experience economy.

**Territorial innovation in the experience economy: an ultimate goal or a promising starting point?**

By analogy, the metaphor of 'bandwagon journey', adopted by Fuglsang and Eide (2013) to describe how the concept of experience economy became a common object of coordination and collective learning among small innovative Norwegian and Danish tourism firms, can be applied to the research community engaged with this same concept, too.

In the past years, several dedicated workshops and publications have acknowledged, explored and established the concept of experience economy in regional and urban studies. Among significant achievements of this process, the edition of two special issues in European journals (Lorentzen and Hansen 2009; Lorentzen and Jeannerat 2013), the publication of a dedicated handbook (Sundbo and Sørensen 2013) and a series of European workshops (for some accounts of these workshops, see Jeannerat 2010; Lorentzen 2011; Grabher and Jeannerat 2012) can be mentioned.

The present edited volume is another important milestone in this research trajectory. Nevertheless, the present volume is not only an additional contribution to the literature on experience economy and territorial innovation. It is also a timely opportunity to evaluate the current state of the reflections and their potential future(s). Again to recall Fuglsang and Eide (2013), providing a reflective account on what has been done is also part of a learning process. It can also help avoid a potential 'lock-in', to adopt another famous metaphor, in the research path initiated for some years now. What are the main achievements of this bandwagon journey?

A first major achievement of this research process has been to overcome the boundaries of different research fields. The concept of experience economy became a 'boundary object' (Star and Griesemer 1989) for researchers coming for instance, from rural, urban, regional or consumer studies. Under this concept, different researchers mobilized theories from economics, geography, anthropology, sociology, marketing or management and provided complementary insights to a common knowledge corpus. The concept also gave the opportunity to address, in a common framework, multiple socio-economic phenomena such as the growing eventification and festivalization of places, the culturalization of traditional productive offerings, or the increasing entanglement of tourism, manufacturing and residential activities in economic life.

Not only a 'boundary object', the concept of experience economy also became an 'intermediary object' (Vinck 2009) in the sense that it was not considered as a finished theory to be empirically tested and implemented in practice. It had a heuristic purpose. Rather than an ultimate theoretical paradigm, Pine and Gilmore's thesis was often utilized as a starting point to question and reconsider the way regions innovate and develop today. Over the years, the concept gained theoretical and empirical thickness, enlarging at the same time the earlier contributions on the subject.

Finally, the experience economy approach developed within broader theoretical debates. This was particularly the case in urban and regional studies where the experience economy approach was positioned against or complemented with, for instance, ongoing debates on the 'knowledge economy' (Lorentzen 2009b), on 'varieties of knowledge bases' (Manniche and Larsen 2013), on 'cultural activities' (Lorentzen 2013a; Power 2009), on 'urban hierarchies' (Jakob 2013) or on 'tourism and destination management' (Richards 2001; Richards and Wilson 2006; Stamboulis and Skayannis 2003). Rather than a positivist and generalizable response to territorial innovation challenges, the concept of experience economy participated to bring alive and evolve debates in regional studies (Lagendijk 2003).

In line with these arguments, the experience economy should be regarded as a promising starting point to revisit territorial innovation models rather than itself an ultimate goal. The primary strength of the approach developed in the past years is not to be found in the achievement of a new encompassing model of territorial innovation. Rather it has been to initiate a new explorative and cross-disciplinary research programme.

## The experience economy as an unachieved agenda in urban and regional studies

But which were then the limitations of the bandwagon journey? If no dedicated and systematic criticisms have formally been addressed to the experience economy approach to territorial innovation, some constructive criticisms can, in my view, legitimately be made.

First, while the 'experience economy' approach carried out new theoretical and empirical insights to territorial innovation, these were rarely interpolated in leading debates within regional and urban studies. Put another way, the scientific knowledge nurtured by this approach has mostly stayed a niche evolving along with external debates but rarely making itself an object of debate in broader literature. The strength of having built on a relatively small community of researchers to develop a renewed understanding of territorial innovation was also a weakness in its lack of impact on a broader research community. For non-initiated scholars, this approach was often and unfairly assimilated to a Nordic and Scandinavian research tradition on cultural and creative economy rather than appraised as a specific theory.

Second, although it was seen as a general ontology, the experience economy approach failed to avoid a certain sectorial bias. Even though it focused the pointer on consumers, the analysis of economic value creation has mostly remained from a production perspective; related to 'experience goods' (Andersson and Andersson 2013; Hutter 2011), 'experience industries' (Nilsen and Dale 2013; Smidt-Jensen *et al.* 2009; Vang and Tschang 2013) or 'experience sector' (Sundbo *et al.* 2013). In this sense, territorial innovation mostly focused on the capacity to relate leisure, entertainment, events or tourism activities to regional production.

Beyond the history of a new economic phase (Pine and Gilmore 1999) and beyond the story of a new theoretical 'turn' in urban and regional studies (Lorentzen and Jeannerat 2013), the experience economy thesis raises research questions that should not be restrained to an analysis of how firms and regions innovate and draw competitive advantage from consumers' experience today. It conveys more profound potentials to reconsider mainstream models of innovation and territorial competitiveness.

## Going beyond without throwing the baby out with the bathwater

In the second half of the past century, a particular vision of economic and territorial development has progressively been established in theories and policy practices based on the argument that successful firms, industries or regions are the ones able to innovate within an increasingly globalized market. Innovation has become the essence of competitive advantage, enabling firms to distinguish themselves from low-cost competitors. From a territorial perspective, regions and nations are most often conceived as particular production and innovation systems, more or less able to turn local factors/resources into competitive commodities (Figure 2.1). Competitiveness is assessed through the capacity to export regional or national goods or services towards external markets and to generate, in turn, new basic revenues for the regions through direct monetary transactions (export sales) (Polèse and Shearmur 2009). Consumption factors and resources engaged in the *territorial valuation* of commodities – that is, how these are actually *valorized and evaluated* (Vatin 2013) in time and space – are rarely specifically examined and theorized.

The experience economy approach developed in the past decades failed, at least partially, to overcome this classical vision. As highlighted above, an important strength of this approach was to propose a new way of approaching economic and territorial development. However, mostly focused on the changing nature of regional offerings to explain new forms of innovation, two critical and interrelated issues have been left mostly unexplored in this research agenda. Addressing these two issues in more systematic and in-depth manner is, in my view, required in order to realize the full potential of an experience economy approach to territorial innovation and competitiveness.

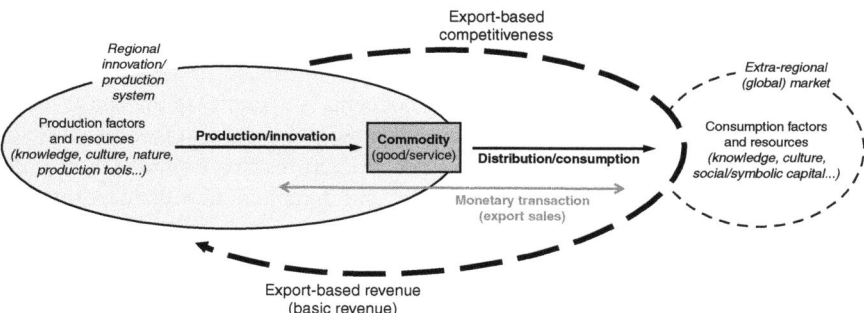

*Figure 2.1* The conventional approach to territorial innovation and competitiveness (source: own elaboration).

The first issue relates to the place of goods and services in market valuation (Jeannerat 2013). Beyond its specific managerial implications, the concept of the experience economy more generally points to the imaginative performance in which market actors engage when valuing particular goods and services (Beckert 2011). An experience is not a finished commodity traded, bought and sold as an object disconnected from its socio-economic context of consumption. It is valued in *prize* and *praise* (Dewey 1939; Stark 2011) within a continuous process whereby stagers and guests (Pine and Gilmore 1999) prepare, anticipate and perform shared imaginaries and common actions in a particular socio-economic framework.

The second question relates to the way monetary transaction(s) and revenue models are organized in the experience economy, that is, how experiential engagement is turned into an economic resource. For Pine and Gilmore, experience is 'what is charged for' and 'admission fees' are what is paid. This provocative thesis remains untenable. If it can be easily adopted for traded leisure or visitor-based activities (festivals, museums, natural/entertainment parks, etc.), it is an oversimplified interpretation for a large number of other activities. In most cases, experiences can hardly be charged as such. Goods and services remain the artefacts of stage setting as they mediate monetary transaction within complex business and revenue models. Their monetary trade-off 'totalizes' (Miller 2005), at a particular moment, the broader social rituals set by an experiential stage. For instance, the purchase of a Swiss watch monetizes at a certain moment a more general process of initiation and experimentation in the valuation process of authentic watchmaking (Jeannerat 2013).

Consequently, a broader and more complex approach should be applied to the analysis of territorial innovation. This cannot be reduced to a dialectical export-based model of regional growth describing, on the one hand, the production of tradable goods within proximity and, on the other hand, their exportation within distance.

Beyond this traditional vision, what could be the next bandwagon journey to depict complex market valuation processes of economic and territorial development *today*?

## Paving the ground for a new concept

For Posner *et al.* (1982), developing new concepts is essential in the construction of scientific knowledge. It enables exploring new empirical and theoretical fields of research beyond the established schemes of interpretation provided by already existing concepts. However, to be pertinent and durable, a new concept must be sufficiently intelligible and plausible to reflect the limits of an existing conceptual corpus and, at the same time, propose a research agenda that can be collectively adopted and co-developed (Posner *et al.* 1982).

The conceptual corpus progressively established by traditional TIMs since the 1980s is largely challenged by current regional studies. Nevertheless, these models still remain the anchorage point of applied theories and policy practices devoted to territorial innovation and competiveness. As many other alternative concepts, the concept of 'experience economy' and its related theoretical apparatus have provided pertinent critical views on these established models but have not provided a systematic alternative to them.

Exploring and co-developing a new boundary and intermediary concept could contribute to exploit the potential of the experience economy approach further. It could also provide a new systematic conception of territorial innovation and competitiveness. The nature of this concept would be explorative and collective. Nurtured by the originality of the experience economy paradigm, it should propose a set of systematic questions leading to accommodate new schemes of interpretation (Posner *et al.* 1982).

To build such an alternative concept, it is necessary to return to the original idea of the experience economy thesis and notably proposed by the Pine and Gilmore headline: 'Work is theater and every business a stage' (Pine and Gilmore 1999). The fundamental message conveyed by this slogan is that the economic value of an entrepreneurial project may not be based primarily on 'producing' goods or services but often also on 'staging' things and people in a particular context. A similar interpretation could be translated to territorial innovation: territorial innovation could be comprehended as a localized ability to stage valuable activities and artefacts rather than as a localized capacity to produce competitive goods and services.

In this view, production resources are not just turned into commoditized goods or services but are mobilized as experiential resources in a process of stage setting (Figure 2.2). Consequently, the market is not perceived as an exogenous selection or information mechanism but as a social stage underlying a situated and dynamic process of valuation (Aspers and Beckert 2011). From this perspective, territorial innovation cannot be reduced to the by-product of a local production system competing on a global and exogenous market. Rather, it is constitutive of a broader *territorial staging system* contributing to economic value generation within and across different territories. What could the concept of 'territorial staging system' (TSS) bring to our current understanding of territorial innovation?

## Exploring the concept of 'territorial staging system'

Building on the seminal contributions mentioned previously in this chapter, an experiential *stage* could economically be defined as a socio-technical context where particular production resources are turned into experiential resources through a particular stage setting, and where particular consumption resources are turned into economic resources through experiential engagement (Figure 2.2). In such a perspective, goods and services are not market ends in themselves. They are props and social perfomances economically valued in particular contexts of experimentation and living.

Following this initial definition, a *staging system* can be regarded as an organizational configuration of actors, objects and activities contributing to turning

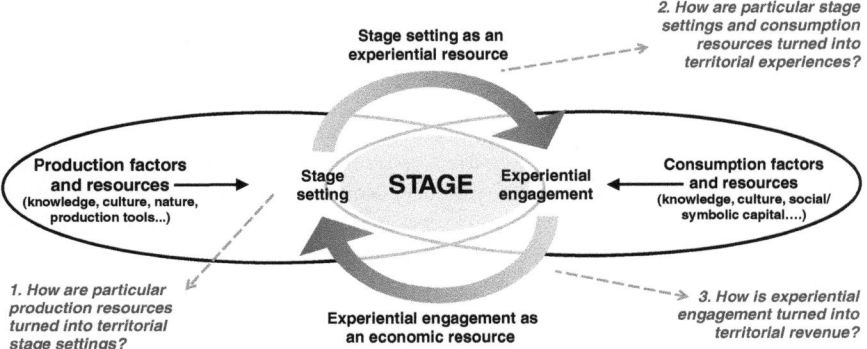

*Figure 2.2* The territorial staging system of experiences (source: own elaboration).

production resources into a particular stage setting and consumption resources into an economically valued experiential engagement. In such a socio-economic system, traded goods and services are conceptualized as revenue drivers rather than as invidual market commodities. For instance, the coffee drunk on St Mark's Square, the night spent at the Hotel Flora, the ticket paid to visit the Doge's Palace and the vase bought in a Murano glass factory would not be just analysed as the 'basket' offering of a touristic destination. They would rather be understood as punctual monetary transactions fueling income into the broader staging system of Venice.

Accordingly, a territorial staging system (TSS) refers to the way production and consumption resources create stages and economic value across time and space. On the one hand, a TSS builds upon the idea of 'territorial production systems'. It conceptualizes how localized stages emerge through spatial dynamics of cooperation, competition, clustering, agglomeration, specialization or diversification, quite parallel to the geography of innovation (for synthetic notes, see Breschi and Malerba 2001). However, a TSS can neither be reduced to a 'cultural cluster' or 'cultural districts' (Cooke and Lazzeretti 2008b), nor to a 'territorial production system of experience'. Such a notion would, in fact, neglect the active role played by consumers' engagement in the valuation of the stage (Lorentzen and Jeannerat 2013). On the other hand, a TSS should also not be restrained to a particular 'consumption site' (for synthetic notes, see Mansvelt 2005: 64–8). Such an approach would resume the spatial valuation of goods and services to consumer places and would elude the role of multiple production resources (enterprises, workers, investors) at the roots of stage setting and of regional growth (Storper and Scott 2009).

In a TSS view, innovation cannot be summarized as a question of how particular regions succeed in producing and exporting competitive commodities in a global market. It implies three inseparable and intertwined questions: (1) How are particular production resources turned into territorial stage settings? (2) How are particular stage settings and consumption resources turned into territorial experiences? And (3) How is experiential engagement turned into territorial revenue? These three questions should be the starting point to explore the concept of TSS.

## How are particular production resources turned into territorial stage settings?

In contrast to main industrial models of innovation, the concept of TSS should not primarily emphasize how local actors innovate in the development of new technologies, processes and designs in the view to produce standalone market goods or services in competition. It should rather point to the way local actors provide symbolic and concrete sceneries through their different and complementary activities to develop, promote and reinforce the coherence of a commercialized stage. In other words, natural, cultural or technological resources are not seen as the inputs of a production chain but as the reinforcing 'cues' contributing to set a 'themed' stage (Pine and Gilmore 1999). This aspect of territorial innovation has already been highlighted around two main issues by most researchers on experience economy mentioned above.

A first type of study has pointed to the strategic activities able to set competitive stages. Different works have shown, for instance, how cultural events and festivals have become contemporary determinant activities in global urban competition and hierarchies (Jakob 2013) as well as in alternative development of peripheral regions (Lorentzen 2013b; Manniche and Larsen 2013). Along the same line of analysis, it has been observed that the local capacity to attract and implement world-famous attractions (e.g. a Disneyland park, a major cultural event, etc.) has become part of urban policies of competitiveness (d'Hauteserre 2013; Jakob 2013).

A second type of research has emphasized how local actors coordinate their activities to set a coherent and specific experiential stage in the governance of a specific stage setting. Various initiatives have been depicted to explain how public and private players mobilize local resources to promote a thematic destination. A broader perspective has been given to tourism activities in regional growth by considering them in relation to the valorization of other regional offerings such as regional cooking and handicraft (Manniche and Larsen 2013). Local innovation is here described as the capacity to give a new and specific content to regional stage setting (Lorentzen 2013b; Marling *et al.* 2009; Richards 2001). Building upon these earlier works, further research avenues can be considered.

A first research avenue is to analyse stage setting as a complex interaction between resident- and visitor-oriented activities. These two types of activities have most often been conceived separately or in opposition to each other. On the one hand, works in the fields of tourism and leisure studies have highlighted how urban or regional experiential stage setting contributes to attract new visitor-based revenues and creates 'windows of opportunity' for local enterprises

(Boswijk 2013; Lorentzen 2012; Smidt-Jensen *et al.* 2009). On the other hand, works on cultural economy and local governance have shown the role of setting experiential stages to enhance creativity and participatory initiatives in local communities of inhabitants (Hallberg and Harslof 2013; Jakob 2013).

Local empowerment achieved through residential stage setting (e.g. a cultural stage) is often opposed to an export-based logic consisting in setting a stage to visitors. A promising research agenda would consist in investigating how these two dynamics co-develop and co-evolve with each other through potential conflicts but also through mutual enrichment. Setting attractive regional or urban stages is about attracting visitors as well as attracting and retaining residents. Posing this research question implies not only identifying the coordinating 'theme' of a local stage setting but also identifying the fundamental social values assigned to this setting and shared by visitors and residents.

A second research avenue deals with the multi-local and multi-scalar dynamics of stage setting. As illustrated by Manniche and Larsen (2013), Bornholm culinary products are not only valued through the stage set on the island of Bornholm, but also relate to the traditional culinary stage of Italy and the event and cooking scene of Copenhagen. More systematic investigations should be promoted to understand how the mobility of knowledge contributes to the development of distant local stages and how the mobility of consumers contributes to the value of various goods and services between different places. In such analyses, the relational complementarities between urban and rural areas should be particularly highlighted. For instance a music festival organized in a rural region should be analysed in relation to an urban cultural stage of music production. Parallel to this, the urban farmers' market is an urban stage setting that can only be understood with reference to a related rural stage setting.

## How are particular stage settings and consumption resources turned into territorial experiences?

Underlined as the most crucial and challenging issue implied by the experience economy approach is the idea that the economic value of goods and services is by nature 'in the hands' of end consumers. A market supply does not have a proven but a 'suggested' value (Schulze 2013) that must be realized by a self-enrolment of the demand. A similar perspective applies to the market valuation of a particular territorial stage setting. As emphasized by Blain *et al.* (2005), the experience-value of a particular destination can be 'promised' but never 'ensured'. To be actually valued, the experience must concretely and symbolically *take place* and the fundamantal questions are how, when and where it can take place within the TSS.

In this view, a first research avenue would be to investigate the 'attraction system' preparing and making possible the engagement of consumers within the stage. Following Richards (2002), an attraction system can be regarded as a configuration of actors and markers 'pulling' (appealing) and 'pushing' (motivating) someone to move to a particular stage setting. The innovation purpose relates here to the territorial value 'suggested' by a particular stage setting and the terri-torial value 'expected' by different consumers. In this interplay, branding geo-graphies (Jansson and Power 2010; Pike 2011; Power and Hauge 2008; Power and Jansson 2011) should be seen as a perpetual game of initiation to and antici-pation of a projected experience. Interpersonal relations should also be studied in depth within this attraction system. For instance, the decision to travel or move to a particular place can be motivated by friends established in this destination or by an earlier experience made there, told and recommended by neighbours. These interpersonal relations create direct links between the stage and a potential guest. They also stimulate anticipation and expectation through an interpersonal sharing of previous experiences related to a particular stage or to other compared stages.

A second research avenue is then, of course, how the TSS enables and makes the realization of a concrete and valuable territorialized experience possible. As already mentioned above, the artefacts and activities of the stage setting frame the experiential engagement of the guests (e.g. a visitor, a resident or a consu-mer). Avoiding negative cues is in this respect crucial (Pine and Gilmore 1999). Yet, guests also contribute to perform the stage among each other (Holt and Lapenta 2013). If this may reinforce a mutual engagment of common ressources in the stage setting (shared imaginaries, common cultural capital, reciprocal per-formances, etc.), the cohabitation of different guests may also be conflictual. For instance, potential conflicts can appear between new and old residents in parti-cular urban stages or between visitors and inhabitants.

As for the question of stage setting, the question of consumer engagement in a TTS should be analysed in relation to its multi-local and multi-scalar dimen-sion. The experience made by a guest on a stage is part of a continual process of initiation, learning and transformation (Pine and Gilmore 2013) taking place in different places and at different moments. As emphasized by Guex and Crevoi-sier (2015) in this volume, a territorial stage is the concretization, at a particular moment, of a symbolic stage.

In this view information techology (IT) should not be seen as alternative and virtual stages to physical stages but rather as complementary to them. The example of the Swiss watch industry could be enlightening (Jeannerat 2013). A consumer does not usually buy an expensive Swiss watch on a whim. He informs himself in online showrooms, initiates himself to complex watchmaking in an initiation workshop organized in his country, visits a trade show in Basel, has a look in a watch shop on the Place Vendom in Paris and buys his watch at the top of the Matterhorn in Switzerland. This stylized example highlights that, in a highly mobile world, a TSS does not end up with an analysis of a particular place or a single experience. It should be studied as a continuum of interrelated contexts of engagement and of multi-located value creation.

## How is experiential engagement turned into territorial revenue?

Deconstructing and understanding complex territorial revenue models is certainly the most unexplored issue addressed by the experience economy approach up to now. As underlined above, specific contributions have been provided by urban and regional studies or by destination management and tourism studies on the question of territorial stage setting, branding and attractiveness. However, very little has been undertaken to understand systematically how monetary exchanges and incomes are generated within an experience stage.

Pioneer works on this issue can be found in management studies on the question of business and pricing models (Chesbrough and Rosenbloom 2002; Ng 2010; Osterwalder and Pigneur 2010; Zott and Amit 2010; Zott et al. 2011) or in ethnographical debates on market commodification (Kaul 2007; Weber 2000). In various ways, this literature underlines the idea that value creation cannot be restrained to the market trade-off of different commodities but should be understood within a complex revenue model implying monetary as well as non-monetary transactions. Investigating a TSS should provide a spatial lens to these pioneer contributions and go beyond a restrictve export-based model of territorial innovation.

The TSS is a model which depicts both a visitor and a residential context of revenue attraction and circulation (Davezies 2009; Segessemann and Crevoisier 2013; Talandier 2008, 2010). Thus, analysing the revenue model of a TSS would not only consist in identifying the local activities bringing new income into the region – the so-called basic activities – but should also examine how this revenue is redistributed and recirculated within the TSS through induced and including activities.

Pointing to the way a stage can be monetized raises the broader question of how particular goods and services become the revenue vehicles of a TSS. Various dimensions of this issue can be highlighted for future research.

A first and quite traditional approach to the monetization of a territorial stage relates to the 'admission to' and 'subsistance in' the stage. Admission is usually monetized through particular fees (taxes, entrance tickets, etc.) and subsistance through traded amenities supporting the realization of a localized experience (hotels, restaurants, cafés, grocery shops, etc.). These monetary trade-offs are already studied as the usual business of touristic destinations. Further research avenues could be to trace more systematically how the monetary income generated by these activities are recirculated within the overall TSS between profit and non-profit-making activities and between private and public spending.

A second issue should be to investigate the 'ritualistic' and 'totemic' value of goods and services traded within the stage (Beckert 2011). To illustrate such an approach, let us recall the examples of coffee bought on St Mark's Square, the vase bought in a Murano factory or the Swiss watch bought at the top of the Matterhorn. In all these examples, traded goods transcend their physical and functional use. They are objects with which buyers interact (Jensen 2013: 198).

In a territorial perspective, the fundamental research issue here is to understand where and when the monetary transaction takes place during the experiential consumption process of the buyer. This monetary transaction marks a 'bracket' (Weber 2000) in the ongoing experimentation of a stage. For instance, buying a coffee may be a ritual point initiating the contemplation of St Marks square or buying a vase a ritual point succeeding to the visit of a glass factory.

Once again, investigating the revenue model of a TSS goes far beyond the examination of revenue flows into a particular export-based region. It implies identifying where and when particular monetary transactions bring income into the system and how this income is recirculated within and between territorial stages.

## Conclusion

Neither a unilitateral proposition nor an achieved model of interpretation, the concept of TSS suggested here intends to continue rather than to conclude the orginal work done by many researchers. It calls for a renewed collective agenda to be retreived in a constant dialogue between theoretical debates and new social challenges.

The experience economy approach developed in the past decade has opened promising avenues to understand territorial innovation and development. It has provided evidence of a necessity to go beyond a productionist and technologist approach to innovation and has formulated alternative solutions for regional development.

However, as for other TIMs, this approach should not be defended in a hegemonic manner. It provides an original lens to understand some challenging contemporary issues often neglected by other approaches, but it should not be arrogantly regarded as the new 'best theory' for the new 'best practices'. A main contribution of this approach is to go beyond the *exchange-value* perspective usually used to explain regional or national competitiveness. It underlines a complex *use-value*, which is socio-economically constructed between producers and consumers, between sectors and between places. Such an approach is to be considered in relation to the challenges that our societies are facing to promote not only highly competitive production regions but also quality places of living and of consumption.

This chapter has proposed a possible interpretation of the current state of theorizing relating to the experience economy concept and has highlighted the necessity to continue the reflection through the broader concept of TSS. Exploring this concept should have the ambition to grasp some challenging research questions mostly left aside by traditional TIMs as well as by recent works on the experience economy. A particular emphasis has been given to the importantance of understanding territorial innovation within a multi-local and multi-scalar system valuing the increased mobility of consumers and residents.

Such an issue is evermore crucial since the consequence of these mobilities is a territorial spread of monetary exchanges. One does not necessarily spend money where one earns it and one may not pay for each experience achieved in different stages. Nevertheless, each experience can contribute to a punctual monetary exchange at a specific moment and in specific places. A systematic examination of monetary transactions reaches, in this sense, far beyond a restrictive interpretation of market exchange and use-values. Our globalized economy is usually considered – both within its primary theorizing as well as in policies/ politics – through the restrictive lens of a global commodity trade. This is, for instance, well illustrated by the World Economic Forum (WEF). The TSS approach leads one to reconsider this restrictive lens, and to take into account complex business models based not only on commodity trading, but also on interrelated spaces of monetary flows and of valued experiences. This implies depicting and understanding complex territorial revenue models. Developing such an approach is ambitious but promising.

## References

Andersson, D.E. and Andersson, Å.E. (2013) 'The economic value of experience goods', in J. Sundbo and F. Sørensen (eds) *Handbook on the experience economy*, Cheltenham: Edward Elgar.

Aspers, P. and Beckert, J. (2011) 'Value in markets', in J. Beckert and P. Aspers (eds) *The Worth of Goods: Valuation and Pricing in the Economy*, Oxford: Oxford University Press.

Beckert, J. (2011) 'The transcending power of goods: Imaginative value in the economy', in J. Beckert and P. Aspers (eds) *The Worth of Goods: Valuation and Pricing in the Economy*, Oxford: Oxford University Press.

Bille, T. (2011) 'The Scandinavian approach to the experience economy – does it make sense?', *International Journal of Cultural Policy*, 18(1): 93–110.

Blain, C., Levy, S.E. and Ritchie, J.R.B. (2005) 'Destination branding: Insights and practices from destination management organizations', *Journal of Travel Research*, 43(4): 328–38.

Boswijk, A. (2013) 'The power of the economy of experiences: new ways of value creation', in J. Sundbo and F. Sørensen (eds) *Handbook on the experience economy*, Cheltenham: Edward Elgar.

Breschi, S. and Malerba, F. (2001) 'The geography of innovation and economic clustering: Some introductory notes', *Industrial and Corporate Change* 10(4): 817–33.

Chesbrough, H. and Rosenbloom, R.S. (2002) 'The role of the business model in capturing value from innovation: evidence from Xerox Corporation's technology spin-off companies', *Industrial and Corporate Change*, 11(3): 529–55.

Cooke, P. and Lazzeretti, L. (2008a) 'Creative cities: an introduction', in P. Cooke and L. Lazzeretti (eds) *Creative Cities, Cultural Clusters and Local Economic Development*, Cheltenham: Edward Elgar.

Cooke, P. and Lazzeretti, L. (eds) (2008b) *Creative Cities, Cultural Clusters and Local Economic Development*, Cheltenham: Edward Elgar.

Costa, P. (2008) 'Creativity, innovation and territorial agglomeration in cultural activities: the roots of the creative city', in P. Cooke and L. Lazzeretti (eds) *Creative Cities, Cultural Clusters and Local Economic Development*, Cheltenham: Edward Elgar.

D'Hauteserre, A.-M. (2013) 'Val d'Europe: A pioneering turn to "experience" planning?', *European Urban and Regional Studies*, 20(4): 435–46.

Davezies, L. (2009) 'L'économie locale "résidentielle"', *Géographie, Économie, Société,* 11(1): 47–53.

Dewey, J. (1939) 'Theory of valuation', *International Encyclopedia of Unified Science,* 2: vii, 67.

Freire-Gibb, L.C. (2011) 'The rise and fall of the concept of the experience economy in the local economic development of Denmark', *European Planning Studies,* 19(10): 1839–53.

Fuglsang, L. and Eide, D. (2013) 'The experience turn as "bandwagon": Understanding network formation and innovation as practice', *European Urban and Regional Studies,* 20(4): 417–34.

Grabher, G. (2009) 'Yet another turn? The evolutionary project in economic geography', *Economic Geography,* 85(2): 119–27.

Grabher, G. and Jeannerat, H. (2012) 'Report on the 3rd workshop of the RSA research network on experience economy and spatial strategies', *Regions Magazine,* 287(1): 23–4.

Guex, D. and Crevoisier, O. (2015) 'A comprehensive socio-economic model of the experience economy: The territorial stage', in A. Lorentzen, K.T. Larsen and L. Schrøder (eds) *Spatial Dynamics in the Experience Economy,* Abingdon: Routledge.

Hallberg, G.W. and Harslof, O. (2013) 'Experiencing everyday life anew: applied theatrical and performative strategies', in J. Sundbo and F. Sørensen (eds) *Handbook on the Experience Economy,* Cheltenham: Edward Elgar.

Harvey, D. (1989) *The condition of postmodernity,* Oxford: Blackwell.

Holt, F. and Lapenta, F. (2013) 'The social experience of cultural events: conceptual foundations and analytical strategies', in J. Sundbo and F. Sørensen (eds) *Handbook on the Experience Economy,* Cheltenham: Edward Elgar.

Hutter, M. (2011) 'Experience Goods', in R. Towse (ed.) *A Handbook of Cultural Economics,* Cheltenham: Edward Elgar.

Jakob, D. (2013) 'The eventification of place: Urban development and experience consumption in Berlin and New York City', *European Urban and Regional Studies,* 20(4): 447–59.

Jansson, J. and Power, D. (2010) 'Fashioning a global city: Global city brand channels in the fashion and design industries', *Regional Studies,* 44(7): 889–904.

Jeannerat, H. (2010) 'Report on the 1st workshop of the RSA research network on experience economy and spatial strategies', *Regions Magazine,* 278(1): 30–1.

Jeannerat, H. (2013) 'Staging experience, valuing authenticity: Towards a market perspective on territorial development', *European Urban and Regional Studies,* 20(4): 370–84.

Jensen, J.F. (2013) 'IT and experiences: user experience, experience design and user-experience design', in J. Sundbo and F. Sørensen (eds) *Handbook on the experience economy,* Cheltenham: Edward Elgar.

Kaul, A.R. (2007) 'The limits of commodification in traditional Irish music sessions', *Journal of the Royal Anthropological Institute,* 13(3): 703–19.

Lagendijk, A. (2003) 'Towards conceptual quality in regional studies: The need for subtle critique – A response to Markusen', *Regional Studies,* 37(6–7): 719–27.

Lorentzen, A. (2009a) 'Cities in the Experience Economy', *European Planning Studies* 17(6): 829–45.

Lorentzen, A. (2009b) 'Space and place in the experience economy: A proactive approach', in S. Hardy, A. Beauclair and L. Bibby-Larsen (eds) *Understanding and shaping regions: Spatial, social and economic futures,* annual conference of the Regional Studies Association, Katholieke Universiteit, Leuven, April 2009.

Lorentzen, A. (2011) 'Report of the 2nd workshop of the RSA research network on experience economy and spatial strategies', *Regions Magazine*, 283: 27–8.

Lorentzen, A. (2012) 'The development of the periphery in the experience economy', in P. de Souza and M. Danson (eds) *Regional Development in Northern Europe: Peripherality, marginality and border Issues*, Abingdon: Routledge.

Lorentzen, A. (2013a) 'Post-industrial growth: experience, culture or creative economies?', in J. Sundbo and F. Sørensen (eds) *Handbook on the experience economy*, Cheltenham: Edward Elgar.

Lorentzen, A. (2013b) 'The experience turn of the Danish periphery: The downscaling of new spatial strategies', *European Urban and Regional Studies*, 20(4): 460–72.

Lorentzen, A. and Hansen, C.J. (2009) 'The role and transformation of the city in the experience economy: Identifying and exploring research challenges', *European Planning Studies*, 17(6): 817–27.

Lorentzen, A. and Jeannerat, H. (2013) 'Urban and regional studies in the experience economy: What kind of turn?', *European Urban and Regional Studies*, 20(4): 363–9.

Malmberg, A. and Power, D. (2005) 'On the role of global demand in local innovation processes', in G. Fuchs and P. Shapira (eds) *Rethinking Regional Innovation and Change: Path Dependency of Regional Breakthrough?*, New York: Springer.

Manniche, J. and Larsen, K.T. (2013) 'Experience staging and symbolic knowledge: The case of Bornholm culinary products', *European Urban and Regional Studies*, 20(4): 401–16.

Mansvelt, J. (2005) *Geographies of consumption*, Los Angeles: Sage Publications.

Marling, G., Jensen, O.B. and Kiib, H. (2009) 'The experience city: Planning of hybrid cultural projects', *European Planning Studies*, 17(6): 863–85.

Miles, S. and Paddison, R. (2005) 'Introduction: The rise and rise of culture-led urban regeneration', *Urban Studies*, 42(5–6): 833–9.

Miller, D. (2005) 'Reply to Michel Callon', *Economic Sociology: European Electronic Newsletter*, 6(2): 3–14.

Ng, I.C.L. (2010) 'The future of pricing and revenue models', *Journal of Revenue Pricing Management*, 9(3): 276–81.

Nilsen, B. and Dale, B. (2013) 'Defining and categorizing experience industries', in J. Sundbo and F. Sørensen (eds) *Handbook on the Experience Economy*, Cheltenham: Edward Elgar.

Osterwalder, A. and Pigneur, Y. (2010) *Business model generation: A handbook for visionaries, game changers, and challengers*, Chichester: Wiley.

Pike, A. (2011) 'Introduction: Brands and Branding Geographies', in A. Pike (ed.) *Brands and Branding Geographies*, Cheltenham: Edward Elgar.

Pine, B.J. and Gilmore, J.H. (1999) *The experience economy: Work is theatre and every business a stage*, Boston: Harvard Business School Press.

Pine, B.J. and Gilmore, J.H. (2013) 'The experience economy: past, present and future', in J. Sundbo and F. Sørensen (eds) *Handbook on the Experience Economy*, Cheltenham: Edward Elgar.

Polèse, M. and Shearmur, R. (2009) *Économie urbaine et régionale (3ème édition)*, Paris: Economica.

Posner, G.J., Strike, K.A., Hewson, P.W. and Gertzog, W.A. (1982) 'Accommodation of a scientific conception: Toward a theory of conceptual change', *Science Education* 66(2): 211–27.

Power, D. (2009) 'Culture, creativity and experience in Nordic and Scandinavian cultural policy', *International Journal of Cultural Policy*, 15(4): 445–60.

Power, D. and Hauge, A. (2008) 'No Man's Brand – Brands, Institutions, and Fashion', *Growth and Change*, 39(1): 123–43.

Power, D. and Jansson, J. (2011) 'Constructing brands from the outside? Brand channels, cyclical clusters and global circuits', in A. Pike (ed.) *Brands and Branding Geographies*, Cheltenham: Edward Elgar.

Pratt, A. (2008) 'L'apport britannique à la compréhension des fonctions créatives dans les villes globales', in F. Leriche, S. Daviet, M. Sibertin-Blanc and J.-M. Zuliani (eds) *L'économie culturelle et ses territoires*, Toulouse: Presses Universitaires du Mirail.

Richards, G. (2001) 'The Experience Industry and the Creation of Attractions', in G. Richards (ed.) *Cultural Attractions and European Tourism*, Oxford: CABI Publishing.

Richards, G. (2002) 'Tourism attraction systems: Exploring cultural behavior', *Annals of Tourism Research*, 29(4): 1048–64.

Richards, G. and Wilson, J. (2006) 'Developing creativity in tourist experiences: A solution to the serial reproduction of culture?', *Tourism Management*, 27(6): 1209–23.

Schulze, G. (2013) 'The experience market', in J. Sundbo and F. Sørensen (eds) *Handbook on the Experience Economy*, Cheltenham: Edward Elgar.

Scott, A. J. (2006) 'Creative cities: Conceptual issues and policy questions', *Journal of Urban Affairs*, 28(1): 1–17.

Segessemann, A. and Crevoisier, O. (2013) 'L'économie résidentielle en Suisse: une approche par les emplois', *Revue d'Économie Régionale et Urbaine*, 4: 705–35.

Smidt-Jensen, S., Skytt, C.B. and Winther, L. (2009) 'The geography of the experience economy in Denmark: Employment change and location dynamics in attendance-based experience industries', *European Planning Studies*, 17(6): 847–62.

Stamboulis, Y. and Skayannis, P. (2003) 'Innovation strategies and technology for experience-based tourism', *Tourism Management*, 24(1): 35–43.

Star, S.L. and Griesemer, J.R. (1989) 'Institutional ecology, "translations" and boundary objects: Amateurs and professionals in Berkeley's Museum of Vertebrate Zoology, 1907–39', *Social Studies of Science*, 19(3): 387–420.

Stark, D. (2011) 'What's Valuable?', in J. Beckert and P. Aspers (eds) *The Worth of Goods: Valuation and Pricing in the Economy*, Oxford: Oxford University Press.

Storper, M. and Scott, A.J. (2009) 'Rethinking human capital, creativity and urban growth', *Journal of Economic Geography*, 9(2): 147–67.

Sundbo, J. and Sørensen, F. (eds) (2013) *Handbook on the experience economy*, Cheltenham: Edward Elgar.

Sundbo, J., Sørensen, F. and Fuglsang, L. (2013) 'Innovation in the experience sector', in J. Sundbo and F. Sørensen (eds) *Handbook on the Experience Economy*, Cheltenham: Edward Elgar.

Talandier, M. (2008) 'Une autre géographie du développement rural: une approche par les revenus', *Géocarrefour*, 83(4): 259–67.

Talandier, M. (2010) 'Economie résidentielle versus économie productive: inverser le regard'. *Compte rendu de la 6ème controverse de cohérence territoriale de la région urbaine de Grenoble, SCoT 2030*, Grenoble, 25 May 2010.

Vang, J. and Tschang, T. (2013) 'Unpacking the spatial organization of the US video-games industry: lessons for research on experience industry clusters', in J. Sundbo and F. Sørensen (eds) *Handbook on the Experience Economy*, Cheltenham: Edward Elgar.

Vatin, F. (2013) 'Valuation as evaluating and valorizing', *Valuation Studies*, 1: 31–50.

Vinck, D. (2009) 'De l'objet intermédiaire à l'objet-frontière', *Revue d'anthropologie des connaissances*, 3(1): 51–72.

Weber, F. (2000) 'Transactions marchandes, échanges rituels, relations personnelles', *Genèses*, 41(4): 85–107.

Zott, C. and Amit, R. (2010) 'Business model design: An activity system perspective', *Long Range Planning*, 43(2–3): 216–26.

Zott, C., Amit, R. and Massa, L. (2011) 'The business model: Recent developments and future research', *Journal of Management*, 37(4): 1019–42.

# 3 Negotiating and producing symbolic value

*Atle Hauge*

At the heart of the experience economy approach lays the fact that much, if not most, of our consumption is not solely based in covering physical demands. In a world of seemingly endless consumer choices, producers need to add value beyond utilitarian requirements. As maintained by the advocates of the experience economy, a way to do this is to create lasting emotions associated with the product, so the memory or the experience itself becomes the product. Experiences are thus understood as events that engage individuals on different levels (Pine and Gilmore 1999), which are comprised of emotional as well as functional interaction between customers and producers (Beltagui *et al.* 2012). The experience can be entrenched in emotional, sensorial, physical and spiritual engagement (Gentile *et al.* 2007). Memories created can obviously be both good and bad, but most firms strive to create positive ones. Arguably one of the most effective methods to engage customers, create memories, and thus construct a potent experience, is to charge products with symbolic value. However, as no single actor has the power to dictate symbolic value, it is helpful to understand this as decided through a series of negotiations. Negotiation is a useful analytical concept because it highlights the fact that symbolic value is persistently contested and challenged.

Pine and Gilmore (1999) use metaphors from the theatre and claim the experience has to be orchestrated, staged and scripted. They argue that providers orchestrate services as the stage on which to involve customers to create a memorable event. However, they stress that staging experiences surpasses just entertaining. Rather, companies need to engage the customers to be able to charge a premium (Pine and Gilmore 1999: 30). Symbolic value can be a valuable competitive resource in an experience economy setting. This is not just an image but denotes a synergy of many aspects related to products' attractiveness/ desirability to consumers, including expectancy, memory and narratives, in addition to the actual consumption. The staging of the experience is also vital in the construction of symbolic value, because symbolic value is an amalgam of different types of information. Hence, in the following I argue that the staging process needs to go beyond the point of purchase to charge the experience with symbolic value. Three key processes are identified in the staging process: (1) the design and production of the products; (2) marketing, branding and mediating;

and (3) retail and consumption. These processes are purposefully set up to deliver products' symbolic value, and all have a certain spatiality with the aim to place the products in a shared system of meaning. The spatial dynamic has at least two features. First, even though globalization plays a major role here as in most other parts of society, symbolic value is to a certain degree context dependent – it can vary across time and space. Second, space and place are powerful resources in the production process of symbolic value because they are unavoidably imbued with geographical associations (Pike 2011). The role of geography is a major theme and will be discussed throughout the entire chapter.

This is primarily a theoretical chapter and is an effort to encapsulate and refine the analysis of the production of symbolic value. However, there are some empirical examples, which stem from several research projects where symbolic value has been in focus (see, for example, Power and Hauge 2008; Hauge *et al.* 2009; Hauge and Hracs 2010; Hauge 2011, 2012; Hauge and Power 2013; Hracs *et al.* 2013). The chapter's main contribution is the explicit analysis of how symbolic value is produced and maintained, and how this is relevant for the experience economy approach. It will add to and extend the experience economy literature by putting the production of symbolic value at the centre of the analysis. This study is by no means an exhaustive review of how the value of symbolic properties is created; the ambition is rather to illuminate some of the negotiation processes whereby symbolic value is shaped and produced.

## The socio-economic production of symbolic value

Here, symbolic value is understood as a synergy of characteristics related to products' attractiveness/desirability to consumers (Hauge 2011). It is constructed through several dimensions, partly based on social status (socio-economic group preferences), design and materiality (the quality and aesthetics of the product) and individual preferences and taste (even if the social aspect is important, personal readings and understandings of symbolic value will differ) (Hauge and Power 2013). Symbolic value is important when brands and consumer products incessantly try to position themselves in the market. Here, the notion of markets is not just seen as faceless economic mechanisms for the allocation of goods, but rather as social institutions embedded in the socio-economic context in which they operate (see, for example, Aspers and Beckert 2011). Symbolic value is best understood in dynamic terms rather than as a given entity and must be related to contextual conditions and to the dynamics of different actors' interaction (Power and Hauge 2008). The marketplace arrangements are essentially contested in this dynamic process, by competitors, mediators and consumers (Banister and Hogg 2004). This means that a product's symbolic value is not only controlled by the firm itself, but is co-constructed in a socio-economic context in interaction with multiple social actors including, for example, producers, service providers, media, retailers and consumers (Entwistle and Rocamora 2006). This continuous practice of marketplace positioning and repositioning is in this paper conceptualized as a series of *negotiations*. Consumers confirm or negotiate symbolic meanings through the way they behave, but meanings are fleeting and unstable and highly context dependable. The negotiating processes are thus social in character, because symbolic meanings are social signals, which influence the shaping of social identity and affiliation. Negotiations are processes of interpreting experiences and perceptions of the brand (Hollenbeck and Zinkhan 2010). Messages derived from advertising and promotion must be mediated with the living experience of purchase and usage (Elliott and Wattanasuwan 1998), or put differently, users negotiate the relation between the matter and the meaning (Hoyer and MacInnis 2001). In order for consumer products and brands to function as communication symbols, meanings must be socially shared, and continuously produced and reproduced during social interactions (Dittmar 1992). However, the meanings of objects are seldom clear-cut, or essentially controlled by manufacturers and marketers. Negotiation as an analytical concept is helpful because it emphasizes the dynamics of symbolic value, and that the process is collective and subjugated by interaction between various actors. An essential feature underpinning symbolic value is thus that it is partly a social construction. It is a systemic exercise performed by actors involved in economical *and/or* social relationships (Bourdieu 1984).

The consumers and their individual experience is a key point in the experience economy, and there is interdependency between producers and consumers (Andersson and Andersson 2013). As Potts *et al.* (2008: 462) argue, 'consumer co-creation is a redrawing of analytic boundaries, such that production processes now extend into domains previously understood as consumption processes'. The role of the consumer might be of an even greater significance when the experience is charged with symbolic value. Ravasi and Rindova (2008) examine the process of symbolic value creation, and call attention to the role of the consumer. They argue that symbolic value is created in the processes of consumption and exchange, and define symbolic value by its ability to generate meanings related to social identity and status of the user. They emphasize that products have both functional and symbolic value. Accordingly, value creation can be understood as developed along two levels – a material level, where product and process technologies are decisive; and at a cultural level, where resources are combined to accommodate cultural categories and trends. This means that clear divides between products' material and immaterial dimensions as well as their production and consumption dimensions are difficult to maintain (Hauge and Power 2013). The duality between the performance and quality of the material product and aesthetic assessments is essential to understand value creation in most consumer markets.

In this chapter there is a focus on symbolic value shared by larger groups of people, i.e. potential consumers. For producers this means that if their products are understood and appreciated as charged with symbolic value, the potential consumer group can be large. The social nature of the negotiation in the symbolic market implies a high level of uncertainty, because the value is to a high degree based on consumers' experience (Sundbo and Sørensen 2013). Producers might have very good knowledge of what has been successful in the past, but this is no guarantee for the latest product to thrive. The consumers' valuation is unknown until a product is actually consumed or experienced, and one consumer's valuation is not necessarily a good predictor of another's response (Caves 2003). This shows that even if it might be tempting to ascribe universal symbolic meanings to products, one cannot presume that these are the same meanings that guide the actions of consumers acquiring those products (Campbell 1996). Individuals or users can enjoy the intangible qualities of a product/ artefact, even if there is no ambition to signal belonging. People may appreciate the intangible value even without recognizing or taking into consideration the symbolic aspects. The product can, for example, resurrect fond memories; provide enjoyment because one appreciates the skills/creative processes behind it; or simply be valued for its look and aesthetic appeal. These intangible 'reasons' for purchase should not be underestimated.

Places play an important role in the transient activities associated with the production of symbolic value. In particular, certain urban districts function as contexts for fixed meanings; some places encourage the collective production process of symbolic value. The spatial fix can be of different types; a more physical fix in the sense of the enduring fixation of capital in place in physical form; and a more metaphorical 'fix' (Jessop 2006) as the lasting sociocultural character and reputation of certain activities are reinforced by particular loci. The physical and reputational fix is in most cases mutually reinforcing. The spatial fix encourages the collective process of the production of symbolic value because these places operate in multiple networks of exchange – of products, ideas and human capital – with other key sites. Locality as an identifying mark and geographical associations can be pungent properties for products. The geographical origin and association have longstanding and enduring impact on products' symbolic value. Paris fashion, Parma ham, Champagne wines, Hollywood films, German cars, just to mention a few, are all examples of products whose symbolic value is strongly associated with their geography of origin. Reputations of certain localities for certain products influence consumers' assessments of attributes quality, and eventually the interpretation of meaning and value. Geographical connotations and statuses are very slow to change or relocate, and persistently imbue products and producers with symbolic value. However, product quality, performativity and physical appearance are still important in how symbolic value is achieved and sustained (Hauge and Power 2013). Numerous studies, especially in economic geography, have shown how specialized local capacities and innovation processes explain why particular types of firms and industries are prosperous, and why the location of firms is important for their competitiveness (Malmberg and Power 2006).

This is, for example, highly visible in fashion with its global capitals – Paris, London, New York, Milan and Tokyo. The production of intangibles (such as symbolic value) seems to rest heavily on the character of the space, but these cities are also focal points in a global industry with a clustering of corporate power (Gilbert 2006). Big trends are set in motion, reported by media and first picked up by sophisticated consumers in the global fashion capitals. However, despite the intensification of global links and flows, everything in fashion is far from streamlined or evenly integrated (Weller 2008). Social status can be achieved through localized cultural capital, i.e. particular forms of knowledge and skills valued in the group as well as skills in combining and reworking the pool of symbolic resources that are shared by group members (Arnould and Thompson 2005). However, these social dynamics are situated within certain spatial settings. This materializes in the distinct styles local to an area, the variation of shops and range of consumers associated with these local spaces. These processes work at both the levels of production and consumption. There seems, for example, to be a willingness of educated professionals to eagerly take consumption cues from urban artists and other creative individuals/groups (Lloyd 2006). As both of these groups favour certain spatial fixes within the urban context, neighbourhoods are important sites of aesthetic innovation and diffusion. These residents 'thrive on the local ambience of urban cool' (Lloyd 2006: 23).

To summarize the argument so far, one way to engage customers and add value to their consumption experience is to imbue this with symbolic value. However, symbolic value is not free-floating and omnipresent. Rather, it is scarce and can only to a certain degree be produced. Furthermore, symbolic value rests in part on immaterial, socially constructed processes (Lorentzen and Jeannerat 2013). This suggests that the production of symbolic value in addition to being contextually dependent is entrenched in societal and relational processes. These production processes are best understood in systemic terms, i.e. as processes rooted in systems of interrelated actors within specific socio-institutional contexts (Bathelt and Glückler 2003). Underpinning this view is a belief that social processes are crucial to comprehend economic actions as well as how institutions like markets work. Moreover, the consumer and the role consumers play in the staging of experiences are at the centre of the analysis. They are not just seen as passive receivers of stimuli and bystanders of the event, but active participants in the production of their own and others' experience (Boswijk *et al.* 2007; Sundbo and Sørensen 2013). The argument can be summarized as a continuous process consisting of an interaction between the practised experiences and the development of ideas. This embeds the production of experiences in space and time, in addition to opening up for the role of the individual as well as group dynamics of consumers.

The next section will illustrate some of the different processes in the creation of symbolic value, and how they resemble a series of negotiations. I will focus on three interconnected stages: design, marketing and retail. All of these stages have a certain spatial fix and the theoretical argument and empirical examples will illustrate how geography can work as a valuable resource. I will show how place and space is central to the way in which symbolic, and thus in most cases economic, value is constituted.

## Stages: negotiating processes in the creation of symbolic value

As argued above, symbolic value is not to be imposed by a single actor as it is constantly contested, by competitors, mediators and consumers. As such, it is better understood in dynamic terms, as emerging through a series of interconnected negotiating processes. This section identifies three key processes in the production of symbolic value: (1) the design and production of the products; (2) marketing, branding and mediating; and (3) retail and consumption. These negotiating processes are premeditated to charge products with symbolic value, located in a shared system of meaning.

### Designing and creating symbolic value

In the current economy, we have seen a development where the cognitive and creative processes in developing a product trumps the actual production when it comes to determining its symbolic value. In an era where outsourcing of production is more the norm than the exception, this is crucial for firms' competitive advantage. This has at least two implications in context of the experience economy. First of all, we have seen the rise of designers as not only the persons responsible for the creative process behind the naissance of a product or an artefact, but also as the main vehicles in the production of symbolic value. Second, place–product association and experience are focal points for the production of symbolic value (Pasquinelli 2013). The last point is maybe most famously illustrated with Apple's information on their products that they are *designed* in California, and assembled in China. For Apple it is vital to communicate that the origins and the ideas behind the product come from a region renowned for its technological innovativeness. We see this in ever more products; the firms think that it is necessary to inform the consumers about where the products are designed, developed and tested in addition to the required 'made in' tag. The Apple example also illustrates that the production processes of symbolic value are organized through both material and immaterial logics. The idea of what constitutes good taste changes over time, and with it the products that embody tastes change. However, the immateriality of symbolic value cannot be understood without referring to the actual, tangible product. Immateriality is not haphazardly created; it is sustained by a system of organizations and institutions that participate in the constant production and re-production of immaterial value. Firms and organizations are interrelated through a wide range of interactions, which are essential to the performance of the individual firms as well as the system as a whole. Even though this dual production of the material artefact and immaterial symbolic value is best understood in systemic terms, some agents still enjoy a somewhat special position. In particular the actual designers, as they work on different aspects of value creation, both the functional and aesthetic. However, at least for the most renowned, the narration of themselves and the particular place they work are input in the production process of symbolic value. Molotch (2005: 22) argues that design is the intentional use of cultural and material resources to create a valuable product, and is 'where the cultural rubber hits the commercial road'. The idea of designers as creative superpersons is based on a romantic idea that creativity is a sign of genius, that these individuals possess superior skills and are capable of extraordinary inventions (Santagata 2004). In reality there is usually a team involved in supporting the big designers, and how much is done by the actual designer is seldom revealed.

In sum this implies that product development should not only be understood as innovations and improvements of functionality, but also as changes in the aesthetic form and/or symbolic value (Tran 2010). Firms balance novelty with the familiar. On one hand the brand needs to be recognized, but on the other it should still be viewed as innovative. It is an ongoing negotiation with customers how conservative versus innovative the company can be. Marketing is one of the imperative communication channels in this process.

## *Marketing, branding and mediating*

Branding and marketing create added symbolic value because they generate meaning (McCracken 2005). Branded in the right way, products are given meaning (i.e. symbolic value) so that they become, for example, a lifestyle statement – a symbol for what consumers aspire to be and with whom they like to be associated. Marketing and branding are analogous but not the same. Branding is not just an add-on in the marketing process; more exactly it is an attempt to encapsulate a balance between different economic values: quality, utility, symbolic and cultural worth. Lury (2004: 27) argues that branding 'is an abstract machine for the reconfiguration of production'. The aim of branding is to produce a resilient link between the character of an object and its branded image or form (Power and Hauge 2008). This varies with different contexts because symbolic value has no straightforward, singular meaning (Moor 2003). Even though the product is the same, and the marketing strategies are similar, brands' connotations differ in different contexts. One example of this is the Swedish brand J. Lindeberg. At home it is viewed and marketed as a 'preppy' brand chosen by many regulars of Stockholm's trendier nightclubs. When asked about this brand, one of the New York informants (from prior research, see Hauge 2007 for details) working in retail said: 'Yes, it is nice but it is very gay'. This brand was characterized by its slim fit and bold colours and was favoured by male homosexuals, thus giving it a different connotation than on the Swedish home market. On the background of consumer preferences, the meaning of this brand changed with different contexts. Or to use geographers' favourite truism 'geography matters' (see, for example, Massey and Allen 1984).

McCracken (1988) suggests that meaning originates in the culturally constituted world, moving into goods via intermediaries such as media, marketing, peers, etc. Despite the flaws in this one-way direction of transfer, McCracken's model illuminates consumers' efforts to enhance a positive self-image by acquiring products with desirable meanings. Schudson (1984) suggests that we should view advertising as just one of society's awareness institutions. This line of argument evokes that there is a somewhat reciprocal relationship between the purchaser and what is purchased. Consumers are actively creating meaning through their consumption; they are not passive receivers of marketing stimuli. In this sense, consumers and producers negotiate brand meanings. Thus the meaning of a brand is not fixed, but is repeatedly socially constructed (Fournier 1998). Hence, consumers have a central position in the processes of reading products' symbolic value.

In an overcrowded media marketing landscape, firms have to come up with creative and innovative marketing tools to be noticed (Hracs *et al.* 2013). New technology, and in particular the so-called social media, has challenged traditional mass marketing channels such as newspaper advertising, billboards or TV commercials. Non-traditional marketing can give unexpected, but nevertheless interesting outcomes. A preferred strategy is to try to 'tickle' people's curiosity and make the most of the fact that many want to stand out as informed fashion consumers. The marketing campaign prior to the launch of the Swedish fashion brand Odd Molly is a good example of how effective it can be to make use of curiosity in marketing. Odd Molly's entire launch was built on 2,000 handwritten postcards, and the total costs were about 8,000 SEK (fewer than €1,000). The cards were in the form of what one would send to one's friends and relatives, like holiday greetings, birthday cards, etc. However, Odd Molly sent messages to both the press and fashion retailers. After receiving three to four cards, shops and journalists started to wonder who they were, and what they wanted. Odd Molly sent about five cards to every recipient, and in that way built up anticipation and a buzz around their brand. This exemplifies the importance of finding your own voice, not only in design but also in marketing – something that makes you stand out from the crowd. This unorthodox campaign is a good example of this. According to the rhetoric of the one informant (from prior research) from Odd Molly, their campaign was a 'whisper', not the 'shout' often used by bigger fashion firms (Hauge 2007). What is of crucial importance about this distribution process is that it was almost entirely interpersonal; it was targeted to strategically important people in the industry where it aroused feelings of curiosity and anticipation. From these nodes the information diffused to a broader audience. This is an illustration of how individuals have key positions in the diffusion process.

As the example above illustrates, with a sceptical approach towards traditional marketing, other means for consumer communication become even more important. It also illustrates how individuals play a role in the negotiation of symbolic value; certain consumers are used and listened to as trendsetters or in the process of diffusing certain trends or brands. This tendency seems to be propelled by interactive media. However, the actual shopping experience should not be underestimated in the production process of symbolic value.

### *Retail and consumption*

Retail is where the physical and the intangible side of production have their most visible encounter. This is where the intangible promises sustaining the brand become reality, and is a concrete manifestation of how different processes work in charging products with symbolic value. Consumption spaces are produced, governed and used to advance shopping experience, and shops can be pivotal spaces that valorize products (Hracs *et al.* 2013). The retail space is used to boost consumers' experiences with the brand; firms try to engage customers in an essentially personal way (Moor 2003). One example is the collaboration between the famous architect Koolhaas and fashion brand Prada in creating and designing flagship stores. Technology, space and marketing are integrated to provide new and unique customer experiences, and function as the brand's 'epi-centre' (Crewe 2010). These stores offer an expansion of the shopping experi-ence where the commercial functions enrich and expand the territory of shopping with new spatial relationships, materials, technology applications and service strategies (Hracs *et al.* 2013).

However, even for less ostentatious brands, shops are the space in which the messages of symbolic values are translated and transmitted to consumers. Brands are reliant upon the stores that exhibit their products in a (for them) constructive way and that show their products to potential customers (Crewe and Forster 1993). *Where* products are presented and sold is thus important for how consu-mers prize products. The place where the products are sold and which other brands are there are thus very important for the brand. Firms try to balance exclusivity, being in the 'right' stores and accessibility, being in enough stores.

As with other spaces, even consumption and retail spaces are defined through their web of social relationships; the characteristics of a space are created through social action and interaction (Logan and Molotch 1987: 45). The approach loosely labelled 'aesthetic labour' is helpful, because it describes the role of shop assistants as vehicles of production of symbolic value and/or added brand value (Warhurst *et al.* 2000). Aesthetic labour refers to the process whereby retail employees embody the desired visual image of the organization; they are 'branded service workers'. The jobs' primary requirements are 'looking good' and 'sounding right'. Appearance and matching grooming standards for frontline workers have always been a concern for retail, and in particular the upscale segment. Cultural and symbolic associations created are added value (Pettinger 2004). The physical retail space and shops' frontline personnel can have a genuine effect upon the consumer's perceptions of a brand. Sales people act as the physical and symbolic centre points for groups of specific merchandise and customers. In her study of fashion retail, Leslie (2002) argues that despite the high frequency of part-time employment, poor salaries and uncertain working conditions, clerks are 'expected to draw upon a wealth of accumulated fashion knowledge' (Leslie 2002: 63). Retail staff are given a great responsibility in pre-senting the clothes that are on display in the shop; normally they are expected to actually embody the image by wearing products they sell. Hence, the fashion shop workforce 'are more than just representatives of the company, they are models of the product on sale' (ibid.). Clerks both wear and sell clothes and are thus walking advertisements for the store.

## Conclusion

This chapter has analysed how symbolic value is produced, or how a physical product is charged with immaterial attributes in order to engage consumers and create experiences. It is argued that no single actor has the power to dictate sym-bolic value. Rather, it can be seen as decided through a series of negotiations.

The negotiating processes are social in character, and engage actors involved in relationships on different levels. Actors may be directly involved in the industry, like companies, designers and retailers. Or they may be a part of related industries, such as service providers, media or other cultural industries. One important but often overlooked group in these negotiation processes are the consumers. They are not submissive receivers of marketing stimuli, but active interpreters of different marketing messages. A brand image or a new trend is not invented by experts, and then imposed on consumers which in turn swallow the bait whole. Products and brands catch on in the marketplace because enough of us as consumers decide they have a value or meaning (Walker 2008). The consumers are active participants in the creation of an uncertain, reiterative process that produces symbolic value – as such they are a part of the negotiation process that ultimately decides the level of symbolic value. This chapter adds to the experience economy literature by an explicit constructivist view. Consumers actively construct or create their own subjective representations of objective reality, and new information is linked to former knowledge. These representations are partly based on social status and preferences of larger groups, and partly based on the quality and aesthetics of the product. Then again, there are individual variations, special preferences and personal readings. Even if the social aspect is important, symbolic value cannot only be understood as a group conception. Moreover, if we want to understand how products or services are linked to experience we need to look beyond retail and the point of purchase. The whole value chain and production network are entrenched in the production process of symbolic value.

In the movement towards the final destination of end consumers, different products travel through different economic actors and different socio-institutional settings. However, rather than being dependent on sequential production processes, the creation and attribution of symbolic value is produced in the relational spaces between different socio-economic actors. The production of symbolic value thus has a multifaceted relationship with space and place and is produced both at local and global levels. Some places have a more positive connotation for certain products or industries than others, and can as such work as hotbeds for the production of symbolic value.

This chapter places itself in the recent experience economy literature where the role of the consumer is at the centre of attention (Lorentzen and Jeannerat 2013). This is important today, and will probably be even more important in the time to come because digital technologies accelerate consumerism and choice (Currah 2003). This means we have seen a shift in power favouring the consumers, or a speeding up of the 'democratization of consumption' (Hracs *et al.* 2013). Retailers cannot influence the customers in the same way as they used to and the competition will intensify even more. The ability to deliver memorable experiences and create symbolic value will be even more important to stay competitive.

# References

Andersson, D.E. and Andersson, Å.E. (2013) 'The economic value of experience goods', in J. Sundbo and F. Sørensen (eds) *Handbook on the Experience Economy*, Cheltenham: Edward Elgar.

Arnould, E.J. and Thompson, C.J. (2005) 'Consumer culture theory (CCT): Twenty years of research', *Journal of Consumer Research*, 31(4): 868–82.

Aspers, P. and Beckert, J. (2011) 'Value in markets', in J. Beckert and P. Aspers, (eds) *The Worth of Goods: Valuation and Pricing in the Economy*, Oxford: Oxford University Press.

Banister, E.N. and Hogg, M.K. (2004) 'Negative symbolic consumption and consumers' drive for self-esteem: the case of the fashion industry', *European Journal of Marketing*, 38(7): 850–68.

Bathelt, H. and Glückler, J. (2003) 'Toward a relational economic geography', *Journal of Economic Geography* 3(2): 117–44.

Beltagui, A., Candi, M. and Riedel, J.C.K.H. (2012) 'Design in the experience economy: Using emotional design for service innovation', in K.S. Swan and S. Zou (eds) *Interdisciplinary Approaches to Product Design, Innovation, and Branding in International Marketing, Series: Advances in International Marketing 23*, Bingley: Emerald Group Publishing Limited.

Boswijk, A., Thijssen, T. and Peelen, E. (2007) *A new perspective on the experience economy: Meaningful experiences*, Amsterdam: Pearson Education Benelux.

Bourdieu, P. (1984) *Distinction – A social critique of the judgement of taste*, London: Routledge.

Campbell, C. (1996) 'The meaning of objects and the meaning of actions: A critical note on the sociology of consumption and theories of clothing', *Journal of Material Culture*, 1(1): 93–105.

Caves, R.E. (2003) 'Contracts between art and commerce', *Journal of Economic Perspectives*, 17(2): 73–83.

Crewe, L. (2010) 'Wear: where? The convergent geographies of architecture and fashion', *Environment and Planning A*, 42: 2093–108.

Crewe, L. and Forster, Z. (1993) 'Markets, design, and local agglomeration: the role of the small independent retailer in the workings of the fashion system', *Environment and Planning D: Society and Space*, 11(2): 213–29.

Currah, A. (2003) 'The virtual geographies of retail display', *Journal of Consumer Culture*, 3(1): 5–37.

Dittmar, H. (1992) *The social psychology of material possessions: To have is to be*, Hemel Hempstead: Harvester Wheatsheaf.

Elliott, R. and Wattanasuwan, K. (1998) 'Consumption and the symbolic project of the self', *European Advances in Consumer Research*, 3: 17–20.

Entwistle, J. and Rocamora, A. (2006) 'The field of fashion materialized: A study of London fashion week', *Sociology*, 40(4): 735–51.

Fournier, S. (1998) 'Consumers and their brands: Developing relationship theory in consumer research', *Journal of Consumer Research*, 24(4): 343–73.

Gentile, C., Spiller, N. and Noci, G. (2007) 'How to sustain the customer experience: An overview of experience components that co-create value with the customer', *European Management Journal*, 25(5): 395–410.

Gilbert, D. (2006) 'From Paris to Shanghai: The changing geographies of fashion's world cities', in C. Breward and D. Gilbert (eds) *Fashion's World Cities*, New York: Berg.

Hauge, A. (2007) 'Dedicated followers of fashion – an economic geographic analysis of Swedish fashion industry', PhD thesis, Uppsala University, September 2007.

Hauge, A. (2011) 'Sports equipment: Mixing performance with brands – the role of the consumers', in A.J. Pike (ed.) *Geographies of Brands*, Cheltenham: Edward Elgar.

Hauge, A. (2012) 'Creative industry: Lacklustre business – Swedish fashion firms' combination of business and aesthetics as a competitive strategy', *Creative Industries Journal*, 5(2): 105–18.

Hauge, A. and Hracs, B. (2010) 'See the sound, hear the style: Collaborative linkages between indie musicians and fashion designers in local scenes', *Industry and Innovation*, 17(1): 113–29.

Hauge, A. and Power, D. (2013) 'Quality, difference and regional advantage: the case of the winter sports industry', *European Urban and Regional Studies*, 20(4): 385–400.

Hauge, A., Malmberg, A. and Power, D. (2009) 'The spaces and places of Swedish fashion', *European Planning Studies*, 17(4): 529–47.

Hollenbeck, C.R. and Zinkhan, G.M. (2010) 'Anti-brand communities, negotiation of brand meaning, and the learning process: The case of Wal-Mart', *Consumption, Markets and Culture* 13(3): 325–45.

Hoyer, W.D. and MacInnis, D.J. (2001) *Consumer behaviour*, Boston: Houghton-Mifflin.

Hracs, B.J., Jakob, D. and Hauge, A. (2013) 'Standing out in the crowd: The rise of exclusivity-based strategies to compete in the contemporary marketplace for music and fashion', *Environment and Planning A*, 45(5): 1144–61.

Jessop, B. (2006) 'Spatial fixes, temporal fixes, and spatio-temporal fixes', in N. Castree and D. Gregory (eds) *David Harvey: a Critical Reader*, Oxford: Blackwell.

Leslie, D. (2002) 'Gender, retail employment and the clothing commodity chain', *Gender, place, and culture*, 9(1): 61–76.

Lloyd, R. (2006) *Neo-Bohemia: Art and commerce in the postindustrial city*, New York: Routledge.

Logan, J.R. and Molotch, H.L. (1987) *Urban fortunes: The political economy of place*, Oakland, CA: University of California Press.

Lorentzen, A. and Jeannerat, H. (2013) 'Urban and regional studies in the experience economy: What kind of turn?' *European Urban and Regional Studies*, 20(4): 363–9.

Lury, C. (2004) *Brands: the logos of the global economy*, New York: Routledge.

Malmberg, A. and Power, D. (2006) 'True clusters: A severe case of conceptual headache', in B. Asheim, P. Cooke and R. Martin (eds) *Clusters in Regional Development, Regional Development and Public Policy Series*, London: Routledge.

Massey, D. and Allen, J. (eds) (1984) *Geography matters!: A reader*, Cambridge: Cambridge University Press.

McCracken, G. (1988) *Culture and consumption*, Bloomington, IN: Indiana University Press.

McCracken, G. (2005) *Culture and consumption II: Markets, meaning, and brand management*, Bloomington, IN: Indiana University Press.

Molotch, H. (2005) *Where stuff comes from: How toasters, toilets, cars, computers and many other things come to be as they are*, New York: Routledge.

Moor, E. (2003) 'Branded spaces: The scope of "new marketing"', *Journal of consumer culture*, 3(1): 39–60.

Pasquinelli, C. (2013) 'The economic geography of brand associations', *CIND research paper* 2013: 2. Online. Available at: http://uu.diva-portal.org/smash/get/diva2:665281/FULLTEXT01.pdf (accessed 28 October 2014).

Pettinger, L. (2004) 'Brand culture and branded workers: Service work and aesthetic labour in fashion retail', *Consumption Markets and Culture*, 7(2): 165–84.

Pike, A. (2011) 'Introduction: Brand and branding geographies', A. Pike (ed.) *Brands and Branding*, Cheltenham: Edward Elgar.

Pine, B.J. and Gilmore, J.H. (1999) *The experience economy: Work is theatre and every business a stage*, Boston: Harvard Business School Press.

Potts, J.D., Hartley, J., Banks, J.A., Burgess, J.E., Cobcroft, R.S., Cunningham, S.D. and Montgomery, L. (2008) 'Consumer co-creation and situated creativity', *Industry and Innovation*, 15(5): 459–74.

Power, D. and Hauge, A. (2008) 'No Man's Brand—Brands, Institutions, and Fashion', *Growth and Change*, 39(1): 123–43.

Ravasi, D. and Rindova, V. (2008) 'Symbolic value creation', in D. Barry and H. Hansen (eds) *The Sage Handbook of New Approaches to Organization Studies*, London: SAGE Publications Ltd.

Santagata, W. (2004) 'Creativity, fashion, and market behavior', in D. Power and A. Scott (eds) *Cultural Industries and the Production of Culture*, London: Routledge.

Schudson, M. (1984) *Advertising, the uneasy persuasion: Its dubious impact on American society*, New York: Basic Books, Inc.

Sundbo, J. and F. Sørensen (2013) 'Introduction to the experience economy', in J. Sundbo and F. Sørensen (eds) *Handbook on the Experience Economy*, Cheltenham: Edward Elgar.

Tran, Y. (2010) 'Generating stylistic innovation: A process perspective', *Industry and Innovation*, 17(2): 131–61.

Walker, R. (2008) *Buying in: The secret dialogue between what we buy and who we are*, New York: Random House.

Warhurst, C., Nickson, D., Witz, A. and Cullen, A.M. (2000) 'Aesthetic labour in interactive service work: some case study evidence from the "new" Glasgow', *Service Industries Journal*, 20(3): 1–18.

Weller, S.A. (2008) 'Beyond "Global Production Network" metaphors: Australian fashion week's trans-sectoral synergies', *Growth and Change*, 39(1): 104–22.

# 4 Municipalities as experiential stagers in the new economy

## Emerging practices in Frederikshavn, North Denmark

*Jens Kaae Fisker*

## Introduction

Two significant processes of change that have unfolded across the globe in recent decades serve as points of departure for this chapter. First, economic geographies from the local to the global have been restructured, and second, the workings of states and governments have been reconfigured in various ways. Obviously such processes of change do not unfold in isolation from one another; quite to the contrary. They have been deeply intertwined as global capitalism has transformed itself in a continuing effort to overcome the internal contradictions that plunges it into occasional bouts of crisis. The emerging 'new' economy has been given many names, many descriptions and many explanations. Likewise the ways in which state practices and forms of organizing have been described and explained in many different ways. In this chapter I do not intend to argue which theoretical concepts hold more or less explanatory power in these regards. Rather I attempt to provide a contextualized discussion that grapples concretely with the intertwined nature of these omnipresent and continuous discussions, i.e. the intertwined relationship between a changing state system and a restructured global economy. My hope is to shed new light on the interrelations of discursive and functional changes as they unfold in a specific geographic context.

Given that this is a book about the experience economy it is hardly surprising that I turn to this specific interpretation of the new economy. My doing so is not an indication that I believe this to be a more valid interpretation of the new economy than others. It is indicative, rather, of the fact that the experience economy has achieved a privileged discursive position in the geographical context that I have been exploring empirically. When the Danish ministries of industry ('Erhvervsministeriet') and culture ('Kulturministeriet') teamed up in the year 2000 to produce a report on Denmark's creative potential, Pine and Gilmore's (1998; 1999) notion of an ascending experience economy was used as a driving argument. The report positioned culture and experiences as a growth sector that Denmark had to embark on to stay competitive in the future. Accordingly it advocated intensified relations between the business sector and the cultural sector in order to exploit the perceived growth potential (Erhvervsministeriet and Kulturministeriet 2000: 22ff.). In 2003 it was followed up by a government strategy on 'Denmark in the Cultural and Experience Economy' and in 2008 by another report called 'Growth through Experiences' (Regeringen 2003; Erhvervs- og Byggestyrelsen 2008).

These national level strategies and government-sponsored analyses are indicative of a widespread experiential turn that has affected strategies and practices at all levels of the Danish state system (Lorentzen 2013; Bille 2010). The turn, however, has not simply been characterized by the import of experience economy notions into political discourse and strategic action. Rather, an array of mobile ideas has come together in the Danish context of public policy formation. Bille (2010) suggests specifically that notions of experience economy derived mostly from Pine and Gilmore (1998, 1999) have entered into a combination with ideas derived from the UK policy focus on creative industries, and Richard Florida's notions of a creative class. Elsewhere I have suggested that Charles Landry's (2000) ideas about creative city-making have also become part of this mix at the local level of government (Fisker 2013: 90ff.). In Frederikshavn municipality, where this chapter is empirically grounded, the influx of these fashionable ideas is also discernible. Furthermore, the relation to a changing global economy is accentuated by the fact that the experiential turn coincided with the onset of a local economic crisis.

While experience economy explanations of the new economy fall short of delivering complete answers as to where economies are heading, they have nevertheless been able to pinpoint some of the more substantial changes observed today. These include altered spatialities of production and consumption, and more specifically the commodification of experience and of place. Concurrently the adoption of experiential municipal strategies has served to reposition the roles of municipal actors in peculiar ways that influence the interfaces between state, citizens and private businesses. They now actively engage in practices which can be referred to as 'experiential staging' (tentatively introduced by Jeannerat and Crevoisier (2010) and elaborated by Jeannerat (2015) in this volume); a term that may find utility in wider debates on changing structures and practices of government and governance. As the chapter progresses I attend in detail to these particular points through theoretical discussion and empirical insight. Along the way I attempt to clarify the connections that bind these distinct topics.

First, the spatialities of production and consumption are discussed with a point of departure in the particular nature of experiential products and the ways in which they are consumed. This leads me to some wider points about how capitalism transforms itself to find new avenues for capital accumulation, and to a number of questions that arise with regards to redrawings of economic geographies in general. Second, I attempt to open up these geographies by attending specifically to place-based experiential production and consumption. Third, I employ the insights attained thus far as a foundation for discussing the role of municipal actors in a setting, where place-based experiential production and consumption have become integral to the everyday reality that municipal actors have to operate within. It is at this point that the notion of experiential staging comes to the forefront of attention. The small city of Frederikshavn, North

Denmark, is visited at intervals throughout the chapter to discern how all of this can play out locally.

## Spatialities of production and consumption

Production and consumption are not truly separable. They comprise different aspects of the same processes; deeply intertwined, interdependent and ultimately constituted in dialectical tension with one another. This is not new, but perhaps recent developments have served to accentuate it further. The spatial heart of the matter is phrased appropriately by Goodman *et al.* (2010: 25), who assert that 'consumption can be said to produce space and place, while production can be said to equally consume space and place'. Consumption in this sense is not just a functional aspect of the economy, but a set of activities that plays out in place as components of spatial practice, thereby contributing to the production of space and place. Commodity production too implies a set of spatially situated activities which both produce and consume space. Goodman *et al.* (2010: 25) argue furthermore that 'conceptualizing production and consumption in this way allows us to open up these two processes and practices to fruitfully explore their dialectical and situated complexities, relationalities and spatialities'. Not least so where experiential aspects of the new economy are concerned. The treatment of production and consumption as separate entities has been tied up with the structures of industrial societies in which consumer goods were produced in factories far removed (in both absolute and relative space) from their place of consumption. With the production of experiences instead of material goods, the interconnectedness with consumption becomes more apparent and much harder to ignore. Tourism scholars, unsurprisingly, have had to grapple with this for a long time, because this mode of production has been all the more obvious in this sector of the economy. Ateljevic (2000: 371) for instance adopts the notion of 'a nexus of circuits operating within production-consumption dialects enabled by the process of negotiated (re)production', which becomes outspokenly explicit in tourism and experience economy, wherein the production-consumption dichotomy cannot be spatially separated, because often the place of production is also the place of consumption. In this sense components of the new economy have become what Crevoisier and Guex (2014) call presential economies, i.e. regional economies that rely not on their productive base, but on their presential base.

Both tourism and experience economy depend on experiential commodification; they rely on the premise that human experience can be marketed and sold. Exchange value is thus based not on material functionality, even though marketed experiences may be mediated through such (e.g. vehicles for transport or buildings for accommodation), or be supported by the use of material goods (e.g. sports and outdoor equipment). In this sense the frontiers of capital accumulation are advanced further into the spaces of leisure, which were previously reserved primarily for the restitution of workers. They are now made to double as means to generate consumption and hence as mainstream vehicles of accumulation.

Britton (1991: 465) among others (see also Toffler (1970) and Holbrook and Hirschman (1981)) observed early on that this was

> an important recent dynamic: the creation and marketing of experiences is becoming increasingly an overt and conscious avenue for capitalist accumulation.... Increasingly, sensations, feelings, perceptions, sensory stimulations, taste, and style are being packaged and marketed in their own right, as well as indirectly through tangible commodities.

By the end of the 1990s Pine and Gilmore had also picked up this tendency and introduced the metaphor that work had become theatre and every business a stage.

These insights entail a two-fold blurring of dichotomies that extends from production and consumption to include work and leisure. Not only is it increasingly unclear where and by whom production and consumption are undertaken, it is also not always clear whether people partake in these activities as workers or as leisure-time consumers. This is not due to experiential commodification alone, but rests also on changing patterns of lifestyle and work, in which the latter becomes a defining element of the former. For an increasing number of people, working life is not just about retaining their livelihood, but also an endeavour to create and sustain a desired image of the self; something often attributed explicitly to consumption practices. Mansvelt (2005: 7) for instance points out that 'consumption is not simply about the using up of things, but also involves the production of meaning, experience, knowledge or objects'. In this sense consumption is a symbolic act of self-imaging, where people signify their desired affiliation with certain groups and movements through acts of consumption (Goodman *et al.* 2010: 25). But jobs too have come to play a part in this, not least in those segments of the labour force that Florida (2002) identified as core groups of his much-debated creative class.

What can be derived thus far for the current purposes is that understandings of production and consumption that are based on narrowly dichotomous modes of thought fall short of attaining adequate explanatory power. The complex interrelations which are obviously at play must be kept alive by embracing their inherent dialectic tensions. These in turn become most apparent when a spatial perspective is applied in which production-consumption activities are situated in absolute, relative and relational space(time) (see Harvey 2006). In this way it is possible to make visible how the commodification of human experience also produces changes in economic geographies.

## *Place-based experiential production-consumption*

In place-based experience economy the commodification of experience also implies the commodification of place. As Britton (1991: 465) observes places are 'marketed as desirable products: not necessarily as ends in themselves, but because visits to them, and the seeking of anticipated signs and symbols, are a vehicle for experiences which are to be collected, consumed, and compared'. To account for the ways in which experiential production-consumption can be place-based, Smidt-Jensen and Lorentzen (2011: 14ff.) introduce a threefold distinction: (1) place in an experiential product; (2) experiential products situated in place; and (3) place as an experiential product. The first relation ties in with Pine and Gilmore's notion of experience as an attribute that can be infused in any product to generate added exchange value. Place-based experiences of this kind are generally material goods of a more or less conventional nature, which have been infused with place-based narratives and imageries that can convey anything from the origin of the product, over the methods of its production, to its influence and meaning in the locality from whence it came. Material relations with the place in question are not necessarily present. Crevoisier and Guex (2014) refer to transactions of such products as non-presential but referential, because specific places are utilized due to their symbolic qualities.

In the second relation the experiential product must necessarily be consumed in place – consumption is presential. The most obvious examples of such products are theme parks and concerts, which can be described as situated experiences. It also includes events staged by retailers or producers (of material goods) to showcase products. Such activities perform a double role by generating on-site consumption and by constructing and reinforcing marketized images, for instance of authenticity through a visible connection between place and product.

The third relation entails a deeper interrelation between commodity and place, because it implies that place plays a critical role in generating the marketed experiences. Experiential commodification is place specific and relies on the totality of that place. Attempts to identify producers and consumers are close to impossible. The experience of a busy shopping street is produced as much by the hordes of consumers milling about as it is by the retailers who put their products on display, the homeless beggar on the sidewalk, the busker on the corner, and the people just passing through. The producer-consumer dichotomy is dissolved, because the experiential production of this space relies on numerous actors not captured by the dichotomy. Even non-human actors – e.g. weather – can play a decisive role in producing widely different experiences of the same slice of absolute space at different times. The notion that the production process is something inherently under the control of producers has no merit here. That does not mean, however, that actors with an economic interest in the commodification of place do not try their utmost to retain some measure of control over the experiential production of space.

In this way the extension of capitalism into the sphere of human experience also becomes a new battleground in the struggle for the use of and right to space. When place is situated by powerful actors as a commodity, it entails that its exchange value is prioritized over its use-value. Only certain kinds of human experience therefore get to count; specifically those that (affluent) consumers are willing to pay for. Others, and especially those deemed disruptive of profitable experiences, are excluded and fought against. The (violent) removal of undesirables such as the homeless and beggars from shopping districts and other experience-scapes is just one example of how efforts to enhance the experiential commodity of place have serious repercussions for disadvantaged social groups, who are denied their right to space. Such processes of exclusion also take place in less violent but equally powerful guises when, for instance, local residents of popular tourist destinations are alienated by the degree of commodification that the tourism industry wields on the places they call home.

## A rough transition

At this point I turn attention to the locality at hand: Frederikshavn. With an urban population of 23,000 (60,000 in the municipality) Frederikshavn is a small third tier city in the Danish periphery (see Figure 4.1). In this chapter I am concerned with the city itself and not the wider municipality. This is due to certain

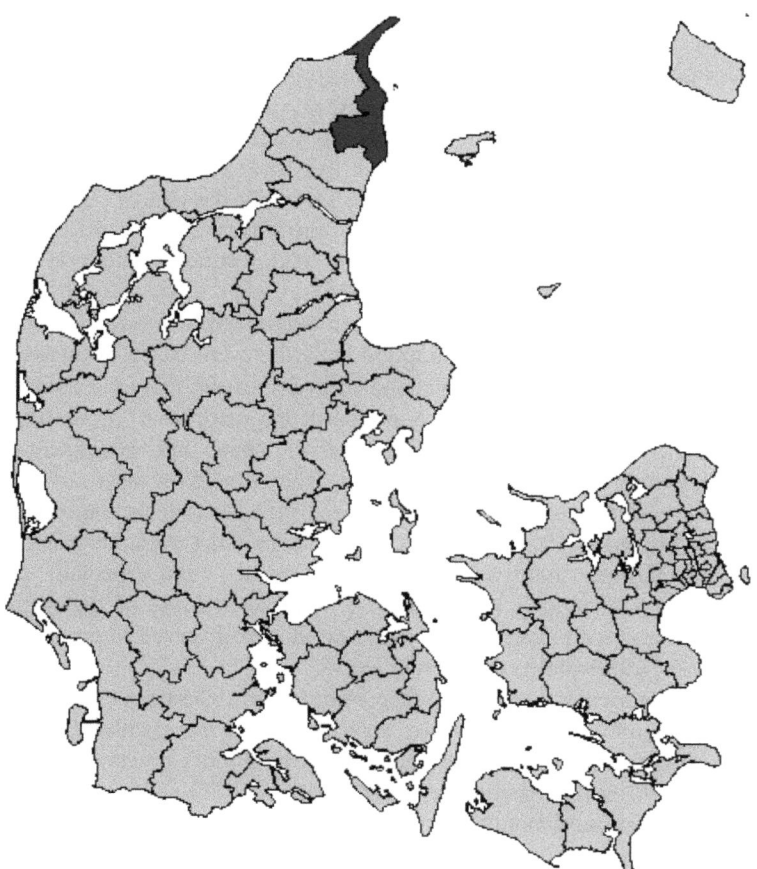

*Figure 4.1* Location of Frederikshavn Municipality (source: Wikimedia Commons 2006).

recent events that I shall return to shortly. Compared to other cities in the national urban system, Frederikshavn's urban history is rather short. It has its roots in changing regional patterns of trade during a string of Scandinavian and European wars fought from the seventeenth to the early nineteenth century that served to reposition the fishing village of Fladstrand as a strategically important location for wartime trade. After its name change to Frederikshavn in 1818, when merchant city status was granted by the king, the strategic location was exploited to attain significant infrastructural upgrades (harbour, railway and better road connections) that proved instrumental in subsequent processes of local industrialization. Because of this history Frederikshavn has stood out in the national urban system as one of the few thoroughly industrialized Danish cities (Nakskov and Elsinore are other notable examples). In the late twentieth century the local economy had essentially evolved into a monoculture based on ship-building industries (see Fisker 2013 for a detailed historical account).

In terms of production-consumption spatialities, the local economy in Frederikshavn has apparently been propelled through a rushed transformation. Before 1998–9 shipbuilding industries dominated the city. Their production practices were far removed from consumption activities as they did not produce for consumers, but catered to the transport needs of other industries. Shipbuild-ing was supplemented by cross-border shopping from Sweden and Norway, enabled by EU legislation that allowed for tax-free trade on international ferry services. Two important events almost coincided towards the end of the 1990s. First, the shipbuilding industries collapsed due to the closure of Danyard around which a shipbuilding monoculture had evolved, and second, changes in EU legislation brought an end to the cross-border retail.

As an economic space Frederikshavn had been dominated by production acti-vities, while the most significant consumption activities were based exclusively on the legislative opportunity that enabled the attraction of shopping guests from Gothenburg, Sweden. It was not based on any particular qualities of place, other than the fact that consumer goods were comparatively cheap and Frederikshavn was readily accessible by regular ferry services. The coinciding losses of pro-duction- and consumption-oriented bases of local livelihoods meant that efforts to cope with the immediate crisis could not be limited to addressing the grievous situation in the maritime industry. The closed shipyard – and especially the massive unemployment among metal workers – attracted most of the initial attention, but the sense of losing on two fronts at once also served to produce a wider awareness of vulnerability to external forces.

Since 1998–9 the local economy of Frederikshavn has experienced structural changes that are significant in at least two aspects: (1) the mono-cultural struc-ture of the maritime industries has been substituted by a more diversified array of specialized small- and medium-sized companies; and (2) service activities have in large parts replaced manufacturing activities (even within the maritime industries, where no new ships are built). The latter shift began before 1998–9, both in terms of employment (minus 6 per cent for industry and plus 5 per cent for service from 1992–7) and exchange value creation (minus 28 per cent for industry and plus 24 per cent for service) (Frederikshavn Kommune 2001). In terms of material realities, then, the transition was not as abrupt as it may appear at first glance. In retrospect interviewees position 1998–9 as a decisive turning point (e.g. Sørensen 2007; Jentsch 2012), but this should be attributed mostly to the ways in which they attempt to construct a meaningful narrative. Furthermore the shock effect did in fact produce a discursive and symbolic turning point. It became the symbolic marker of the shipbuilding era coming to an end, thus allowing local actors to adopt new mindsets regarding possible local futures.

## Roles of the municipality in experiential staging

Given a capitalist society in which the human experience of place has been com-modified, municipal actors are left in a peculiar situation. It is their jurisdiction to plan the materiality of public space and to regulate activities within it. Their decisions in both regards influence which kind of places that emerge and evolve locally. Do they act as the supporting cast of experiential industries by designing and investing in public spaces that serve the interests of this sort of business? Do they, in other words, seek to optimize the qualities of place to increase its exchange value as an experiential commodity? And how do they seek to balance these aspirations with other (social, cultural and environmental) concerns? Observation of local practices reveal that this is partly the case, but a focus on the local scale is not sufficient to understand the ways in which practices are entangled in a wider web of practices and rationalities. The roles that municipal actors play in the new economy, and specifically in the experiential commodifi-cation of place, are thus tied up with more pervasive transformations of state structures and governance practices.

The term 'governance' has attained prominence as an analytical concept due to perceived deficiencies in the term 'government' to provide a meaningful depiction of the processes through which society is governed. The state has ceased to be the only relevant actor to behold, because decision-making proces-ses now include an array of non-governmental actors. Still the state holds a pri-vileged position in governance processes, because formal power continues to be vested in the institutions of the state. As Allen (2009: 201) notes, however:

> the privatization of authority, the shift from government to governance and the proliferation of regulatory bodies are among those changes that have made it altogether more difficult to pin down the institutional geography of power, especially when it comes to tracking the decision-making processes that shape political outcomes.

The study of power relations, then, becomes all the more pertinent when a shift from hierarchical government to more complex governance landscapes occurs. Hierarchical features have been supplemented and partly substituted by various horizontal and cross-scale relations. With this in mind Torfing *et al.* (2012: 10f.) assert that governance does not replace but merely supplements government, through 'an uneven and combined development of traditional forms of government and new forms of governance that varies from country to country, from policy area to policy areas, and between different scales'. More specifically they argue that increasingly the new role of government is the governing of governance – or meta-governance.

The transition from government to governance has been thoroughly politicized, first by calls for public participation and citizen empowerment and second by the neo-liberal wave that has swept through public policy. This is essentially what David Harvey (1989) describes, when he identifies an entrepreneurial turn in local governments across the US context. In his narrative of change the rise of governance has been closely associated with a transformation of local government practices designed specifically to serve the interests of capital. Local governments across Europe and North America are increasingly expected to engage in interlaced competition; an expectation that has been built into the state apparatus itself. As Jones and Ward (2002: 137) conclude: 'a cornerstone of neo-liberalism has been the state's internalizing and subsequent creation in institutional form of interurban competition'. This has also been the case in the Danish context. Pedersen (2011) has chronicled how the Danish welfare state has transformed itself into a competitive state, and Carter (2011) shows how municipalities are being 'compelled to compete'. It is into this emerging competitive setting that the experience economy concept is introduced as a way for municipalities (and for the country as a whole) to generate competitive advantage.

## Municipal staging practices

The experiential turn in public policy, institutionalization of inter-place competition, and emerging entrepreneurial attitudes have combined to produce a setting in which municipalities are situated as key players in the production of commodified experience spaces. The new governance landscape offers a convenient match between the experiential form of capitalist production and the governance mechanisms currently available, because it allows for the economic actors that rely on the production of attractive experience spaces to be involved in decision-making around issues of public space. The practices that emerge when this match is exploited can be referred to through the notion of territorial staging. Jeannerat and Crevoisier (2010) introduced the term tentatively to aid the construction of an experience economy counterpart to territorial innovation systems. They held that such theories were inept at grasping the specific ways in which experiential aspects of regional economies call for an integrated understanding of production and consumption. Instead they suggested conceiving of territorial staging systems in which production resources are employed to perform diverse acts of stage setting, while consumption resources are directed towards various forms of experiential engagement. In accordance with points made earlier in this chapter, they do not conceive of production and consumption as spatially separated activities. Rather they conceive of them as sharing a common (territorially underpinned) stage on which experiences are co-produced and co-consumed.

It is into this complex set of production-consumption activities that municipalities insert themselves, when they become involved in experiential staging practices. Their specific involvement centres around stage setting activities. The complexity of this practice is not only given by the fact that multiple heterogeneous actors are involved, but also by the diverse nature of the involved activities. These include at least the three following forms:

1 Material staging: the provision of cultural sector infrastructure and facilities (e.g. theatres, concert venues, museums, sports stadia and arenas, congress centres, etc.);
2 Symbolic staging: activities directed at place branding (extra local) and identity (re)production (local);
3 Institutional staging: initiatives with the purpose of forging, developing and maintaining alliances across the public, private and civic spheres of local communities through the establishment of new, or development of existing, institutions.

Throughout the 2000s Danish municipalities have engaged in place-making practices in the interest of experiential production, i.e. experiential staging with a territorial underpinning. They have been engaged in place branding aimed at the construction and communication of place-based images, which position their locality or region as particularly suitable for experiential engagement (Smidt-Jensen 2012; Jensen 2007). They have invested in cultural infrastructure, either on their own or through public-private partnerships, and thereby literally built stages for experiential purposes (Lorentzen 2011b; Jensen 2007). In other cases they have been more or less directly involved in experiential production, when they invest financial and human resources in local events such as festivals, sporting events and conventions (Galland and Arthur 2010; Lorentzen 2013). And finally they have redesigned and refurbished public spaces with perceived experiential potentials (Skot-Hansen 2007; Jensen 2007). In a detailed study of municipal strategies in the North Denmark Region, Lorentzen (2013: 469) finds that all municipalities in the region 'have embarked on experience-based urban strategies as a response to serious challenges of industrial restructuring and a shrinking population. They hope to attract new citizens, boost tourism and develop new branches of industry'. However, she also concludes (2013: 470) that these strategies 'only very indirectly approach the structural challenges of the demography, employment and skills bases of the small cities'. If this is indeed the case, important questions emerge: how have these experience-based strategies interacted with other approaches to local development? Have efforts aimed at traditional local sectors been supplanted by experiential strategies or have they entered into some kind of coexistence?

### *Material, symbolic and institutional staging*

Since the late 1990s Frederikshavn municipality has also become involved in various forms of experiential staging practices. This has been shown in earlier studies that provide detailed accounts of the changes in municipal practice that have occurred. Lorentzen (2007, 2011a, 2011b, 2013) illuminates how Frederik-shavn has been rebranded with the direct involvement of municipal actors. She also accounts for the ways in which experiential aspects have been introduced in the local economy through events, tourism and urban amenity investment (Lorentzen 2011b). And finally she shows how 'the experience economy has been formally institutionalized in Frederikshavn with the introduction of the experience economy concept in many parts of the municipal strategy' (Lorentzen 2013: 468). Additionally, Therkildsen (2007) details the introduction of experi-ences into local planning documents in the early 2000s, and provides an analysis of how innovative practices of urban planning were induced during the local crisis by creating a period marked by 'fruitful panic' – and characterized by Lorentzen (2011b: 108) as a window of opportunity. Finally my own study of municipal practice in the Centre for Culture and Leisure from 1998 to 2013 shows how the changing practices of municipal actors, and gradual institutionali-zation of experience economy thinking, has unfolded through a number of phases in which underpinning rationalities have been continually de- and recon-structed, while changing material conditions have resumed to alter spaces of the possible for municipal actors (Fisker 2013: 103ff.).

Municipal involvement in staging practices can be broken down according to the three aspects of staging identified in the previous section (see Table 4.1 for an overview of staging activities in Frederikshavn). In terms of material staging, the municipality has invested heavily in cultural infrastructure and urban ameni-ties, especially in the first five years after the economic crash. In this period a regional concert venue was erected next to city hall, the city centre was redesig-ned and refurbished according to a distinctly maritime theme, and a sports and events arena was constructed through a public-private partnership. Apart from such conventional material staging, an array of more creative initiatives was taken as well. A Norwegian developer enquired about the possibility of planning for an artificial ski slope on the outskirts of town, and the idea received support among both politicians and public servants. Extensive planning measures were taken to facilitate the project, which eventually failed to materialize. Today the small road Skicentervej ('ski centre road') serves as a material reminder of the scrapped ski slope. The absence of mountains and reliable snowfall in winter means that Denmark has almost no traditions for domestic skiing, which made the proposal stand out as something of an oddity.

The exotic nature of the project was echoed by the establishment in 2004 of an artificial palm beach north of the harbour. Once again the idea challenged the physical geography of Denmark, thereby implicitly transmitting the message that nothing is impossible. The idea was realized through entrepreneuring practice by a few public servants in the Centre for Parks and Roads, who secured political backing during the annual 'green tour', where public servants take politicians on a tour of ongoing projects. During an intermission they made a gimmicky demonstration of their idea, which was well received by politicians. Public ser-vants reacted quickly and implemented the idea immediately, because as one of

Table 4.1 Significant municipal involvement in experiential staging (see also Lorentzen 2011: 105)

|  | *Municipal involvement in staging* |
| --- | --- |
| Material | Det Musiske Hus (regional concert venue) |
|  | Arena Nord (sports and events arena) |
|  | Iscenter Nord (arena for ice sports) |
|  | Palmestranden (artificial palm beach) |
|  | Skibakken (artificial skiing centre) |
|  | Maskinhallen (cultural centre in an old power plant) |
|  | Palm City (golf course, holiday homes, hotel and entertainment facilities) |
| Symbolic | From Shipyard City to Host City (rebranding and communication strategy) |
|  | Experience Economy as one of four 'growth tracks' |
|  | Rolf Jensen's *Dream Society* as compulsory reading among public servants in the technical department |
| Institutional | Establishment of the Centre for Culture and Leisure |
|  | Frederikshavn Event (semi-public events bureau) |
|  | Karizma (programme for experiential and entrepreneurial municipal practice) |

them observes in retrospect: 'we knew that with this one, it's a matter of getting it executed before anyone finds out what it is they've agreed to' (Heftholm 2012, Interview). Other actors have since contributed to the staging of 'tropical' experiences. Ferry company Stena Line invested in tropical-themed The Reef Hotel and Resort, while utilizing the palm beach heavily in their Swedish marketing campaigns. And private developers approached the municipality with the project Palm City, a resort-style development featuring a golf course, holiday homes, hotel and entertainment facilities. Just like the ski slope, however, this project never left the drawing board; this time because investors pulled out during the global financial crisis. Once again the municipality had already contributed with the necessary physical planning to allow development to go ahead.

The municipality became involved in symbolic forms of staging. Most significantly rebranding of the city and restoration of local pride was on the agenda. To this end an alliance of municipal actors, local businesses and communication consultants (local and extra local) was loosely created. Efforts were directed at disseminating the message that Frederikshavn was changing in a positive direction, and that the many negative stories that had flourished during the crisis belonged entirely to the past. In 2004 consultants were hired to develop a new communication strategy. They came up with six key messages that they advised the municipality to emphasize in both local and extra local communication. Among them was the message that 'Frederikshavn moves from shipyard city to host city' (Gaardbo Comm 2004: 13). This caught on in media reports and public debate as an appropriate label to apply to the local experiential turn. The symbolic significance of experience economy discourse has since been strengthened by its positioning as one of four 'growth tracks' – along with maritime industries, energy and food – in the municipal strategy for economic development. Internally in the municipal organization it is also noteworthy that the technical director made Rolf Jensen's book *Dream Society* (1999) compulsory reading for his employees. The book is a Danish counterpart to Pine and Gilmore and was published around the same time. It also played a part in the establishment of the annual local cultural festival Days of Tordenskjold in 1998; one of the most obvious examples of experiential activities in Frederikshavn. The idea was born in the midst of the crisis and was an attempt to salvage some local pride by staging fictionalized theatrical accounts about the Danish-Norwegian naval war hero Tordenskjold, who had a brief spell at the local fortress in the early eighteenth century. It was staged on the harbour next to the shipyard and theatre was supplemented by other experiential activities. The event has become a success both in terms of the attracted audience and the citizen mobilization required to stage it.

Institutionally the municipality aided the establishment of experiential stages early on by creating the Centre for Culture and Leisure in 1998 as an initial reaction to the local crisis. Headed by the mayor, local politicians were intent on boosting this policy area, and the many acts of material staging accounted for earlier were made possible by this institutional foundation. With the physical stages in place, municipal actors took the next step in institutional staging by entrepreneuring a semi-public events bureau – Frederikshavn Event ApS – the purpose of which was to make sure that high-profile events would be staged in Frederikshavn's new facilities. More recently, the entrepreneurial culture of practice that had emerged in the municipal organization was intended to be institutionalized, specifically with reference to the experience economy, through the Karizma programme. This was a policy experiment in which the Centre for Culture and Leisure sought to make space for deinstitutionalized (creative) practice within the organization, while also establishing a platform for citizen outreach. Essentially Karizma was supposed to support the creation of an experience-related entrepreneurial culture that reached across municipality, citizens and local businesses.

It should be clear thus far that Frederikshavn municipality took on the role of experiential stager. Their actions, however, have been headed in two separate directions. Local politicians mostly viewed the experience economy as a new supplement to the maritime industries. Their primary focus was still on restoring these industries to their former glory. The experiential turn did not imply a turn away from maritime industries; it was merely an addition, which was pursued only in ways which did not conflict with industrial interests. This is evident from the political attention to spatial segregation of experiential staging and maritime industrial activities. Debates within city council and various subcommittees show that politicians were extremely cautious of the new practices, which they feared could be a threat to the continuation of industrial activities. In 2005 a new plan for physical development of the harbour was made in which it is repeatedly made clear that the harbour is meant for industrial purposes, and that 'softer' activities will only be allowed to a very limited degree and in specially designated areas. During the final debate, in which the plan was passed through the council, all parties made it explicit that they too saw the harbour first and foremost as an industrial space, which, in the words of one councillor, 'had to be protected from the city'.

The idea that such a harbour could be used for other – purportedly more lucrative – purposes in the new economy had been introduced to councillors when the planning committee sought inspiration for their new plan. It was not well received. One councillor lamented that 'there have been forces attempting to use parts of the harbour … to build housing' and concluded that the new plan was good, because 'it has now once and for all been rammed home that Frederikshavn Harbour is an industrial harbour' (Frederikshavn Kommune 2005 – council meeting audio). Yet the majority of councillors were not against the experiential turn as long as it did not conflict with industrial interests. They wholeheartedly supported projects such as the ski slope and the palm beach, because they kept a healthy distance from the industrial harbour. The only example to date of experiential staging that has been able to break this segregation is the cultural festival Tordenskioldsdage, which was situated on the harbour from 1998 to 2012. Even this event, however, had to relocate when its usual site was occupied by industrial activities in 2013.

## Conclusion

The case of municipal practice in Frederikshavn as it evolved from 1998 to 2013 bears witness to an experiential turn through which municipal actors took on the role of experiential stagers. They attempted in various ways to pave the way for a thorough transformation of place that would enable it to be marketed and sold as an experiential commodity to tourists, visitors, as well as old and new citizens. To achieve this they utilized their privileged position to cater for private developers who shared their aspirations. They also allowed public servants to entrepreneur spectacular projects that matched the experiential visions. In several cases the proactive approach meant that municipal resources were wasted on projects that never materialized, because private developers backed out at a later stage. On the other hand, the realization of other projects might not have taken place without the change in attitude that occurred. This ties back to Patsy Healey's (2004: 100) assertion that:

> a mode of urban governance which encourages creativity has to learn to experiment and therefore to learn from failure as well as success, and to recognize that redundancy in resource use is as much a positive quality, spreading access to opportunity and support, as it is a negative inefficiency.

The question that remains unanswered, however, is where to draw the line. How much risk is acceptable for a municipal organization to commit to? In the context of experiential staging this is a distinctly relevant problematic to consider, where material staging processes are concerned, as these are generally both the most costly and the ones where public actors take on most of the risk (as shown for instance by Harvey (1989)).

Denmark may not be the most critical case for studying the commodification of experience and of place, at least not when it comes to the repercussions for different social groups that this transformation within capitalism can be expected to have. What does stand out is that such concerns are nowhere to be found in the government strategies and reports that deal with the ascendancy of a Danish experience economy. Despite the fact that some of these are co-authored by the Ministry of Culture, their focus seems to be exclusively growth oriented. They ask not how 'experiensation' (as Smidt-Jensen (2012) refers to it) can be regulated and controlled. On the contrary, their concerns seem only to lie with questions of how the process can be promoted, encouraged and accelerated. As such, these publications are overt examples of the kind of thinking that the shift from welfare state to competitive state has given rise to. The challenges of generating and retaining competitiveness outweigh all other concerns. This does not mean that other concerns (welfare, environment, etc.) are not taken seriously, but only if they do not conflict with the aspiration for competitiveness. This is also where my main concern with the insights from Frederikshavn lies. Experimental municipal practices in this small city have proven able to produce remarkable policy outcomes, but have also continually been legitimized through discourses of competitiveness. The palm beach, for instance, was not legitimized because it recreated a social meeting place for local citizens that had vanished with industrial infrastructure construction in the 1970s. It was legitimized as a valuable component of ongoing place branding activities designed to enhance Frederikshavn's competitiveness as an experiential product.

## References

Allen, J. (2009) 'Three spaces of power: territory, networks, plus a topological twist in the tale of domination and authority', *Journal of Power*, 2(2): 197–212.

Ateljevic, I. (2000) 'Circuits of tourism: stepping beyond the "production/consumption" dichotomy', *Tourism Geographies*, 2(4): 369–88.

Bille, T. (2010) 'The Nordic approach to the Experience Economy – does it make sense?', *Creative Encounters*, Working Paper #44, Copenhagen: Copenhagen Business School.

Britton, S. (1991) 'Tourism, capital, and place: towards a critical geography of tourism', *Environment & Planning D: Society & Space*, 9: 451–78.

Carter, H. (2011) *Compelled to compete? Competitiveness and the small city*, Aalborg: Department of Development and Planning, Aalborg University.

Crevoisier, O. and Guex, D. (2014) 'Beyond production: the presential economy', paper presented at RSA Global Conference 2014, Fortaleza, 26–9 April 2014.

Erhvervs- og Byggestyrelsen (2008) *Vækst via oplevelser – en analyse af Danmark i oplevelsesøkonomien*, Copenhagen: Erhvervs- og Byggestyrelsen.

Erhvervsministeriet and Kulturministeriet (2000) *Danmarks kreative potentiale*, Copenhagen: Erhvervsministeriet and Kulturministeriet.

Fisker, J.K. (2013) *The challenged locality and the entrepreneurial local state*, unpublished PhD thesis, Aalborg: Department of Development and Planning, Aalborg University.

Florida, R. (2002), *The rise of the creative class*, New York: Perseus Book Group.
Frederikshavn Kommune (2001) *Kommuneplan for Frederikshavn Kommune år 2001–2012*, Frederikshavn: Teknisk Forvaltning, Frederikshavn Kommune.
Gaardbo Comm (2004) *Kommunikationsstrategi – Frederikshavn*, Frederikshavn: Gaardbo Comm.
Galland, D. and Arthur, I.K. (2010) 'The Experience Economy as a tool for urban and rural development in North Denmark: Exploring current means', paper presented at RSA Workshop: 'The Experience Turn in Economic Development and Planning', Aalborg University, 16–17 September 2010.
Goodman, M.K., Goodman, D. and Redclift, M. (eds) (2010) *Consuming Space – Placing Consumption in Perspective*, Farnham: Ashgate.
Harvey, D. (1989) 'From Managerialism to Entrepreneurialism – The transformation in urban governance in late capitalism', *Geografiska Annaler*, 71(b): 3–17.
Harvey, D. (2006) 'Space as a keyword' in N. Castree and D. Gregory (eds) *David Harvey: A Critical Reader*, Antipode Book Series, Malden, MA: Wiley-Blackwell.
Healey, P. (2004) 'Creativity and urban governance', *Policy Studies*, 25(2): 87–102.
Heftholm, S. (2012) Interview conducted by J.K. Fisker (26 June 2012).
Holbrook, M. and Hirschman, E. (1981) 'The experiential aspects of consumption: Consumer fantasies, feelings, and fun', *Journal of Consumer Research*, 9: 132–40.
Jeannerat, H. (2015) 'Towards a staging system approach to territorial innovation', in A. Lorentzen, K.T. Larsen and L. Schrøder (eds) *Spatial dynamics in the experience economy*, Abingdon: Routledge.
Jeannerat, H. and Crevoisier, O. (2010) 'Experiential turn and territorial staging system: What new research challenges?', paper presented at Regional Studies Association Workshop on the experience turn in local development and planning, Aalborg University, Aalborg, September 2010.
Jensen, O.B. (2007) 'Culture stories: Understanding cultural urban branding', *Planning Theory*, 6(3): 211–36.
Jensen, R. (1999) *Dream Society*, New York: McGraw-Hill.
Jentsch, M. (2012) Interview conducted by J.K. Fisker (5 February 2012).
Jones, M. and Ward, K. (2002) 'Excavating the Logic of British Urban Policy: Neoliberalism as the "Crisis of Crisis-Management"', *Antipode*, 34(3): 473–94.
Landry, C. (2000) *The creative city: A toolkit for urban innovators*, London: Earthscan.
Lorentzen, A. (2007) *Frederikshavn indtager 'the global catwalk'*, Aalborg: Institut for Samfundsudvikling og Planlægning, Aalborg University.
Lorentzen, A. (2011a) 'Lokal udvikling i oplevelsessamfundet', in A. Lorentzen and S. Smidt-Jensen (eds) *Planlægning i oplevelsessamfundet*, Aarhus: Aarhus Universitetsforlag.
Lorentzen, A. (2011b) 'Frederikshavns forvandling', in A. Lorentzen and S. Smidt-Jensen (eds) *Planlægning i oplevelsessamfundet*, Aarhus: Aarhus Universitetsforlag.
Lorentzen, A. (2013) 'The experience turn of the Danish periphery: The downscaling of new spatial strategies', *European Urban and Regional Studies*, 20(4): 1–13.
Mansvelt, J. (2005) *Geographies of Consumption*, London: Sage.
Pedersen, O.K. (2011) *Konkurrencestaten*, Copenhagen: Gyldendal.
Pine, B.J. and Gilmore, J.H. (1998) 'Welcome to the experience economy', *Harvard Business Review*, 76(4): 97–105.
Pine, B.J. and Gilmore, J.H. (1999) *The experience economy: Work is theatre and every business a stage*, Boston: Harvard Business School Press.
Regeringen (2003) *Danmark i kultur- og oplevelsesøkonomien – 5 nye skridt på vejen*, Copenhagen: Regeringen.

68    *J.K. Fisker*

Skot-Hansen, D. (2007) *Byen som scene: kultur- byplanlægning i oplevelsessamfundet,* Frederiksberg: Bibliotekarforbundet.

Smidt-Jensen, S. and Lorentzen, A. (2011) 'Planlægning i oplevelsessamfundet', in A. Lorentzen and S. Smidt-Jensen: *Planlægning i oplevelsessamfundet,* Aarhus: Aarhus Universitetsforlag.

Smidt-Jensen, S. (2012) 'Making a micropole: the experiensation of Vejle', in A. Lorentzen and B. Van Heur (eds) *Cultural Political Economy of Small Cities,* London: Routledge.

Sørensen, E. (2007) Interview conducted by H.P. Therkildsen (13 June 2007).

Therkildsen, H.P. (2007) *Nytænkning i Byplanlægningen – Frederikshavns forvandling,* unpublished master's thesis, Aalborg: Aalborg Universitet.

Tofler, A. (1970) *Future Shock,* New York: Random House.

Torfing, J., Guy Peters, J.P. and Sørensen, E. (2012) *Interactive Governance: advancing the paradigm,* Oxford: Oxford University Press.

Wikimedia Commons (2006) *Map DK Frederikshavn,* Wikimedia Commons. Online, Available at: http://commons.wikimedia.org/wiki/File:Map_DK_Frederikshavn.PNG (accessed 15 August 2014).

# Part III
# Relations in the experience economy

# 5 Selling the stage

## Exploring the spatial and temporal dimensions of interactive cultural experiences

*Brian J. Hracs and Doreen Jakob*

## Introduction

> The Internet is the greatest force of commoditization ever known to man, for both goods and services.
>
> (Pine and Gilmore 1999: 10)

Imagine for a second that you had just formed a band. After writing and rehearsing a few songs you decide to do some recording with your laptop and free software. At this point you may be marvelling at how digital technologies have transformed these capital intensive and highly specialized tasks into relatively affordable and accessible activities. However, when you decide to post, promote and sell your songs online, the real challenge becomes apparent: with declining entry barriers, digital technologies and global integration, the marketplace for cultural products – including music and craft – has become saturated and highly competitive. Indeed, Apple's iTunes music store offers over 37 million songs and Etsy listed over 34 million new cultural products in 2013 (Apple 2014; Etsy 2014). This 'dilemma of democratization' curtails the ability of independent cultural producers to command monopoly rents and increases market volatility. Between 2001 and 2006, for example, the annual incomes of musicians in Toronto declined by 25.9 per cent to $13,773 (CAD) (Hracs and Leslie 2014) and craft makers often take on additional work to support their income (Jakob 2013). In response, cultural entrepreneurs are developing innovative and spatially rooted strategies to market and monetize their products and to 'stand out' in the crowded marketplace (Hracs *et al.* 2013).

As Pine and Gilmore (1999) anticipated, many of these strategies involve adding experiential elements. However, experiences are often considered as a means of complementing existing goods and services or as a way to build brand recognition and loyalty rather than as products in their own right. Moreover, existing studies tend to focus on large global firms such as Prada and their efforts to use space and technology, through their flagship stores and websites, to enhance the shopping experience and to build and differentiate the aura of their brand (Crewe 2010). As such, this chapter contributes to our understanding of the experience economy, consumption and entrepreneurship by examining the ways in which poorly understood independent cultural producers are using experiences as standalone products to help supplement and promote their goods and services. In so doing, we demonstrate how local producers are manipulating four different aspects of their experience offerings (exclusivity, interactivity, space and time) and harnessing consumer desires for symbolic value, authenticity and creative expression.

Here, independent or 'indie' refers to individuals or small groups who produce cultural goods, services and experiences. Within this broad group we focus on individual musicians who are not affiliated with record labels and craft makers who produce customized items or single collections in small numbers (for a detailed definition of craft and craft makers see Jakob 2013). Although this mode of do-it-yourself (DIY) production is often dismissed as a niche alternative, it is rapidly becoming a significant source of economic activity, employment and value in the cultural sector. In Canada, for example, over 95 per cent of all musicians operate as independent entrepreneurs (Hracs *et al.* 2013) and Etsy.com, the online handmade goods retail platform, reported a 5,000 per cent sales increase between 2008 and 2011 (Jakob 2013).

The chapter begins by reviewing the relevant literature on the experience economy and the evolving nature of consumer demand. After outlining our field-work, it offers a four-part analysis of how independent musicians and craft makers structure and enhance cultural experiences by manipulating (1) exclusivity; (2) interactivity; (3) space; and (4) time. The chapter concludes by considering the effectiveness and sustainability of using experiences to generate distinction, value and loyalty.

## The experience economy

As the cultural economy continues to globalize and markets become increasingly integrated and competitive, the impetus to create and exploit new forms of value is intensifying. In geography, the competitiveness of firms is often linked to the production of new knowledge and products through innovation. For city regions, competitiveness is said to flow from the ability of places to develop and exploit local production, milieus and cultural activities (Scott 2000). Recently, however, this productionist perspective has been critiqued (Grabher *et al.* 2008; Power and Hauge 2008) and alternative frameworks for understanding value creation and the relationship between production and consumption have arisen. Originating from studies in consumer behaviour (Holbrook and Hirschman 1982; Schmitt 1999) and strategic management (Pine and Gilmore 1999), the experience economy perspective – which asserts that consumption and consumer engagement are central to the creation of economic value – has gained currency in economic geography (Lorentzen and Jeannerat 2013). Here spaces are not mere production sites or containers of economic activity but rather important sites of consumption and 'stages' that shape exchanges between producers, intermediaries and consumers and the outcomes of such interactions (Lorentzen and Jeannerat 2013).

Thus, according to Pine and Gilmore (1999), contemporary firms must transition from providing products to offering experiences that enhance existing goods and services and constitute new consumption opportunities and sources of value. Swiss watchmakers, for example, use interactive experiences such as workshops, exhibitions, museums and factory visits to legitimize and educate consumers about the value of their products (Jeannerat 2013). For producers, the benefits of offering experiences are obvious but why are consumers compelled to spend time and money on them? More importantly, as the volume and range of deliberately staged experiences in the marketplace increases, how do consumers choose between the competing alternatives?

## 'I speak through my experiences' – the evolving nature of consumer demand

The pioneering works of Veblen ([1899] 1912) and Simmel (1904) demonstrate that consuming cultural products allows people to communicate characteristics such as class, status, occupation and individuality through a system of codes, symbols and signs. Today, the desire for social distinction, prestige and personality via consumption and style is intensifying (Bourdieu 1984). For Zukin (2004), shopping is the primary strategy for creating value and way for individuals to define who they are and what they want to become. Indeed, choosing certain products over others allows consumers to exercise their judgement of taste and articulate their sense of class and cultural identity (Shipman 2004).

As Trigg (2001) points out however, the search for status through consumption is never-ending and products that once conferred status can lose that ability. Whereas fashion used to be the quintessential signifier of class and distinction from the masses, cheap knock-offs and counterfeit copies are eroding the value of luxury goods. This has compelled consumers to shift their focus from goods to authentic and exclusive experiences that are more difficult to replicate (Gilmore and Pine 2007; Zukin 2010). Indeed, when cultural products become available to all, sophisticated consumers can maintain their exclusivity by getting a better view (Shipman 2004).

In general, the attractiveness and value of experiences rests with their participatory nature but of course not all experiences are created or consumed in the same way. For example, Pine and Gilmore (1999) outline a four-part typology of experience realms (entertainment, education, escapism and aesthetic), which features varying levels of intensity and engagement from consumers. Whereas entertainment or aesthetic experiences often entail passive participation from consumers, escapist or educational experiences are often more active and participatory in nature. An entertainment experience, for example, may involve listening to a story about a product but an escapist experience may involve actively creating a personalized or entirely new product. To cater to a range of tastes, firms endeavour to 'stage' environments, artefacts and contexts that facilitate interaction and allow consumers to co-create their own experiences.

As a result, experiences allow contemporary consumers to create unique identities, display social status and pursue self-actualization through learning, doing, trying and making (Boggs 2009; Lorentzen and Hansen 2009). In *The Rise of the Creative Class* (2002), Florida argues that members of the so-called creative class prefer 'authentic and participatory experiences' to passive and staged experiences such as those provided by Disney. Thus, unlike Veblen's 'leisure class' contemporary creatives constitute an 'active class' who replace time-killing activities with a more purposeful utilization of leisure time and covet experiences that fire their creative impulses and generate new opportunities for workplace creativity (Banks 2009).

## Fieldwork

The empirical evidence and conceptual understanding of exclusive and interactive cultural experiences presented in this chapter comes from seven separate research projects (Figure 5.1). The projects were planned and conducted

**Brian J. Hracs**

**Prince Edward County (Ontario) 2004–5**
Interviews with artists and craft makers: 19
Observation (studios, stores, venues)
Analysis of relevant media

**Toronto 2007–9**
Interviews with musicians: 51
Interviews with key informants: 14
Observation (concerts, bars, studios, music stores)
Participation (performing and recording with bands)
Analysis of relevant media

**Stockholm 2012–13**
Interviews with musicians and record store employees: 11
Observation (record stores)

**Doreen Jakob**

**New York City 2005–7**
Interviews with musicians: 16
Interviews with craft makers: 15
Interviews with key informants: 74
Observation (studios, galleries/stores, markets/events/festivals, clubs)
Participation (gallery work, member of local artist collective, workshops)
Analysis of relevant media

**Doreen Jakob**

**Berlin 2005–7, 2011**
Interviews with musicians: 8
Interviews with craft makers: 16
Interviews with key informants: 40
Observation (studios, galleries/stores, markets/events/festivals, clubs)
Participation (member of local artist collective)
Analysis of relevant media

**Durham (North Carolina) 2011, 2013–14**
Interviews with craft makers: 30
Observation (studios, galleries/stores, markets/events/festivals)
Participation (member of two local craft markets, craft festival participation and organization, classes and workshops, studio artist at local ceramics centre, studio technician)
Analysis of relevant media

**South West England 2012–13[1]**
Interviews with craft makers: 19
Interviews with key informants: 13
Observation (studios, galleries/stores, markets/events/festivals, craft guilds)
Participation (guild membership meetings, classes and workshops)
Analysis of relevant media
[1]with Nicola J. Thomas

*Figure 5.1* Summary of fieldwork.

independently but subsequent discussions and data comparison between the authors revealed that the projects featured remarkably similar objectives, data collection methods and findings.

In addition to conducting over 300 interviews (combined), each author observed how products were marketed and experienced by visiting retail shops, fairs, marketing events and music performances. The authors also participated directly in local markets as a musician and a craft maker. This personal engagement and familiarity, as noted by Valentine (2005), proved useful in establishing rapport with respondents and interpreting the rich results of the interviews and observation.

Although we freely acknowledge the lack of complete uniformity between the cases, the high degree of overlap convinced us that combining our data would generate a better understanding of cultural experiences and a more original contribution to the field. Such a combination allowed us to construct our arguments from a larger sample of in-depth interviews and years of observation and participation. Moreover, because this sample includes interviews with independent musicians and craft makers we were able to extend our analysis beyond one single industry. As these respondents operate in a variety of locations ranging from rural South West England and medium-sized Durham (USA) to the metropolises of Toronto, Stockholm, Berlin and New York City, the combination also allowed us to consider the use of experience-based strategies in various places of cultural production. At a time of increasing globalization, labour mobility and hyper-competition, bringing together responses from many independent producers yields a more nuanced account than either of the authors could have produced on their own. As such, we believe that any methodological unevenness is outweighed by the value of exploring these phenomena and establishing a foundation for future research.

## Selling backstage passes – generating value through exclusive experiences

As digital technologies continue to spur the industrialization and democratization of cultural production, the cultural marketplace is becoming saturated. Concomitantly, consumer demand is increasingly reflexive, sophisticated and volatile. As a result, independent musicians and craft makers face intensifying competition, market volatility, precarious working conditions and ultimately struggle to attract and retain the attention and patronage of fickle consumers. To circumvent mass-produced or illegal substitutes, our research indicates that some cultural producers generate distinction and value through traditional artisanal production techniques and exclusivity. For instance, it is common for independent musicians to produce handcrafted albums that feature hand-painted artwork, photographs of the band, poetry, individual numbering and handwritten thank-you cards. These albums are marketed as unique products that contain layers of value that are not offered by digital downloads or mass-produced CDs. As one respondent explained:

People want to be part of the club [and] they want to have the limited edition stuff.... We have done releases in vinyl, which had been hand numbered. We offer hand etchings on the fourth side of the vinyl and add additional or extended tracks. It ends up being a package that you wouldn't normally see. It is not a mass-produced package and with all of the handcrafted detail we only issue about 300 units. We take it on the road and sell it for $25 instead of $15 (CAD) so we are selling them for a premium. When people start talking about the limited edition albums you get some buzz going and it helps promote the album and the live show. People start saying 'I was one of the few to snag this new cool album'.

As consumers must display high levels of cultural, social and economic capital to find and afford unique products, limiting supply allows indie producers to generate distinction and value.

In addition to selling exclusive goods, some independent musicians enhance the exclusivity and value of their live shows. Instead of targeting big venues and large audiences, some respondents are offering exclusive 'salon' style experiences that are limited to 25 people. Musicians interact directly with fans, through their websites and social media, to arrange small private shows performed at the houses of fans. These exclusive experiences can generate over $500 (CAD) a night for musicians. This is particularly impressive given that the majority of the musicians in Toronto reported that because of high levels of competition, it is difficult to earn more than $50 (CAD) for a live performance.

Independent craft makers also offer consumers opportunities to participate in exclusive private previews before the opening of craft shows and/or craft gallery exhibitions. Previews are usually invitation-only events hosted the night before the general opening for a selected audience of donors, collectors, buyers, senior politicians and representatives of arts and cultural institutions. They often feature public speeches, the presentation of special awards, live music and signature cocktails. For craft makers, previews offer the opportunity to pamper clients and mingle with potential customers in an exclusive setting. For consumers, being invited to previews is valuable because they symbolize membership to an exclusive club (Shipman 2004). Respondents in Europe and North America reported that exclusive previews generate higher sales than general admission.

Exclusive experiences allow consumers to 'get a better view' of the stage (Shipman 2004) and to cultivate and communicate their taste and individuality (Veblen [1899] 1912; Simmel 1904; Bourdieu 1984) which in turn generates distinction and additional value for cultural producers. Yet, as consumer experiences are controlled and staged by the producers, the relationships are one-sided. The following demonstrates that more balanced and intimate interactions between producers and consumers and hands-on experiences with products, production processes and producers add even greater levels of exclusivity and appeal to consumer desires for authenticity and self-actualization.

## Co-creating onstage – generating value through interactive experiences

While exclusivity and value can be generated through limitation, customization and uniqueness, providing additional products and special events may not be enough to sustain the attention of more ambitious consumers. Thus, some cultural producers cater to consumers with immersive, participatory and interactive, rather than passive, experiences. These offerings build on the long-acknowledged relationship between cultural producers and consumers. Indeed, in 1908 Charles Ashbee wrote that the ideal working life of a craftsman consists of:

> some collective grouping, a number of workmen practicing different crafts, carrying out as far as possible their own designs, coming into direct contact with the material, and so organized as to make it possible for the workmen to be wherever necessary *in touch with* the consumer.
>
> (Ashbee [1908] 1977: 18, emphasis added)

Yet, interactions between producers and consumers appear to be accelerating for a variety of reasons. As the number of 'desk jobs' that eschew physical and creative aspects increases, individuals crave 'hands on' and mentally stimulating activities outside of work. In some cases this overlaps with do-it-yourself (DIY), maker, environmental and anti-capitalist movements. Thus, handmade and artisanal production is regaining its appeal as a form of self-fulfilment and authenticity (for a discussion about the resurgence in craft production and consumption see Jakob 2013). By involving consumers in the production process and facilitating 'co-creation' (Potts *et al.* 2008), producers are able to generate exclusivity, value and loyalty by blurring the boundaries between the previously distinct processes of production and consumption (Hracs *et al.* 2013).

Our research shows that interactions between producers and consumers can take different forms. While live music performances showcase the production of music, craft makers demonstrate the skills and the many steps it takes to turn raw materials into craft objects. Experiences that encourage consumer education and interaction have long been critical elements for developing consumer appreciation for fine craft. In our interviews, craft market organizers, gallery managers and individual craft makers all talked about the enhanced value and connection that consumers feel towards the craftwork through watching the making process which in turn leads to greater sales for the makers. In addition, Web 2.0 technologies allow for demonstrations to be 'on demand' via video and social media. For instance, the craft blog network craftgossip.com curates the 20 best newly posted craft tutorials and distributes them to its membership every day. Similarly, the website nowplayit.com sells recorded tutorials where established and emerging musicians teach viewers how to play their songs. To illustrate how popular tutorials are becoming, a simple search for 'music tutorial' on YouTube produced over ten million results.

Although these interactive experiences help independent producers to educate consumers, market their products and generate income, their effectiveness is curtailed by their increasing ubiquity and passive nature. Indeed, consumers are increasingly interested in 'getting their hands dirty' and experiencing direct interaction with producers and materials. Thus, personal instruction, in the form of classes and workshops, is being offered as intense and intimate experiences that feature higher levels of exclusivity, interactivity and value for consumers.

As our interviews and personal participation revealed, classes and workshops come in many forms and no two experiences are alike. While most feature personal or group instruction by an expert, some develop or advance specific skills (e.g. learning to play a selected instrument), while others focus on specific projects (e.g. designing and making a dresser) or mastering a specific technique (e.g. pulling and throwing ceramic handles and lids). Despite their individual dynamics, these classes and workshops share a common structure that enables and encourages consumers to directly interact, engage with and learn from cultural producers.

Consumers are drawn to these experiences because they are considered more authentic, facilitate creativity and self-actualization and result in a 'story' that can be converted into social and cultural capital (Zukin 2004; Gilmore and Pine 2007; Boggs 2009; Lorentzen and Hansen 2009). As one consumer explains:

> I made our wedding bands from some gold that was in my family.... Not being artistically inclined or crafty myself, and not working in a profession that really allows me to use my body creatively, I also like opportunities to do something with my hands.... Our jeweler uses a lot of hand-based techniques, which we felt made the wedding ring more special. Making the bands myself represents another notch down the spectrum of meaningful ringdom, so to speak. It all creates a great story that we can tell forever.

Similarly, a lawyer in New York City emphasizes the emotional and therapeutic benefits of 'making' and taking classes with cultural producers when she says that these experiences make her feel like 'a very complete person'. She further explains: 'Everyone else in my office just gets drunk to deal with the stress of the job ... and I do woodworking' (cited in Ryzik 2010: C1).

For cultural producers conducting classes and workshops has numerous benefits. In addition to providing an extra (sometimes substantial) income stream, which helps them to diversity their revenues and cope with market volatility, the act of teaching can be immensely rewarding. For the ceramic artist Demetria Chappo, teaching classes is 'so inspiring as well as so grounding. Getting back to basics, reiterating technique and process is fruitful for my own work and often translates to the business side' (Design Sponge 2014). Teaching also provides ample opportunities to introduce one's own work to a new audience and to cultivate future customers. In fact, introducing its new 'Craft in an Age of Change' report at a presentation event in Bristol, UK, in 2012, the UK Crafts Council explained that their programme to teach ceramics in schools is not only meant to introduce children to making but more importantly raise them to be passionate future consumers and collectors of craft.

This statement supports the recent work by Jeannerat (2013) who demonstrates that watchmaking companies educate and 'initiate' consumers, journalists and brand ambassadors through interactive experiences (e.g. workshops, exhibitions, factory visits). Through these staged encounters consumers experience the idealized origin of the product, which is then legitimized and appreciated as real. Interestingly, whereas large global firms postpone the monetary transaction until the final purchase of the product and do not typically charge consumers admission for these experiences (Jeannerat 2013), independent cultural producers are selling interactive experiences as stand-alone products.

## Locating the stage – enhancing experiences through the manipulation of physical and virtual space

Geographers have considered how consumption spaces are produced, governed and used, but, as this edited volume suggests, the ways in which specific spatial dynamics shape and enhance experiences can be further unpacked. There is a need to move beyond the examination of flagship stores (Crewe 2010) and retail spaces of connoisseurship (Jeannerat 2013) to consider how independent producers manipulate and benefit from physical and virtual spaces in much less resource-intense ways. This section will demonstrate that as experiences become more common, some independent cultural producers are staging experiences with specific spatial dynamics to enhance their exclusivity and interactive value. By providing examples of how specific activities and events are being staged in physical as well as online environments, it also highlights the diverse spatial spectrum of cultural experiences.

In line with Currid (2007), who argues that fashion shows, music venues and art galleries are pivotal social settings that valorize cultural products and the identities of audience members, some cultural producers intentionally limit access to physical spaces such as parties, sales events and workshops to produce scarcity as well as social and cultural capital.

Our research suggests that musicians and craft makers stage cultural experiences in 'secret spaces', including publicly unknown music venues, bars, galleries, clubs and studios, to enhance their attractiveness, exclusivity and value. In New York City, for example, secret places resurrect nostalgic memories of prohibition. To stage the experience of secrecy, many venues eschew signage and require secret passwords from their patrons. In some cases managers verify the authenticity of a code word or invitation before granting access. We found similar venues in Berlin and Toronto, including an experimental jazz club located in a difficult-to-find industrial unit next to a furniture showroom. According to the owner, this venue was designed to offer an intimate and exclusive setting and facilitate interactions between performers and audiences.

Secret places represent an additional layer of geography in which economic capital is trumped by the social capital of 'who you know' and the cultural capital of 'what you know' (Bourdieu 1984; Currid 2007). The mystique and exclusivity of these spaces can generate buzz and value but maintaining this status can be challenging. Once secret spaces become exposed and popularized they usually lose their cachet. Popularity also intensifies the pressures of gentrification, which often reduce the short lifecycles of these establishments (for a review of these tensions see Zukin 2010). Moreover, given the volatility of local cultural scenes, property values and consumer perceptions of place, it is difficult and risky for businesses to make long-term investments in their shops and spatially entangled brands.

While secret clubs can literally restrict access and insiders can visually verify their exclusive membership, these strategies must be amended for use in online environments. As Currah (2003) points out, in cyberspace the power dynamics have been reworked and producers must deploy new methods of display to entice consumers. For musicians, simple websites that promote traditional products, like recorded music and live performances, are evolving to include virtual products and exclusive and interactive experiences (Denegri-Knott and Molesworth 2010). Websites provide platforms to attract, reward and stay connected with consumers, and bands often sell the experience of joining an exclusive 'members only' club. In Toronto, many independent musicians offer members the experience of previewing new material (songs, videos, live shows, photos, contests) before it is officially released to the public and provide access to exclusive 'members only' content (rare demos, behind the scenes footage and photos, private performances). According to Choi and Burnes (2013) the value that music fans gain from their participation in online communities comes from the sense of identity that being a member of the community gives them.

Traditionally, the ability of music consumers to co-create value was limited by the need for direct interaction between producers and consumers. However, the advent of the Internet and especially Web 2.0 offers the potential to overcome the need for spatial proximity and temporal synchronicity and opens up new opportunities for interaction (Choi and Burnes 2013). For example, to tap into the growing demand for interactive experiences bands stage remix contests that allow consumers to express their own creativity by reconfiguring the band's audio and video content. An illustrative case of this much-emulated practice comes from the UK rock band Radiohead. In 2008, Radiohead created a remix on its website. Fans were invited to download (from iTunes for $0.99 each) five different stems – the bass track, the drum track, the vocal track, the guitar track and an FX track – to create a remix of the song 'Nude' which would be judged by the band and fan community. In one month over 2,000 remixes were uploaded to the band's website. Despite being conducted completely online, offering this interactive experience helped Radiohead to deter the illegal downloading of its songs and sell five tracks at $0.99 instead of one to a horde of fans who were eager to interact with the band. Thus, the commercial success of this album was made possible by harnessing the desire to be part of an exclusive club and in this case the production process itself (Van Buskirk 2008).

Although consumers can never be sure how exclusive virtual spaces and digital content are, their willingness to believe constructed images suggests that virtual interaction and imagined exclusivity are powerful tools to create authentic and valuable experiences for consumers.

## Choreographing the stage – enhancing experiences through the manipulation of time

To enhance the distinctiveness and value of cultural experiences, cultural producers can blur the boundaries between physical and virtual space and strategically grant or limit access to specific settings. Increasingly, however, the staging of space is being combined with the strategic choreography of time. Music and craft festivals both embrace the heightened customer experience generated from temporality. For example, the first night bazaar held in Brooklyn, New York City, in 2011 featured independent craft makers as well as independent musicians for one night only, from 5 p.m. to midnight. The event generated crowds so large that people lined up for up to four hours.

Many of the aforementioned demonstrations and workshops also strategically limit their duration and producers endeavour to enhance value by offering experiences that are not only 'one of a kind' but also 'one time only'. One particularly illustrative example of how different elements can be layered to generate increased authenticity comes from the handmade online retail platform DaWanda.com. When it organized its first physical craft market in 2011 it limited the event to one day only and held it in a hip hotel in downtown Berlin. It also showcased selected craft makers, their work and individually designed wallpaper by each maker for each hotel room. By combining exclusive and interactive experiences and enhancing them with specific spatial and temporal elements DaWanda.com created a truly unique and highly valuable spectacle (cf. also designlifeberlin.de 2011).

With the success of these events, placing temporal limits on experiences has become a popular strategy of staging cultural experiences. Recently, for example, a growing number of so-called pop-up shops have been erected in both crowded and secret locations in many cultural metropolises including New York City, Berlin and Toronto, as well as in rural counties (e.g. Devon, UK). In December 2012, for example, Etsy.com opened its first ever retail space in SoHo, New York City, as a pop-up shop for ten days during the Christmas season. Much like the DaWanda event, Etsy did not stop at opening a conventional retail shop. Instead, the shop provided an environment curated by nine star designers and stylists that also changed every day as new artists made work within the shop for daily display. It continuously offered different events from the time it opened to the time it closed including talks, discussions, concerts, performances, tastings and workshops.

Most intriguing to consumers, however, were the numerous opportunities to observe the making process and interact with the makers of the products displayed. As a customer explains: 'What we really loved about the shop was that you had the letterpress set up and you had the sewing machines. So it was really hands on', while another states: 'You feel like this is a place where artists can flourish and you can actually see their work and make a connection with them' (quoted in Etsy 2013).

In addition, the shop offered Etsy an opportunity to transcend the spatial boundaries between its permanent online business and short-term offline activities. Indeed, one visitor talked about the opportunity to physically engage with makers: 'The neat thing about here is having the interaction face-to-face with the makers. I have had lots of online interactions with people but it is nice to have that face-to-face interaction as well'. While another is looking forward to extending her experience to the online shop: 'I'll probably go home and go online and look up some more stuff' (cited in ibid.). Given its first success, Etsy has meanwhile organized more pop-up shops in New York City as well as in other cities (e.g. Atlanta, Chicago, Seattle, Portland, Salt Lake City).

Interestingly, different geographies do not necessarily lead to different business strategies. In our research, pop-up shops in rural England, medium-sized Durham (North Carolina, USA), New York City or Berlin all employed similar entrepreneurial approaches to attract and entertain audiences. Although entrepreneurs in these different spatial settings constructed and exploited a range of local imaginaries, from the idyllic countryside to gritty, post-industrial urban quarters, the underlying organizational logic of their strategies and the specific mechanisms through which they generate distinction and value are remarkably similar – a noteworthy finding given the geographic preoccupation with local specificity and uniqueness.

While short-term spectacles are certainly exclusive, their authenticity, appeal and strategic effectiveness may decrease as one-of-a-kind events 'pop up' on every street corner. Moreover, staging these experiences requires resources, logistics and coordination that are beyond most independent entrepreneurs who already struggle to complete a range of creative and non-creative tasks (Hracs and Leslie 2014). Indeed, organizers have to be very effective in finding an appropriate audience (in size, purchasing power and interest). This is especially important in less urban areas with fewer drop-in customers. For instance, in rural South West England successful pop-up shops tend to be located in places with an established craft clientele, at tourist destinations or coinciding with other special events and festivals. Moreover, staging shows and workshops increases the risk that independent producers will have their unique designs and techniques stolen and duplicated by 'copycats' (MacCall 2008).

Thus musicians and craft makers are also developing longer-term and repetitive experiences for consumers that generate value through personalization, trust, loyalty and repeat business. With social media, continuous engagement between producers and consumers is easier than ever. By 2007, 80 per cent of all musicians maintained a MySpace page (Antin and Earp 2010). Today, using online spaces such as iTunes and personal websites to sell and promote products has become a necessity for success. Modern social media applications such as Facebook and Twitter allow cultural producers to engage directly with consumers on increasingly personal levels and have fundamentally altered and blurred the relationship between these individuals. Through the practices of 'friending' and 'following', producers invite consumers to experience their creativity, businesses and private lives. Our research finds that 'creating conversations' and making 'meaningful emotional connections' with consumers, also dubbed 'friends' and 'fans', is vitally important to building a stable client base and surviving the volatile marketplace (Hracs and Leslie 2014).

As social media sites become saturated with information, however, maintaining connections with consumers becomes more difficult. Indeed, keeping consumers engaged requires cultural producers to constantly update their creative and personal content and this requires more and more time, energy and aesthetic labour. In some cases, producers resort to using scripted templates and for this, and other reasons, information and interactions available online can be judged to be less authentic and valuable than experiences that transpire through face-to-face interactions.

In addition to the intimate spatial settings offered by the aforementioned classes, regular retail events, including the growing number of craft markets and local music events, offer opportunities for establishing and maintaining producer–consumer relationships. For instance, at the Durham Craft Market, craft makers report that the market's regularity (every Saturday morning from April to November) fosters a continuing relationship with consumers who regularly visit to buy but also to chat about new products and life in general. Through these interactions, producers learn about their consumers' tastes, their favourite forms and colours and intimate details about their lives including where their kids go to college and where they spend their holidays. Over time, trusting relationships are forged and maintained which allow producers to develop personalized, and thus more valuable, products for an increasingly loyal group of consumers. Our findings echo recent work by Ocejo (2012) who examined similar relationships between bartenders, barbers and butchers and their customers. As he notes:

> [Consumers] seek high-touch experiences in public places to acquire knowledge and goods that transcend the everyday experience of shopping and leisure consumption. Building 'trust' over time (to be able to serve someone a new drink they'll like, or suggest a new hairstyle or different cut of meat, all based on their prior orders and tastes), building 'confidence' as a worker to integrate cultural knowledge, technical skill, and interpersonal communication (head, hand, and heart) into their work, and taking control of the production process to create the 'right' product and service are all part of that and all strongly feature deliberate temporality.
>
> (Ocejo 2012)

Given the volatility of the market for cultural products and the precarity of independent production, consumer trust and loyalty are the most important resources and basis for sustainability.

Although the temporal aspects of cultural experiences remain under-theorized, it is clear that independent producers are strategically manipulating the duration of events, activities and relationships. While short or limited time horizons heighten the perception of exclusivity for fickle consumers, sustained interaction over time can build more trusting relationships and meaningful experiences for 'regulars'. In the age of short attention spans and fast-fashion, building a base of loyal friends and fans helps independent producers to weather the cyclical trends and volatility in the marketplace.

## Conclusion

This chapter contributes to our understanding of the experience economy, consumption and entrepreneurship by examining how independent musicians and craft makers use experiences as stand-alone products to help supplement and promote their goods and services. The four-part analysis highlights the ways in which these entrepreneurs stage exclusive and interaction experiences that cater to the evolving demands of contemporary consumers. Whereas consumers value exclusive experiences for their symbolic properties, interactive experiences attract consumers who want to develop and express their own creativity. Crucially, to make these experiences more authentic independent producers combine these dominant properties and enhance them with specific spatial and temporal elements.

On the surface, developing exclusive and interactive cultural experiences appears to bring great benefits to independent musicians and craft makers but there is a danger of romanticizing the economic effectiveness of these strategies and ignoring their physical and emotional consequences. As the literature on the precariousness of creative work and our own research highlights (MacRobbie 1998; Hracs and Leslie 2014; Jakob 2013), independent cultural producers face a battery of risks and challenges including self-exploitation, temporal and spatial fragmentation, and extremely uncertain and low incomes. For instance, in 2006 musicians in Toronto earned average annual incomes of $13,773 (CAD), which places them below the 'low-income cut-off' of $20,778 (CAD) (Hracs *et al.* 2013). Moreover, the ability of online spaces to blur the boundaries between producers and consumers and facilitate intimate interactions brings benefits and challenges. Websites and social media allow independent cultural producers to establish relationships with fans, build brand loyalty, crowd source creative ideas and secure funding for new projects (using sites such as Kickstarter.com). Yet, these activities require investments of aesthetic labour, which limits the resources these entrepreneurs can allocate to developing new creative content and contributes to what MacRobbie calls the 'corrosion of creativity' (2002: 61). Therefore, although offering cultural experiences may help independent cultural producers become economically self-sufficient, the majority are destined to fail (Banks 2007).

As independent cultural producers allocate more resources to exclusive and interactive experiences it is also important to question the sustainability and ongoing effectiveness of these commercial strategies. With the marketplace for cultural goods, services and experiences becoming even more saturated and competition intensifying, producers and consumers are locked into a never-ending cycle of discovering and discarding sources of uniqueness and value. Against this backdrop, critics may contend that given their limited resources it may only be a matter of time before independent cultural producers lose their ability to offer authentic and valuable experiences. Yet, as the chapter demonstrates, enduring relationships with consumers can help producers mediate market volatility and digital technologies are constantly providing new ways to extract value from the desire of consumers for symbolic value, exclusivity, creative expression and self-actualization. Therefore, we submit that future research should examine the sustainability and ongoing effectiveness of using experiences to market and monetize cultural products and how these commercial strategies can be differentiated and enhanced with specific spatial settings and temporal choreography.

## References

Antin, J. and Earp, M. (2010) 'With a little help from my friends: Self-interested and pro-social behavior on MySpace Music', *Journal of the American Society for Information Science and Technology*, 61: 952–63.

Apple (2014) 'iTunes features'. Online. Available at: www.apple.com/itunes/features/ (accessed 22 January 2014).

Ashbee, [1908] (1977) *Craftmanship in competitive industry*, New York and London: Garland Pub.

Banks, M. (2007) *The politics of cultural work*, Basingstoke: Palgrave Macmillan.

Banks, M. (2009) 'Fit and working again? The instrumental leisure of the "creative class"', *Environment and Planning A*, 41: 668–81.

Boggs, J. (2009) 'Cultural industries and the creative economy: Vague but useful concepts', *Geography Compass*, 3: 1483–98.

Bourdieu, P. (1984) *Distinction: A social critique of the judgement of taste*, Cambridge, MA: Harvard University Press.

Choi, H. and Burnes, B. (2013) 'The internet and value cocreation: The case of the popular music industry', *Prometheus: Critical Studies in Innovation*, 31(1): 35–53.

Crewe, L. (2010) 'Wear: where? The convergent geographies of architecture and fashion', *Environment and Planning A*, 42: 2093–108.

Currah, A. (2003) 'The virtual geographies of retail display', *Journal of Consumer Culture*, 3: 5–37.

Currid, E. (2007) *The Warhol economy: How fashion, art, and music drive New York City*, Princeton: Princeton University Press.

Denegri-Knott, J. and Molesworth, M. (2010) 'Concepts and practices of digital virtual consumption', *Consumption Markets and Culture*, 13: 109–32.

designlifeberlin.de (2011) 'Jubel, trubel, design – Volles haus beim Dawanda-Kreativmarkt', *Design life berlin: Magazin für designkultur*. Online. Available at: www.designlifeberlin.de/5/jubel-trubel-design-volles-haus-beim-dawanda-kreativmarkt (accessed 22 January 2014).

Design Sponge (2014) 'BIZ ladies profile: Demetria Chappo', *Design Sponge*. Online. Available at: www.designsponge.com/2014/01/biz-ladies-profile-demetria-chappo.html (accessed 22 January 2014).

Etsy.com (2013) 'The Etsy holiday shop', *Etsy News Blog*. Online. Available at: www.etsy.com/blog/news/2013/the-etsy-holiday-shop/ (accessed 22 January 2014).

Etsy.com (2014) 'Weather report'. Online. Available at: www.etsy.com/blog/news/tags/weather-report/ (accessed 22 January 2014).

Florida, R. (2002) *The rise of the creative class: And how it's transforming work, leisure, community and everyday life*, New York: Basic Books.

Gilmore, J.H. and Pine, B.J. (2007) *Authenticity: What consumers really want*, Cambridge, MA: Harvard Business School Press.

Grabher, G., Ibert, O. and Flohr, S. (2008) 'The neglected king: The customer in the new knowledge ecology of innovation', *Economic Geography*, 84: 253–80.

Holbrook, M.B. and Hirschman, E.C. (1982) 'The experiential aspects of consumption: consumer fantasies, feelings, and fun', *Journal of Consumer Research*, 132–40.

Hracs, B.J. and Leslie, D. (2014) 'Aesthetic labour in creative industries: The case of independent musicians in Toronto', *Area*, 46(1): 66–73.

Hracs, B.J., Jakob, D. and Hauge, A. (2013) 'Standing out in the crowd: The rise of exclusivity-based strategies to compete in the contemporary marketplace for music and fashion', *Environment and Planning A*, 45: 1144–61.

Jakob, D. (2013) 'Crafting your way out of the recession? New craft entrepreneurs and the global economic downturn', *Cambridge Journal of Regions, Economy and Society*, 6: 127–40.

Jeannerat, H. (2013) 'Staging experience, valuing authenticity: towards a market perspective on territorial development', *European Urban and Regional Studies*, 20: 370–84.

Lorentzen, A. and Hansen, C.J. (2009) 'The role and transformation of the city in the experience economy: Identifying and exploring research challenges', *European Planning Studies*, 17(6): 817–27.

Lorentzen, A. and Jeannerat, H. (2013) 'Urban and regional studies in the experience economy: What kind of turn?', *European Urban and Regional Studies*, 20: 363–69.

MacCall, S. (2008) *The Savvy Crafter's guide to success*, Cincinnati: North Light Books.

MacRobbie, A. (1998) *British fashion design: Rag trade or image industry?*, Abingdon: Psychology Press.

MacRobbie, A. (2002) 'Clubs to companies: Notes on the decline of political culture in speeded up creative worlds', *Cultural Studies*, 16: 516–31.

Ocejo, R.E. (2012) 'Craft and the reinvention of working-class jobs', paper presented at Association of American Geographers Annual Conference, New York, February 2012.

Pine, B.J. and Gilmore, J.H. (1999) *The experience economy: Work is theatre and every business a stage*, Boston: Harvard Business School Press.

Potts, J., Hartley, J., Banks, J., Burgess, J., Cobcroft, R., Cunningham, S. and Montgomery, L. (2008) 'Consumer co-creation and situated creativity', *Industry and Innovation*, 15: 459–74.

Power, D. and Hauge, A. (2008) 'No Man's Brand—Brands, institutions, and fashion', *Growth and Change*, 39: 123–43.

Ryzik, M. (2010) 'Urban artisans: A collective thrives in Brooklyn', *New York Times* 2 July. Online. Available at: www.nytimes.com/2010/07/03/arts/design/03third.html?pagewanted=all (accessed 22 January 2014).

Schmitt, B. (1999) 'Experiential marketing', *Journal of Marketing Management*, 15: 53–67.

Scott, A.J. (2000) *The cultural economy of cities*, London: Sage.

Shipman, A. (2004) 'Lauding the leisure class: symbolic content and conspicuous consumption', *Review of Social Economy*, 62: 277–89.

Simmel, G. (1904) 'Fashion', *International Quarterly*, 10: 130–55.

Trigg, A.B. (2001) 'Veblen, Bourdieu, and conspicuous consumption', *Journal of Economic Issues*, 35(1): 99–115.

Valentine, G. (2005) 'Tell me about...: Using interviews as a research methodology', in R. Flowerdew and D. Martin (eds) *Methods in Human Geography: A Guide for Students Doing a Research Project*, Harlow: Longman.

Van Buskirk, E. (2008) 'Radiohead "Nude" contest generates more than 2,200 remixes online'. Online. Available at: www.wired.com/listening_post/2008/05/radiohead-nude/ (accessed 22 January 2014).

Veblen, T. [1899] (1912) *The Theory of the Leisure Class*, New York: A.M. Kelley.

Zukin, S. (2004) *Point of Purchase: How Shopping Changed American Culture*, New York: Routledge.

Zukin, S. (2010) *Naked City: The Death and Life of Authentic Urban Places*, New York: Oxford University Press.

# 6 Qualifying aesthetic values in the experience economy

## The role of independent fashion boutiques in curating slow fashion

*Deborah Leslie, Taylor Brydges and Shauna Brail*

## Introduction

Recent years have witnessed the growth of 'slow fashion'. This movement has emerged as a challenge to 'fast fashion', a model of clothing production which is premised on bringing the latest styles to the consumer as quickly as possible and at low cost (Reinach 2005; Tokatli 2008). In order to reduce the price of clothes, production is typically located overseas in low wage countries. Recent media attention has highlighted the extreme costs of this model. In 2013, for example, 1,129 workers died and numerous others were injured with the collapse of a building that housed multiple garment manufacturers in Bangladesh (Liljas 2013; Wong 2013). The company was making clothes for a number of retailers, including the Canadian fast fashion label Joe Fresh. Despite campaigns and protests, Joe Fresh and many other international fashion retailers continue to manufacture fast fashion clothing.

However, as the controversy surrounding fast fashion continues to grow, many designers, retailers and consumers are advocating an alternative model of 'slow fashion' (Clark 2008; Holt 2009; Wood 2008; Leslie *et al.* 2014). The slow fashion movement is observed in cities around the world, and is characterized by the growth of small independent boutiques. These boutiques differentiate themselves from mainstream fashion retailers by offering customers an alternative retail experience. Independent retailers are focused on the qualification and curation of fashion apparel and lifestyle amenities through the provision of customized service, deep supplier, labour and client relationships and an emphasis on locally produced, environmentally sustainable and ethically sourced goods.

In this paper we contribute to the literature on the geography of the experience economy by exploring the role of small independent retail boutiques in qualifying slow fashion goods, and in carving out alternative relationships, experiences and spaces. We highlight a growing role for new actors in aesthetic economies and examine how independent fashion boutiques develop closer relationships with consumers (through education, special events and online activities). We argue that in fashion aesthetic value is especially important and that these values constantly are being contested by actors in a range of spaces (Hauge and Power 2012). Space is both a site for staging experiences, but also a site of networking and negotiation in the assessment of quality.

We examine the movement towards slow fashion in Toronto, Canada, focusing on the role of small independent retailers in curating slow fashion products. The fashion industry in Canada continues to grow and has adjusted to global shifts in fashion production. In Toronto, there are more than 25,645 designers, marking the city as having the third largest design workforce in North America (Design Industry Advisory Committee, n.d.). The city is also home to the second largest fashion week in North America (Key industry sectors, n.d.). The location quotient for the fashion industry in the city is 1.96, indicating a high degree of specialization in the sector (Labour force survey data, n.d.). Within the sector, there is a growing subset of independent designers and retailers. These actors have not received as much attention in the literature compared to their mainstream counterparts. However, independent retailers constitute an extremely dynamic and innovative sector of the fashion industry in Toronto.

Our research draws on 69 interviews with independent retail owners, salespeople, fashion designers and government representatives. In this paper, we draw mainly on the interviews with fashion retailers located in a number of down-town neighbourhoods known for specialized style curation, personalized attention and creative retailing formats (such as Queen West and Dundas West). Interviews were conducted between 2007 and 2013.[1] Interviews were one to two hours in length and were digitally recorded, transcribed and coded according to theme. In these interviews, we examine how customer focused experiences are integrated into retail strategies – from innovation and processes that aim to attract consumers, to the creation of place-based strategies that promote interaction amongst retailers, customers and neighbourhoods. We seek to understand the role of stores in qualifying aesthetic values (Entwistle 2009; Callon *et al.* 2002), and in presenting a mix of alternative retail experiences for consumers who are interested in local, ethical and community-based consumption experiences.

Organized into two main sections, we first begin by examining the emergence of the experience economy, paying particular attention to the manner in which slow fashion continues to evolve into a cultural industry guided by aesthetics, symbolic meaning and complex global and local interactions. In the second section, we present our empirical case study. In particular, we explore the role that small independent fashion boutiques play in curating slow fashion products. We examine the close relationships they establish with customers, educating them about the benefits of slow fashion. This education takes place across a range of spaces, including the store and online spaces. With the rise of slow fashion, we see a growing role for a new generation of cultural mediators, such as small independent boutiques.

## Qualifying aesthetic values in the experience economy

The growing importance of experiences is well established in the literature on consumption (Lorentzen and Hansen 2009). In this paper, we highlight the role played by new actors and spaces such as small independent fashion boutiques.

In the experience economy, 'success of a product or service is when the consumer keeps a pleasant memory of his/her meeting with the product or service' (Lorentzen and Hansen 2009: 819). There is a high degree of involvement on the part of the consumer, and experiences become a key vehicle through which the consumer constructs their identity (Lorentzen and Hansen 2009).

Experience-based industries tend to be concentrated in large cities, although they can be located across an array of smaller centres and rural areas as well (Lorentzen and Hansen 2009; Therkildsen *et al.* 2009). In this new economy, the centres of cities serve as spaces of consumption and leisure, offering a variety of amenities and experiences. Many experiences are place-bound, and as a result, the experience economy is often associated with changes in the physical landscape of cities. Place often becomes part of the stage in the experience economy, and it is also the site of complex networks and exchanges between actors in a sector.

Rather than competing on price, firms add value to products and services by enhancing their aesthetic and experiential dimensions. Pine and Gilmore (1998: 97–8) argue that, 'from now on, leading-edge companies – whether they sell to consumers or businesses – will find that the next competitive battlefield lies in *staging experiences*' (emphasis added).

Decisions of what to make and what to buy increasingly hinge upon aesthetic considerations (Holbrook and Hirschman 1982). Firms pay particular attention to the sensory, aesthetic and emotional influences that affect buying and cultural consumption more generally (Holbrook and Hirschman 1982; Havlena and Holbrook 1986; Schmitt 1999). Holbrook and Hirschman (1982) propose an experiential model in order to understand consumer behaviour that places a priority on symbolic meanings, hedonic response and aesthetic values that may be detached from logical considerations.[2]

Callon *et al.* (2002) trace the way in which goods are transformed into products through processes of qualification and requalification. They define a good as an item that satisfies economic needs. A good tends to be associated with a stabilization of its characteristics (including quality, location, time, availability) into a particular state. A product, on the other hand, is an economic good seen from the vantage point of the entire circuit of its production, circulation and consumption. As Callon *et al.* (2002: 197) argue, the notion of a product encompasses

> a sequence of actions, a series of operations that transform it, move it and cause it to change hands, to cross a series of metamorphoses that end up putting it into a form judged useful by an economic agent who pays for it.

During this process of transformation, stretching from the research laboratory to the sales brochure, the characteristics of the product change (Callon *et al.* 2002: 199). A product is thus comprised of the various networks and agents that define it (Callon *et al.* 2002: 198). The qualities of a product are established through a linking and co-construction of the dynamics of supply and demand. Actors on the supply side do not simply impose their understanding of the qualities of a good on consumers. Consumers also qualify products, using and evaluating them and comparing differences. Interactions are therefore complex and reciprocal (Callon *et al.* 2002: 201). As distinctions in fashion have expanded in terms of price, brand awareness, ethical considerations, as well as other aesthetic attributes, consumer decisions regarding fashion purchases have become increasingly experiential in nature, in line with Andersson and Andersson's (2013) notion of experiences as multi-dimensional.

In their examination of the winter sports industry, Hauge and Power (2012) explore the ways in which quality is a key source of competitiveness and product differentiation in a crowded marketplace. Notions of quality and value are the product of interactions between producers, intermediaries and consumers (often in the form of lead-users). The authors argue that products should be understood as resulting from a complicated and continuous process. In this process, geography plays a distinct role. Not only do conceptualizations of quality vary from place to place, but they are impacted by locally embedded factors and networks of meaning. Particular places have developed powerful reputations for quality, such as couture fashion from Paris (Scott 1997). In other words, as function and aesthetics play increasing roles in the creation of places, 'the quality of places and the quality of products, in such a view, become the two inseparable sides of the same coin in economic and territorial valuation processes' (Lorentzen and Jeannerat 2012: 364).

One actor who plays an important role in qualifying products in the fashion sector is the buyer. Fashion buyers work for department stores or major retail chains and are responsible for selecting the mix of products to be sold in the store. Entwistle (2009: 150) explores how

> buyers are active in defining, shaping, transforming, qualifying and requalifying products. Through this qualification process, buyers act upon markets – their selections resulting in the particular assemblage of products on the shop floor that constitute fashionable clothing for that particular retailer at any particular time. Of course, the process of qualification does not stop there, since buyers monitor the effects of their decisions and in due course, the results (in the form of sales figures) are monitored, digested and translated into the formal and informal knowledge that will form the basis of next season's buying. The circuitry of this process is itself evidence of the way in which production and consumption are interlinked or interwoven precisely through the actions of buyers.

Fashion buyers are responsible for selecting goods and presenting them in the marketplace (Entwistle 2009: 150). Their work involves calculating the market through analysis of trends. Buyers need to have their 'fingers on the pulse', but they cannot simply follow demand because fashion knowledge is constantly changing (Entwistle 2009: 129). As Entwistle (2009: 164) describes it, 'tomorrow's "supply" depends upon the active interpretation of this fluidity – upon buyers' active interpretation and mediation of tastes'. The decision of what to buy, and in what quantity, hinges upon numerous practices of calculation.

This calculation involves risk and trade-offs. Buyers balance economic and cultural values (Entwistle 2009: 102).

Not only do buyers choose what products to stock, but they also shape the look and feel of the retail floor and the ways in which products are placed, displayed and promoted. Through these actions, buyers both communicate and also shape fashion trends (Entwistle 2009: 154). This illustrates that the meanings and identities of products are constantly being altered.

In the next section we discuss how independent fashion retailers shape the values and meanings attached to slow fashion goods. Like buyers for large department stores, the owners of independent fashion boutiques select what items to buy and how to present them to consumers. Moreover, it is during the customer service experience that independent fashion retailers play an important role in mediating their customers' tastes and values, by educating them about the ethos and identity of slow fashion.

## Analysing the spatial dynamics of slow fashion

### *Slow fashion: an alternative fashion experience*

As Callon *et al.* (2002) argue, markets are constantly evolving over time: 'economic markets are caught in a reflexive activity: the actors concerned explicitly question their organization, and based on an analysis of their functioning, try to conceive and establish new rules for the game' (Callon *et al.* 2002: 194). Slow fashion has evolved out of a process of questioning, and in particular, out of a critique of fast fashion.

Fast fashion refers to a system where companies copy the latest trends spotted at fashion shows, transforming them into low-cost versions in a matter of weeks (Reinach 2005: 48). There is thus a rapid speed in turnaround time from design to shop floor (Barry 2004). Traditionally, fashion buying was season based. With fast fashion, however, firms adopt a just-in-time approach, dividing the buying process into multiple stages and leaving a significant portion of buying until they have a chance to determine how consumers are reacting to current trends (Barry 2004; Bhardwaj and Fairhurst 2010).

Fast fashion incorporates high fashion at low cost (Tokatli 2008). It is considered part of a new trend towards 'disposable fashion' since products are typically of low quality. In order to produce clothing at low cost, production is typically located offshore in low wage labour countries. As Tokatli (2008) demonstrates, countries such as India and Morocco are increasingly seen as ideal manufacturing locations, as their factories are able to produce garments with the flexibility, speed and cost fast fashion retailers demand.

### *Slow fashion and its ties to slow food and slow cities*

In order to challenge this system, many designers and retailers have adopted a more localized and ethical model that some refer to as 'slow fashion' (Clark

2008; Holt 2009; Wood 2008; Pookulangara and Shepard 2013). The notion of slow fashion has its origins in the slow food movement, and is dedicated to the creation of a more sustainable approach to fashion, which encourages greater knowledge about the product being consumed. Slow fashion promotes greater bonds between producers and consumers (see Table 6.1). Parallel to slow food, there is a heightened attention to quality, detail and techniques of production. Local production is encouraged, as are environmentally friendly and sustainable processes (Leslie *et al.* 2014). The emphasis on higher quality, often locally pro-duced goods and environmentally friendly products, often translates into higher price points. The idea is to buy less clothing, but to make better choices. Similar to Sundbo *et al.*'s (2013) focus on how the Nordic Cuisine Movement exempli-fies meaning-creation and innovation in a local food industry, the emergence of slow fashion draws on local strengths and authentic experiences.

At the core of this movement is an alternative set of experiences tied to con-cepts of 'slow living' and 'slow cities' (Knox 2005; Mayer and Knox 2005). Parkins (2004: 364) defines slow living as 'the conscious negotiation of the dif-ferent temporalities which make up our everyday lives, deriving from a commit-ment to occupy time more attentively'. Slow living cultivates pleasure in everyday life (Parkins and Craig 2009). It encompasses a high degree of reflexi-vity, whereby one constantly reflects upon the impacts of one's actions (Parkins 2004: 369). It is also premised upon an ethic of care – a concern for the materials that go into the goods we consume, the longevity of products, and the lives of those involved in their production. Of great importance is the idea that slow

*Table 6.1* Comparison of fast and slow fashion

|  | Fast fashion | Slow fashion |
|---|---|---|
| **Quality** | Low | High |
| **Production** | Global | Local |
| **Customer interaction** | Low | High |
| **Customer knowledge** | High (based on sales figures not experience) | High |
| **Innovation** | Fast, constant style changes | Slow, 'timeless' designs |
| **Product range** | Large selection of products | Smaller selection of carefully chosen |
| **Design and aesthetic value** | High | Very high |
| **Fabrics** | Low quality | High quality, sustainable and alternative fabrics |
| **Labour costs** | Low | High |
| **Retail environment** | Chain stores | Independent boutiques |
| **Retail location** | High streets, malls | Alternative, 'bohemian' neighbourhoods |
| **Marketing** | Traditional advertising | Word of mouth, customer events, online |

fashion is more embedded than fast fashion. Aesthetic values are cultivated to a larger degree, and customer relationships are of a completely different character.[3]

### Curating slow fashion

One dimension of slow fashion that is of concern is how the curation or qualification process might differ for slow fashion. In the mainstream and fast fashion industry, fashion buyers, editors and magazines play a central role in setting trends and mediating tastes. While these actors are still important in slow fashion, we argue that small independent boutiques play a key role as style curators. These retailers cultivate closer relationships with suppliers and consumers, and are often (although not always) more locally focused. They also have a strong online presence and are associated with bohemian neighbourhoods, known for alternative retailing experiences. In the next section we provide a case study exploring the relationship between independent retail boutiques and their consumers across space.

### Establishing innovative customer relationships

In her study of mainstream department stores, Entwistle (2009: 160) suggests that buyers rarely interact with garment makers, designers or consumers. They often know very little about the origins of clothes they are selling, and 'buyers rarely, if ever, directly meet their customers' (Entwistle 2009: 163). Consumers are known mainly through merchandising statistics, which provide buyers with a portrait of demand for different types of products. Another way that buyers acquaint themselves with customers is through weekly floor walks, where buyers go through the store with shop-floor managers, discussing sales and consumer feedback (Entwistle 2009). Thus, in this traditional model, direct contact with the consumer is minimal. As we argue in this section, this presents a contrast with slow fashion retailers.

### Product selection and buying

Like buyers for major department stores, the owners and employees of independent slow fashion boutiques play an important role in selecting and presenting a range of styles that reflect their own tastes and their perceptions of trends in the market. As one retailer puts it, 'We look for things that reflect the store and our vibe, and what we love. We look for brands and styles that compliment what we already have' (Interview, retailer). The task of selecting products encompasses aesthetic evaluations, which are based on assessments of what customers will buy.

Interviewees consistently stress the importance of educating their customers on the brands in the store and how items purchased one season could be worn next season, in the vein of building a classic or timeless wardrobe that would not go out of fashion overnight. Unlike fast fashion, retailers stock, and encourage customers to purchase, items as investment pieces that customers can wear for a long time. Many retailers reported a shift in some customers' perceptions of fashion toward a smaller, curated closet of items that were higher quality. This requires a process of educating the consumer. As Sundbo and Sørensen (2013) argue experience is more than entertainment, it also involves learning. As one retailer argues, 'That's really where I come in. I have to do a lot of educating with my consumers and say, "you can put yourself together this way, and give this impression"' (Interview). Another retailer reiterates this point, arguing that

> for the contemporary brands, I go to trade shows, such as those in Paris and New York City. I look for what's new and what brands we do not already have in Toronto. The downside to that is you need to educate your customer on brands they won't immediately recognize, but so many small businesses in Toronto need to differentiate themselves somehow.
>
> (Interview)

As argued, slow fashion garments are positioned as the antithesis of fast fashion. The ethos encouraged by slow fashion retailers is to invest in and build a wardrobe that will last, instead of purchasing fast fashion clothing for short-term wear and disposal. This mentality lends itself to the style found in many of the independent retailers, which is classic rather than trendy, but still quirky and original. As one retailer describes it,

> The clothes are classic with a bit of a twist.... Our clothes have longevity, because they have a bit of a vintage feel. But we also do things that are incredibly modern and that aren't vintage, but it coordinates.... You can buy something from this season that goes with something from five years ago.
>
> (Interview, retailer/designer)

It also becomes apparent that slow fashion retailers must take into account their personal style and the ethos/identity they are trying to create in their store, combining it with an understanding of their customer base. Through high levels of personalized customer service and extensive product knowledge, the retailer can create a retail experience that encourages the consumer to purchase slow fashion clothing.

In order to accurately 'read' their market and differentiate themselves, independent fashion boutiques cultivate an alternative retail experience. They go out of their way to establish close relationships with their customers. They apply a number of strategies to strengthen the contact with the customers and thus forge a feedback loop, whereby the consumption patterns and desires of customers become an important component of the calculations of buyers. This involves not only the provision of better service. The strategies consist of the deliberate use and development of place, time, relationship and experiential engagement and education.

*Personalized customer service through relationship building and style curation*

One of the most important features differentiating an independent fashion boutique from a fast fashion outlet is the level of customer service. The retail employee makes suggestions and pulls together complete outfits for the consumer. Hracs *et al.* (2013) argue that the key way in which local cultural producers 'stand out in the crowd' is through the use of exclusivity-based strategies. In a marketplace where there are lots of shops – and lots of clothing to be purchased – slow fashion retailers use their customer service and style curation skills to add value and generate customer loyalty. Experiential components of the product thus become very important (Hauge and Power 2012).

Interestingly, while global luxury brands pride themselves on providing sophisticated, elite and exclusive customer service, fast fashion retailers offer a no-frills environment with minimal staff. But, with the growth of the slow fashion movement, we note a return to the importance of customer service, whereby retail workers act as style curators for their customers. Both the clothing and the time spent in the store are investments, for consumer and retailer. For the consumer and the retailer, the shopping experience is more of a personal experience that requires engagement.

Service can include things as small as remembering a customer's name, helping a customer put together an outfit, or coordinating goods with items from the customer's closet. In return, many of the retailers interviewed reported having a small (yet growing) and loyal customer base that they depend on for the vast majority of their sales. As one retailer argues, '[we] are very much geared towards the one-on-one relationship built with customers, so that's really been the ticket to our success in the past couple of years' (Interview, retail owner).

Several retail owners have previous experience in the fashion industry, as stylists or fashion buyers for television, movies and magazines, and use this expertise when they help customers. This is one example of the ways in which the curation abilities of the retailer and their employees are a vital tool that they use to stand out in a competitive retail landscape:

> I've tried to cater the shopping experience to what I like when I go shopping. If you've been to New York and other parts of the world, you know that shopping is a completely different experience. It's not like here. You are treated like a queen, from the minute you walk in until the minute you leave. A salesperson that does not know their brands would never happen in a really well run boutique. It will happen in a really big store where the staff doesn't learn the product, but it's one of my biggest pet peeves. If I ask about a garment, I want to know everything about it.
>
> (Interview, retail owner)

This retailer provides a detailed explanation of the curation and customer service process that she provides during a typical customer interaction:

If a customer comes in, I ask how they are doing and get a bit of a story about who they are, because it helps me serve them better.... I then can very easily go through the racks and can start pulling things that would work for them. Within a few pieces, it's very easy more or less to pull things and know their style.... I feel like for them, walking into my space, it's not just a retail store, but also a bit of a styling service.... I'm always telling my clients to bring in their own clothes or they have a piece they don't know how to style, for them to bring it in and we can style it.

(Interview, retail owner)

Through this description of a customer interaction, it becomes apparent that for the alternative fashion retailers, personalized and attentive customer service is of paramount importance. Retailers must manage their performance and energy, providing high levels of customer service and meaningful client interactions. This is critical to differentiating themselves from mainstream retailers.

Many retailers create an environment where they become friendly with their customers. The retailers work exceptionally hard to cultivate a relationship with their customers and work very hard to maintain it. Slow fashion retailers effectively model Schmitt's (1999) experiential marketing characteristics by focusing on the customer's overall experience. The following example further demonstrate this as one retailer reported:

With a lot of our customers, we've developed a pretty friendly relationship. We might go for dinner together or the rest. We have a nice relationship we've built over time, and they love to get involved with the store.

(Interview, retail owner)

### Events as alternative retail experiences

The majority of retailers reported hosting events, such as parties, in their retail spaces as an opportunity to build relationships and dialogue. Through these events, a retailer strengthens their bonds with customers, which builds loyalty to their establishment. As the example below demonstrates, customers are selected by the retailer to be invited to an exclusive fashion show:

We do customer nights, where customers come for a fashion show with the designers. And they get a gift with purchase. They are invitation only, so there is limited space. We start at the top customer and when it's full, we're done. We do invite new customers, because we try to have a mix of customers, but it's not a mass email. We couldn't afford to do that.

(Interview, retail manager)

Retailers host events designed to introduce new fashion seasons or new product launches. As this retailer describes:

> We've done events like the [fashion brand] party for the [x] launch. We did
> one for this brand [name].... It's a higher-end brand from the United States.
> It is exclusive to three stores in Canada, and we're lucky enough to be one
> of them, so we did an event for customers to come in and see ... the quality.
>
> (Interview, retailer)

These events provide an opportunity to see your customers and get a sense of
their needs and reactions:

> [A]nother thing is we are just doing a fall launch for our best clients and it's
> not like you always have a good product and you put it in a store and it
> sells.... It's a status kind of business, so everything you do has to sort of
> really suit your clients and suit their lifestyle and status and all that kind of
> thing. There's a lot of money that goes into the marketing of it.
>
> (Interview, retailer/designer)

In these events, the store itself becomes a site for the staging of experiential
encounters relating to slow fashion goods.

Relationships built up at events are often continued in virtual spaces:

> Photo shoots, pop-up shops, and social media – these things helped us build
> our brand. Our brand was everything. So of course we had awesome clothes
> and a fun party with champagne, but it's about building that brand, so our
> website has these amazing, beautiful photo shoots. I think that really gave
> us a level of professionalism, which meant that our customers trusted us.
> Then we saw that they would come to the parties and buy clothing, and that
> cycle has continued.
>
> (Interview, retail owner)

As this example demonstrates, the decision to become a retailer in a competitive,
style-driven industry involves work across a range of spaces. It involves relations of understanding and trust between actors. These relations are strengthened
through their attachment to memorable experiences and are thus tied to the experience economy (Hauge and Power 2012: 387–8).

### Building a slow fashion community

In their efforts to build a market for slow fashion, individual retailers often collaborate with one another to educate the consumer. Independent boutiques make
attempts to ensure the products they are selling have a different aesthetic and
clientele than for other retailers in their neighbourhood. Neighbourhoods such as
Queen West and Dundas West in Toronto become known as alternative fashion
retailing districts, known for their quality and 'ethical' products. Independent
retailers often act as an integrated cluster that sells complementary products,
which allows for mutual benefit. The retailers see themselves in competition

with mainstream and fast fashion retailers, rather than with each other. As one retailer describes it, retailers form part of an alternative retail cluster:

> Everyone knows everyone. It makes it so much easier [to open up a store)] because it feels like you're joining the community. It's great.... Everyone's so supportive, or they seem to be at least. I've constantly referred people to other [neighbourhood] retailers and they refer customers to me. And it's not so much that we compete with each other, but that we compete with big box stores.... We're trying to get people to shop local and shop small.
>
> (Interview, retail owner)

Another retailer argues that in her neighbourhood,

> I feel like it has a great vibe. The other day, a girl came in and said, 'I think you have some competition down the street'. And I said, 'Who? The place next door?' First of all, no because I'm not selling the same stuff, but it's not even about that. It's all women who own stores, which is straight up girl power. It doesn't get any better. It's a tightknit community. If I don't have what you're looking for here, let me help you check out the next best thing. It's all different, all cool vibes here, I'm so happy to be a part of this community. I live here. I work here.
>
> (Interview, retail owner)

These positive community connections impact both the retailers and their customers, and provide a broader style community, offering alternative retail experiences. Stores and the products within them also gain value by being in alternative neighbourhoods, (such as Queen West and Dundas West) known for slow fashion boutiques, community-based economies and alternative experiences. These neighbourhoods develop a reputation over time for selling high quality and locally embedded products. In this way, narratives about place add value to their products (Scott 1997, 2006).

## Conclusion

In this paper, we examine the role of independent retailers in curating slow fashion products. The independent retailers under examination emphasize high quality and locally sourced products, and play a central role in educating their customers about the ethical and aesthetic values associated with these products. They cultivate a unique experience for the customer, hosting special events and parties, and reaching out in virtual as well as physical space. In these encounters, the store becomes a site for staging alternative experiences, as well as a site of networks involved in the negotiating of quality and value. The mediating role played by independent retailers illustrates the increasingly close ties between retailers and consumers, and the complex interdependencies between the two.

The qualities of a product are established through the co-construction of supply and demand (Callon *et al.* 2002).

This paper contributes to the literature on style curation and experience economies by arguing that with the rise of slow fashion, there is a growing role for a new generation of cultural curators such as small independent boutiques. With this shift, curation is less concentrated in the hands of large actors such as buyers, editors and magazines. Rather, in the current environment, many of the traditional and exceptionally powerful actors in the fashion industry (for instance, fashion houses and magazines) are facing intense scrutiny and challenges from new players, such as street-style aficionados and small independent boutiques. In this context, new spaces have been opened up for smaller-scale actors, who play a role in disseminating alternative fashion values and experiences. Rather than mainstream retail strips and malls, these retailers are associated with alternative neighbourhoods. These neighbourhoods develop a reputation for quality, illustrating the tight links between quality and place (Hauge and Power 2012). What remains to be seen, however, is the extent to which these local actors can compete with global fashion brands, and continue to carve out unique retail experiences and spaces in the city.

## Notes

1 Interviews are the primary research method utilized in our case study. Interviews include older independent boutiques that have been in existence since 2007, but also stores that have opened more recently. The longer time period for the interviews was meant to capture new players on the scene. There has been a rapid growth in independent retail boutiques in Toronto. All interviews are with separate stores. However, two interviews were conducted at one retail boutique. Most interviews were with the store owner, who also serves as the main buyer. However, a few interviews were with employees of the store rather than owners. Participants were asked the same questions, although participants were also invited to raise themes and issues that they viewed as relevant to the project. In this way, interviews were led as much by the participant as the researcher. Interviews focused on the types of products being sold and why, as well as on how relationships with suppliers and customers were established. Questions also explored the strategies that independent fashion boutiques use to compete with fast fashion chains, and the methods they use to choose goods and present them to the customer.

2 The traditional and most pervasive model used to understand consumer behaviour is focused on the logic and rationality of the consumer, and is referred to as the 'information processing model'. Under this model, the consumer is seen as 'a logical thinker who solves problems to make purchasing decisions' (Holbrook and Hirschman, 1982: 132). The information processing model is similar to the theory of 'economic man' in which perfect information is available and used to make economic decisions. Holbrook and Hirschman (1982) propose that elements from both the information processing model and the experiential view together influence consumer behaviour and that in making consumption decisions that elicit a hedonic, emotional, sensory or symbolic response, the experiential view may predominate (Holbrook and Hirschman 1982; Havlena and Holbrook 1986).

3 Given the higher price points and quality of garments, slow fashion consumers are typically middle to high income, opening up the sector to criticisms of elitism. While this is certainly the case, there are also examples of young, lower income consumers

opting to buy fewer clothes, but higher quality pieces. Often these consumers are motivated by ethical and environmental concerns. (Please note that this comparison is a generalization and is not true of all firms in each category).

## References

Andersson, D.E. and Andersson, Å.E. (2013) 'The economic value of experience goods', in J. Sundbo and F. Sørensen (eds) (2013) *The Handbook of the Experience Economy*, Cheltenham: Edward Elgar.

Barry, N. (2004) 'Fast fashion', *European Retail Digest*, 22 March, 1–8.

Bhardwaj, V. and Fairhurst, A. (2010) 'Fast fashion: Response to change in the fashion industry', *The International Review of Retail, Distribution and Consumer Research* 20(1): 165–73.

Callon, M., Méadel, C. and Rabeharisoa, V. (2002) 'The economy of qualities', *Economy and Society*, 31(2): 194–217.

Clark, H. (2008) 'SLOW + FASHION – an oxymoron – or a promise for the future…?', *Fashion Theory: The Journal of Dress, Body & Culture*, 12(4): 427–46.

Design Industry Advisory Committee, n.d. *Greater Toronto area: A design value proposition*. Online. Available at: www.diac.on.ca/research/quick-facts/ (accessed 16 May 2014).

Entwistle, J. (2009) *The aesthetic economy of fashion: Markets and value in clothing and modelling*, Oxford: Berg.

Hauge, A. and Power, D. (2012) 'Quality, difference and regional advantage: The case of the winter sports industry', *European Urban and Regional Studies*, 20(4): 385–400.

Havlena, W. and Holbrook, M. (1986) 'The varieties of consumption experience: Comparing two typologies of emotion in consumer behaviour', *Journal of Consumer Research*, 13: 394–404.

Holbrook, M. and Hirschman, E. (1982) 'The experiential aspects of consumption: Consumer fantasies, feelings, and fun', *Journal of Consumer Research*, 9(2): 132–40.

Holt, T. (2009) 'Is the time right for slow fashion?', *Christian Science Monitor*, 10 February. Online. Available at: www.csmonitor.com/2009/0210/p17S01-lign.html (accessed 17 September 2013).

Hracs, B., Jakob, D. and Hauge, A. (2013) 'Standing out in the crowd: The rise of exclusivity-based strategies to compete in the contemporary marketplace for music and fashion', *Environment and Planning A*, 45(5): 1144–61.

Key Industry Sectors, n.d. 'Fashion/Apparel'. Online. Available at: www1.toronto.ca/wps/portal/contentonly?vgnextoid=2436c1b5c62ca310VgnVCM10000071d60f89RCRD&vgnextchannel=401132d0b6d1e310VgnVCM10000071d60f89RCRD (accessed 17 June 2014).

Knox, P. (2005) 'Creating ordinary places: Slow cities in a fast world', *Journal of Urban Design* 10 (1): 1–11.

Labour Force Survey Data, n.d. Industry profiles. Online. Available at: www.toronto.ca/investintoronto/labour force industry employment.htm (accessed 17 June 2014).

Leslie, D., Brail, S. and Hunt, M. (2014), 'Crafting an antidote to fast fashion: the case of Toronto's independent fashion design sector', *Growth and Change* 45(2): 222–39.

Liljas, P. (2013) 'In Bangladesh, Rana Plaza victims still await compensation', *Time Magazine*, 16 September. Online. Available at: http://world.time.com/2013/09/16/in-bangladesh-rana-plaza-victims-still-await-compensation/ (accessed 17 September 2013).

Lorentzen, A. and Hansen, C.J. (2009) 'The role and transformation of the city in the experience economy: Identifying and exploring research challenges', *European Planning Studies*, 17(6): 817–27.

Lorentzen, A. and Jeannerat, H. (2012) 'Urban and regional studies in the experience economy: What kind of turn?', *European Urban and Regional Studies*, 20(4): 363–9.

Mayer, H. and Knox, P. (2005) 'Slow cities: Sustainable places in a fast world', *Journal of Urban Affairs*, 28(4): 321–34.

Parkins, W. (2004) 'Out of time: Fast subjects and slow living', *Time & Society*, 13(2–3): 363–82.

Parkins, W. and Craig, G. (2009) 'Culture and the politics of alternative food networks', *Food, Culture and Society: An International Journal of Multidisciplinary Research*, 12(1): 77–103.

Pine, B.J. and Gilmore, J.H. (1998) 'Welcome to the experience economy', *Harvard Business Review*, 76(4): 97–105.

Pookulangara, S. and Shepard, A. (2013) 'Slow fashion movement: Understanding consumer perceptions—An exploratory study', *Journal of Retailing and Consumer Services*, 20(2): 200–6.

Reinach, S.S. (2005) 'China and Italy: Fast fashion versus prêt à porter. Towards a new culture of fashion', *Fashion Theory: The Journal of Dress, Body & Culture*, 9(1): 43–56.

Schmitt, B. (1999) 'Experiential marketing', *Journal of Marketing Management*, 15(1–3): 53–67.

Scott, A. (1997) 'The cultural economy of cities', *International Journal of Urban and Regional Research*, 21(2): 323–39.

Scott, A. (2006) 'Creative cities: Conceptual issues and policy questions' *Journal of Urban Affairs*, 28(1): 1–17.

Sundbo, J. and Sørensen, F. (eds) (2013) *Handbook on the Experience Economy*, Cheltenham: Edward Elgar.

Sundbo, B., Sundbo, D. and Jacobsen, J. (2013) 'Concept experiences and their diffusion: the example of the New Nordic Cuisine', in J. Sundbo and F. Sørensen (eds) (2013) *Handbook on the Experience Economy*, Cheltenham: Edward Elgar.

Therkildsen, H.P., Hansen, C.J. and Lorentzen, A. (2009) 'The experience economy and the transformation of urban governance and planning', *European Planning Studies*, 17(6): 925–41.

Tokatli, N. (2008) 'Global sourcing: insights from the global clothing industry—the case of Zara, a fast fashion retailer', *Journal of Economic Geography*, 8(1): 21–38.

Wong, K. (2013) 'Bangladesh factory collapse: Can Gap and others pin down worker safety?' *Guardian* 10 September. Online. Available at: www.theguardian.com/sustainable-business/rana-plaza-gap-worker-safety (accessed 17 September 2013).

Wood, Z. (2008) '"Slow fashion" is a must-have ... and not just for this season', *Observer* 3 August. Online. Available at: www.guardian.co.uk/business/2008/aug/03/retail.fashion1/print (accessed 17 September 2013).

# 7 The 'Airbnb experience' and the experience economy

## The spatial, relational and experiential in-betweenness of Airbnb

*Ole Kjær Mansfeldt*

## Introduction

This chapter is concerned with examining how users of Airbnb, both hosts and guests, experience and use the Airbnb platform for sharing space for travel accommodation. While tourism accommodation is usually either commercial (hotels, hostels, holiday apartments, camping sites, etc.) or non-commercial (staying with friends and family, Couchsurfing, HomeExchange, etc.), Airbnb is a platform for sharing space that portrays itself as commercial and non-commercial at the same time. Arguably, Airbnb simultaneously allows for commercial exchange, for human relations between hosts and guests and for contributing to a potentially great experience. Through this perspective, Airbnb has been portrayed as a company belonging to the so-called sharing economy (Gansky 2010; Botsman and Rogers 2010), an economy that is based on consumers engaging directly with each other. Airbnb can also be perceived to be part of the experience economy (Pine and Gilmore 1999; Prahalad and Ramaswamy 2004; Boswijk *et al.* 2007) with Airbnb's strong focus on delivering what Brian Chesky, Airbnb's Chief Executive Officer, terms as 'the perfect experience' (Fast Company 2012).

Thus, Airbnb seems to be an exemplary phenomenon of ongoing transitions within tourism. These transitions are mainly driven by how consumers, the tourists, want to experience a destination. Maitland (2010) has analysed tourists' motivations for experiencing everyday life in the city and found that some tourists are attracted by places that are not touristy, out of the way, less crowded, etc. Maitland (2010: 176) observes that city tourism 'can no longer be simply seen as a separate activity, focused on well-defined tourism precincts, where comparatively passive visitors consume carefully designed tourism products'. Similarly, Larsen (2008: 179) has argued that the dualism between tourism and everyday life does not apply since 'experienced travellers may find the exotic in the everyday, in the real life of the city to be found off the beaten track'. Boswijk *et al.* (2007) argue how the experience economy has developed towards a more consumer-oriented version compared to the first generation introduced by Pine and Gilmore (1999), which had a strong focus on the company's role in staging and delivering experiences. It is the understanding of this transition towards a more user-oriented approach to experiences that the present chapter wants to contribute to with a study of Airbnb hosts and guests.

More specifically, the focus of the chapter is on getting an in-depth understanding of how the Airbnb experience unfolds. The underlying expectations for 'the Airbnb experience' and its relations to the experience economy and the sharing economy are central to this understanding. The chapter seeks this understanding through an interview-based study of Airbnb hosts and guests in Copenhagen. Here, I have aimed to get close to understanding the spatial, relational and experiential implications of using Airbnb. For this inquiry, I use the concept of in-betweenness, inspired by authors such as Löfgren (2008), Edensor (1998), Bærenholdt *et al.* (2004) and Larsen (2008). In-betweenness is used in three different meanings. Experiential in-betweenness gives a perspective on the ambiguous ways of experiencing, with guests being tourists and locals at the same time. Relational in-betweenness offers a perspective on the ambiguous relations between hosts and guests. Spatial in-betweenness gives a concept for the places that are in-between the defined and designed tourist places: places that are not developed for tourism, but attract tourists looking for experiences. As such, the current chapter is inspired by and draws upon ideas of analysing and understanding experiences as performative, as doings, not as fixed or given (Bærenholdt *et al.* 2004; Larsen 2008; Urry and Larsen 2011). I do this by empirically testing some of the dualisms associated with the tourist experience and with the Airbnb experience, such as everyday vs tourism (e.g. Larsen 2008) and must-see attractions vs off-the-beaten-track (e.g. Judd 1999). In this sense, the chapter contrasts the 'stereotypical' Airbnb experience with the actual Airbnb experiences by hosts and guests. Based on the Airbnb experiences by guests and hosts, the chapter calls for a more ambiguous and multi-dimensional understanding of how experiences unfold.

The chapter sets out to investigate how Airbnb affects the spatial, relational and experiential aspects of tourists visiting a destination, and how the users evaluate their experience of using Airbnb. I introduce Airbnb and analyse it through notions of the experience economy and the sharing economy and compare these perspectives with those found in existing research on Airbnb. Then follows a brief introduction to the term of 'in-betweenness' before applying the concept to my analysis of the Airbnb experience by hosts and guests. I end up by discussing the implications of this study for tourism planning.

## Airbnb and the Airbnb experience

Airbnb is a website that allows people (hosts) to earn money from renting out space, while it allows other people (guests) to find a place to stay. Three co-founders established the company in 2008 and have managed the business in a way that has led to the company being ranked as the sixth most innovative company in the world (Fast Company 2014a). While Airbnb is a rather new phenomenon, it has had more than 11 million guests since the first guests checked in (Airbnb 2014). Actually, the very first guests checked in with one of the co-founders in his apartment during a conference in San Francisco (Airbnb 2011). The three founders refer to Airbnb as a community marketplace for space and claim that Airbnb 'has blossomed into this open marketplace of space, much like eBay did with stuff' (Airbnb 2011). According to Chief Executive Officer Brian Chesky, the 'product isn't just our website; it's also our hosts, listings, users, photographers, and employees' which lead to the statement that 'our product is the entire community' (Fast Company 2013). Following this statement, the concept of Airbnb, as described by the co-founders, is not just 'where you stay, but what you do – and whom you do it with – while you're there' (Fast Company 2014a).

The community, which the co-founders refer to, consists of all the hosts and guests of Airbnb plus the local offices, photographers, etc. The relations between hosts and guests represent an important aspect of the offering and of the success. In fact, one of the reasons for the ranking as the sixth most innovative company was due to Airbnb 'making the most of its hosts' (Fast Company 2014b). Host testimonials found on Airbnb's website include words and statements such as 'gratitude', 'best parts of our daily life', 'forever friends', 'memorable stay', etc. (Airbnb 2012c). In a short video, a host states that 'One amazing thing is that I get to help people live their dreams' (Airbnb 2012c). Thus, Airbnb wants to be about much more than spare space, for the hosts as well as for the guests. As an example, Airbnb has introduced the guest service 'Airbnb Neighborhoods', which they coin as 'the definitive guide to experiencing neighborhoods around the world [with] rich content from a local perspective' (Airbnb 2012a, Airbnb 2012b). A similar initiative is called 'Local Lounges' where Airbnb 'has partnered with iconic coffee shops to bring you a welcoming neighborhood experience' (Airbnb 2013). Both 'Neighborhoods' and 'Local Lounges' show how the founders behind Airbnb want to actively influence the experiences of guests (and hosts). Here, Airbnb wants to take the guests away from the major tourist districts (where the hotels are) and let them explore the local, off-the-beaten-track places (where most of the Airbnb units are). Here, both the individual hosts and the services offered assist the local experience. To understand these dimensions of the Airbnb experience, the next section will deal with them in relation to the experience economy and the sharing economy.

### Airbnb in the perspective of the experience economy and the sharing economy

A central feature of the experience economy is, following Pine and Gilmore (1999: 170), that the economy is moving from goods and commodities through services to experiences. Instead of selling goods and commodities at a low price, companies sell services and experiences at a higher price through the principles of staging. This could describe Airbnb's proposition to customers, since they have transformed the original B&B concept with a global reservation system combined with a community approach. Airbnb definitely wants to offer something more than just spare space, namely an Airbnb experience, through the combined efforts of the Airbnb company, the community of people, and other initiatives like 'Neighbourhoods' and 'Local Lounges'. However, it is not possible to create a consistent Airbnb experience since the people staging the experience, the hosts, are not employees of Airbnb, but part of the community. The importance of the relations between hosts and guests, with Airbnb as an intermediary, makes it a different model.

A more recent conceptualization of the experience economy focuses more on the user and less on the company. Boswijk *et al.* (2007, 2012) name Pine and Gilmore (1999) as the first experience economy generation with 'staging' as the keyword. The second generation with Prahalad and Ramaswamy (2004) has 'co-creation' as the keyword. Hence, the third generation with Boswijk *et al.* (2007: 10) focuses on 'communicative self-direction'. In the third generation of the experience economy, focus changes from the company to the user. Companies need to understand that individuals are in charge and not see them as consumers and customers they can control (Boswijk *et al.* 2007: 198). In the third generation, thus, the experience economy becomes less centred around how companies can stage experiences and more centred on how individuals themselves ascribe meanings to things and experiences. Similarly to the perspective above, Lorentzen and Jeannerat (2013: 364) describe what they term as an 'experience turn' in the economy. In this perspective, the experience turn implies a shift from a production perspective to a perspective addressing the (relations to) consumers. Here, the point of departure for the understanding of the experience is the consumers rather than the producers. Another implication of this experience turn is that we need to consider the spaces and places of the experience economy primarily from the perspective of the consumers, since the consumers, and not companies, are the major resources of value creation (Lorentzen and Jeannerat 2013: 364). This is also at the core of Sundbo and Sørensen's (2013a) edited volume on the experience economy, which argues that firms do not deliver experiences, and that the ones experiencing are in charge (Sundbo and Sørensen 2013b: 4). In the same line of thought, Svabo *et al.* (2013: 311) argue that while producers of experiences 'are powerful in framing experiences they do not determine how experiences actually take place'.

The experience economy (regardless of which generation) primarily focuses on how companies can stage experiences and earn profit to get success. In contrast, the sharing economy uses examples of companies like Airbnb (Botsman and Rogers 2010: ix–xiv), Zipcar (Gansky 2010: 9–15) and Roomarama (Gansky 2010: 24–5) to describe this new era. A major difference between the perspectives is that while the experience economy has 'staging', 'co-creation' or 'communicative self-direction' as the criteria for success, facilitating and sharing experiences is key to success in the sharing economy. The sharing economy and its businesses 'are thriving on the growth of social media, the Internet, wireless networks and mobile phones.' (Gansky 2010: 15–16). Interestingly, Botsman and Rogers open their book with a more than five pages long example (2010:

ix–xiv) on how Airbnb started and got successful. The key for Airbnb was the use of social media with reviews and recommendations as a primary strategy to drive business: 'In other words, one traveller picking where to stay on Airbnb rather than booking a cheap hotel on Expedia makes Airbnb a more attractive choice to others' (Botsman and Rogers 2010: 202). The sharing economy, arguably, seems to take the users more seriously compared to the experience economy's original focus on designed and sold experiences.

### Existing research on Airbnb

Existing research on the experience economy and the sharing economy both focus on the business model and operating principles behind Airbnb and similar companies. Similarly, existing research is focused on the company rather than on the use of the services. A review of research about Airbnb identified only few research contributions (Luchs *et al.* 2011; Yannopoulou *et al.* 2013; Guttentag 2013). Luchs *et al.* argue that Airbnb is just one example of how 'both companies and consumers discover new ways to make consumption sustainable' (2011: 2), in ways that do not limit or increase costs for the consumers. The article states that Airbnb 'provides expanded options and benefits to consumers' (2011: 10) since they introduce a new value proposition to the market, different from the buyer/seller logic that the sharing economy also points to. Thus, this perspective positions Airbnb as an opposite to typical tourist consumption. Yannopoulou *et al.* (2013) study Airbnb and Couchsurfing as examples of user-generated brands. Building on research into social media, marketing and consumers, it is argued that the user-generated brand narrative of Airbnb is largely based on the host that rents out spare space (2013: 87). It is emphasized how Airbnb and Couchsurfing differ on different levels, including how people are to interact with each other. Contrary to Couchsurfing, which is characterized by a high degree of interaction between guests and hosts, Airbnb 'hosts can, but do not need to interact with guests.' (2013: 88). Nevertheless, the article concludes that Airbnb, as well as Couchsurfing, is different to 'mainstream' consumption. Guttentag (2013: 2) analyses Airbnb as an example of disruptive innovation due to its 'innovative internet-based business model and its unique appeal to tourists'. Guttentag continuously refers to the unique appeal of Airbnb and the guests' quest for local experiences (2013: 6) and compares this quest to what MacCannell (1999) refers to as 'back regions' (Guttentag 2013: 7). In sum, existing research deals with analysis of the business model, with less attention to the role of guests and hosts.

## The in-betweenness of the Airbnb experience

I will now turn to report findings from my study of the Airbnb experience based on in-depth interviews with 11 Airbnb guests and 5 Airbnb hosts in Copenhagen. The study aimed to understand the Airbnb experience seen from the users' perspectives. The Airbnb guests and hosts (see Table 7.1 and Table 7.2 at the end of the chapter) studied here represent different age groups (from early twenties to late sixties). The guests were on different types of stays (business, short breaks, around-the-world trips and summer holidays). Moreover, the hosts practised different ways of renting out (entire home, a room in their private home and a separate apartment).[1] Thus, the different uses of Airbnb add more nuanced perspectives on the way it works.

One of the ways that I used to understand the Airbnb experience as it unfolds in practice was by application of different dichotomies when interviewing the guests. The guests were asked to place themselves and their way of experiencing on binary scales (e.g. from must-see to off-the-beaten-track). The scales were inspired by a previous study that used similar scales to study more than 5,000 tourists (Ek *et al.* 2008; Mansfeldt *et al.* 2008). While the previous study was quantitative, the current study has a qualitative approach, thus allowing room for discussion of the dichotomies. During the interviews, it was obvious that some guests explicitly wanted to avoid ticking off only one point on the scales. Hence, some guests questioned the binaries and argued that they were complementing each other rather than opposing each other. Moreover, a couple remarked that they 'do see must-see attractions, but in an off-the-beaten-track way' (Guest 4), implying that one end of a scale does not rule out the other. Others drew larger figures spanning over several points on the scales (e.g. Guests 1 and 10), arguing that they shifted positions during their stay. Four of the interviews included two people (all couples), and in these interviews the couples did not agree on where they should place the marks on the scales (Guests 4, 6, 7, 11), resulting in at least two marks. Therefore, the figure below (see Figure 7.1) only indicates where the guests eventually marked their positions on those scales.

Throughout the empirical analysis, the notion of in-betweenness helped to describe how the Airbnb guests (and hosts) were doing their Airbnb experience.

## The spatial in-betweenness of the Airbnb experience

Spatial in-betweenness refers to the spaces and places in-between must-see attractions. In-betweenness has been connected to places of immobility such as airports, waiting rooms, etc. where the otherwise mobile visitors are immobile

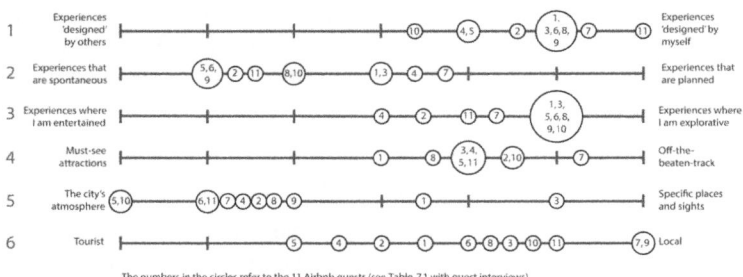

The numbers in the circles refer to the 11 Airbnb guests (see Table 7.1 with guest interviews)

*Figure 7.1* Six scales on the guests' ways of experiencing.

(Bærenholdt *et al.* 2004: 149–50). Löfgren (2008: 47) conceptualizes in-betweens as the situations where tourists are doing nothing. Both Bærenholdt *et al.* (2004: 149–50) and Löfgren (2008: 47) use the concept about places that are in-between the designed and defined tourist places. In-between places, for both contributions, are said to be specific places such as train stations and airports, where people wait in line and do nothing. The notion of in-betweenness in a spatial context signifies that the place or the activity was not designed or intended for experiencing. The notion of spatial in-betweenness is able to bridge the usual focus on, for example, tourist bubbles (Judd 1999) and urban tourism precincts (Hayllar *et al.* 2008a, 2008b) on the one hand and another focus on off-the-beaten-track experiences (Maitland 2008, 2010) and everyday experiences of tourists (Larsen 2008). People actually do search for experiences outside of the defined and designed places. Consider the following quotes from two of the Airbnb guests:

> I only see must-sees by accident. I will not be heartbroken if I don't go there. It will not be mind-blowing for me to see a must-see.
>
> (Guest 2)

> The things like museums and sightseeing is the whipped cream of the city. But that is not the reason to come. That is atmosphere, people.
>
> (Guest 10)

Looking at Figure 7.1, and in particular on scales 3, 4 and 5, the guests seem to be having experiences of the city that are 'explorative', revealing the 'city's atmosphere' in 'off-the-beaten-track' areas. That is, the guests place themselves away from the designed tourism experiences and near the end points. A phrase like 'people-watching' (Guest 8) is used in different ways by many guests (Guests 10, 2, 7), indicating that people and atmosphere are more important than attractions. However, almost all the Airbnb guests still prioritize seeing certain places because of 'cultural significance' (Guest 11) or 'just to snap a picture of it [The little Mermaid]' (Guest 9). Some use advice from hosts to find must-sees, although the advice of hosts is not always helpful: 'We sometimes pass by the top things that hosts advise us to do, but those are not always our must-sees' (Guest 7). When the guests were asked to draw the places they have visited on a map of the city, many had actually visited the major attractions, but argued that they did so because of their own interest in that particular place (Guests 5, 6, 9, 10). These perspectives are interesting because the Airbnb segment was introduced as an alternative segment doing sustainable consumption (Luchs *et al.* 2011), different from mainstream consumption (Yannopoulou *et al.* 2013) and, thus, mainstream tourism. However, the Airbnb guests are, probably not unlike many other tourists, ambiguous in their ways of spatially exploring the city. Many find their way to what can be termed as 'alternative' must-sees, for example the freetown of Christiania (e.g. Guests 1, 6, 7, 10, 11) and the Meatpacking District, a creative district that used to be an industrial area (e.g. Guests 2, 4, 5, 9, 10, 11). Both places have been referred to as interesting off-the-beaten-track places to visit in media, guide-books, on websites, etc. so they can arguably be termed as must-sees.

Another important spatial aspect is the location of the Airbnb unit which one guest talks about as a 'trendier spot than the downtown commercial location' of hotels (Guest 3), and that the Airbnb location provides a way 'to get a local perspective' (Guest 9). The guests want to go to both alternative and conventional must-sees and appreciate the city both as what they themselves term as locals and as tourists. Thus, the places and spaces of the city they visit are to a certain extent less important than the way through which they do it. Instead of following specific routes and having a set itinerary, many prioritize time to walk, not being sure about where to go. For example, Guest 5 explains how he 'just walks around and gets lost, and then eventually finds a map to find my way back'. Almost all guests are using similar spatial strategies. However, the guests did mainly explore the central, medieval district of Copenhagen, although they specifically had ambitions to go where locals went. They also talked about experiences that were non-touristy even in or around what could be termed as tourist places. It was interesting that often their best experiences were not staged and did not take place within specific experience-scapes.

In sum it seems fruitful to describe guests' ways of experiencing by the notion of spatial in-betweenness. They are not quite tourists, not quite locals.

## The relational in-betweenness of the Airbnb experience

The notion of relational in-betweenness describes how tourism and experiences happen in relations between different people, places, etc. Relational in-betweenness emphasizes how these relations are not given or fixed. Relational in-betweenness also refers to new ways of being in dialogue, involving producers, intermediaries as well as consumers. I use relational in-betweenness to describe how the roles of, for example, producers and consumers are gradually changing. In my study of Airbnb hosts and guests, the relations were both mentioned as positive and negative, often by the same guest, as seen below:

> A big pro for Airbnb is that you can connect to the host … the host can be somebody that you get advice from.… One of the big cons is that you are inside someone's house.
>
> (Guest 11)

> I am not really using hosts for advice. Our host here recommended a terrible place, so I am not gonna use that advice. I prefer to do research myself.
>
> (Guest 1)

> Meeting this guy in Odense and going to Kerteminde with him and his dad, having afternoon tea with his family, and so on. Oh my God, those are magical, life-changing experiences.
>
> (Guest 6)

The relations between guests and hosts seem quite ambiguous, varying from the stereotypical (sharing economy) Airbnb relationship, characterized by mutual experiences of meaningful interaction to more straightforward host–guest exchanges. Host 1 thus referred to her first guest, a young Frenchman who stayed in her place for a month; they are still in contact months after his stay. With the rest of her guests, this has not been the case. Host 2 has a similar story with a couple from Ireland that he connected with on Facebook afterwards, but it is more the exception than the rule that relations develop into long-term relationships. Another host thus states that while he tries to make a friendly relation to all guests, the guests are 'the type of people that can themselves, that do things on their own' (Host 2). Still, the hosts represented in the research are, in general, satisfied with their guests, although they all mention that they get very tired and exhausted by having guests and that they sometimes 'need a break from guests after a few visits' (Host 5). Similarly, Guest 7 states: 'When it is for a longer period, it can be tiring for us and for the hosts. It feels like we are imposing ourselves in their lives. Sometimes we need a break from living with someone'.

The guests share some reservations regarding the aspect of staying in someone's home. One guest mentions the sense of awkwardness upon meeting each other and moving into someone else's place (Guest 9). Another guest talks about her special situation where the host is renting out her own bedroom and, while the guest is there, has to sleep in her daughter's room (Guest 10). One guest has to share just one bathroom with the host and the host's big family, but again the guest states that 'this is the only problem, and on the positive side I get a look into their life as a family' (Guest 5). The typical relation, according to one of the frequent users, is that 'we meet, we get rules and guidance, and then we separate' (Guest 7). One of the guests has a similar way of interacting with the hosts, since they 'are not here to make friends with the host; we have no need for that' (Guest 4). Guests are generally not interested in making friends for life, but as Guest 3 comments: 'Even if you don't interact with the host, it is still nice to stay with someone else' (Guest 3).

The notion of relational in-betweenness grasps the blurred guest–host relation described here: a relation that is both a buyer–seller relation and a friendly relation at the same time. The relations include both the logic of monetary transactions and the logic of sharing. Airbnb seems to be perceived as not quite a hotel, not quite a home. The sharing economy's approach to Airbnb as a special form of collaborative consumption, where hosts and guests are sharing in new ways, seems to be just a stereotypical ideal, while the reality seems much more blurred.

## The experiential in-betweenness of the Airbnb experience

The notion of experiential in-betweenness intends to denote how experiences play out from an individual point of view. The experiences of a given place can vary greatly from person to person; one tourist's experience can be completely different from that of another, depending on culture, milieu, weather, etc. (as, for example, shown by Edensor 1998). People with anti-tourist attitudes (Jakobsen 2000) or post-tourist attitudes (Feifer 1985) for example, tend to distance themselves from the designed and spaced experiences, even when visiting them. Hence, the notion of experiential in-betweenness refers to *how*, not *what*, the guests experience and the strategies they use to find interesting experiences. Experiential in-betweenness also refers to the combination of everyday activities with visiting must-see attractions.

> We are so not tourists.... Tourists are blind. Tourist is a negative.... People are lining up, tramping on things, blindly ignoring culture and human energy – tourism is an intrusion in my opinion.
>
> (Guest 7)

> It is more satisfying to find something for yourself.... It is nice to see tourist spots but also nice to see surprising places.... I don't forget that I am a tourist. I am an outsider, and I like that feeling.
>
> (Guest 4)

The above approaches to experiencing can fruitfully be described as experiential in-betweenness. Some guests place themselves on the local end of the scale, while others are around the mid-point. A handful of guests use statements like 'we are not interested in seeing the standard tourist sights. We like the slightly more interesting spots.' (Guest 6), or contrasting oneself to the 'good' tourist: 'I am a really bad tourist. I am not planning; I am not taking pictures' (Guest 2). However, as the second statement above shows, the guests are not seeing the dichotomies as black and white. Some guests discuss the notions of local and tourist, for example: 'I don't like to feel that I am a tourist.... But I also don't want to be a complete local who does not appreciate the city' (Guest 3). It is also underlined how being a local can be very difficult: 'In general, I like to see the city as a local.... But I acknowledge that I can't be a local. The ambition is to be a local but it is hard to be so' (Guest 11). A statement that was repeated in other words by other guests.

There seems to be a certain balance between how the guests want to experience the local spots and hang out with the locals, and how they want to experience unique must-see places and appreciate the city as tourists do. Hence, it is more about the way they experience both must-sees and off-the-beaten-track places than choosing one or the other. Even though almost all the guests tend to favour the self-designed, explorative experiences to planned and designed experiences, they also do something planned in designed places and activities. The research thus suggests that being spontaneous and explorative does not rule out planning and being entertained. Experiential in-betweenness signals that both tourist experiences and other forms of experiencing motivate Airbnb guests in their approaches when travelling.

## Conclusion

This chapter has examined how Airbnb is experienced by guests and hosts The main focus of the chapter was to investigate the spatial, relational and experiential aspects arising from Airbnb, based on users' evaluations of their experiences.

When analysing Airbnb, the term of 'in-betweenness' was used to describe the new dynamics of tourism in general and the use of Airbnb in particular. While Airbnb has been investigated mainly as a business model and a way to organize business, this study has turned the focus towards the users. Airbnb represents some of the principles of the experience economy and the sharing economy, but the chapter argues that the experiences by Airbnb users are quite multifaceted and ambiguous. The chapter has argued that the concept of in-betweenness seems fruitful in understanding the Airbnb experience as ambiguous and multifaceted. While Airbnb has been understood as an opposite to traditional tourism (and, for example, staying in hotels), the chapter shows that there may not be any opposition. The difference is rather that Airbnb is approached in many different ways, which makes it difficult to define one unifying principle of use. Therefore the chapter suggests to characterize the use of Airbnb by the notions of spatial, relational and experiential in-betweenness, a notion which captures the way that Airbnb guests visit, relate and experience the city in a relatively, but not completely, independent way.

The Airbnb guests seek both the designed and defined tourist places and the more unknown places. Hence, rather than analysing Airbnb users as a new segment, different from traditional tourists, the guests are both 'touristy' and 'non-touristy' (like many other tourists). The present study implies that experiences cannot be ready-made and designed. Spaces also cannot be completely designed for specific purposes. Likewise, the quality, intensity and durability of relationships depend on actual encounters and practices of tourists and locals, of guests and hosts, and can only to some extent be orchestrated or designed. Sometimes the relation turns out magical and life-changing; other times it is just pure business. Most often, however, the Airbnb experiences are somewhere in-between.

The 11 guests' background information is seen in Table 7.1:
The five hosts' background information is seen in Table 7.2:

*Table 7.1* The interviewed Airbnb guests

| Guest no. | Gender | Age | Travel group | Previous bookings | Nationality | Stay |
| --- | --- | --- | --- | --- | --- | --- |
| 1 | Man | 30s | Group | 11–20 | Norway | Entire home/apt. |
| 2 | Woman | 20s | Family | 3–5 | USA | Private room |
| 3 | Woman | 20s | Alone | 3–5 | New Zealand | Private room |
| 4 | Woman | 40s | Couple | 1–2 | Holland | Entire home/apt. |
| 5 | Man | 20s | Alone | 6–10 | Russia | Private room |
| 6 | Man | 30s | Couple | 3–5 | USA | Entire home/apt. |
| 7 | Woman | 40s | Couple | 11–20 | Canada | Private room |
| 8 | Woman | 30s | Alone | 1–2 | Canada | Private room |
| 9 | Man | 30s | Alone | 21– | USA | Private room |
| 10 | Woman | 30s | Alone | 1–2 | Germany | Private room |
| 11 | Man | 30s | Couple | 3–5 | Canada | Entire home/apt. |

*Table 7.2* The interviewed Airbnb hosts

| Host no. | Gender | Age | Household | Number of guests | Listing |
|---|---|---|---|---|---|
| 1 | Woman | 60s | Single | 11–20 | Private room or entire home/apt |
| 2 | Man | 30s | Single | 11–20 | Entire home/apt. |
| 3 | Man | 30s | Family | 6–10 | Entire home/apt. (2nd home) |
| 4 | Woman | 40s | Family | 21– | Private room or entire home/apt. |
| 5 | Man | 30s | Single | 11–20 | Private room |

## Note

1 The Airbnb office in Copenhagen helped contact guests and hosts between June and September 2013. None of the interviewed hosts and guests were actually hosts and/or guests to each other. All participants volunteered for the study but did, however, get a good coffee during the interview.

## References

Airbnb (2011) *Joe Gebbia: The Airbnb story*, talk at the PSFK Conference. Online. Available at: http://vimeo.com/23275754 (accessed 25 November 2013).

Airbnb (2012a) *Neighborhoods*. Online. Available at: https://www.airbnb.com/locations?locale=en# (accessed 26 November 2013).

Airbnb (2012b) *Introducing Airbnb neighborhoods*. Online. Available at: http://vimeo.com/53386231 (accessed 26 November 2013).

Airbnb (2012c) *Hosts love using Airbnb*. Online. Available at: www.airbnb.com/info/why_host?locale=en (accessed 26 November 2013).

Airbnb (2013) *Local lounges*. Online. Available at: www.airbnb.com/locations/local-lounges?locale=en (accessed 26 November 2013).

Airbnb (2014): *About Airbnb*. Online. Available at: www.airbnb.com/about/about-us (accessed 21 March 2014).

Bærenholdt, J.O., Haldrup, M., Larsen, J. and Urry, J. (2004) *Performing Tourist Places*, Aldershot: Ashgate.

Boswijk, A., Peelen, E. and Olthof, S. (2012) *Economy of Experiences*, Amsterdam: European Centre for the Experience and Transformation Economy.

Boswijk, A., Thijssen, T. and Peelen, E. (2007) *The Experience Economy: A new perspective*, Amsterdam: Pearson Education Benelux.

Botsman, R. and Rogers, R. (2010) *What's mine is yours: How collaborative consumption is changing the way we live*, London: Collins.

Edensor, T. (1998) *Tourists at the Taj: Performance and meaning at a symbolic site*, London: Psychology Press.

Ek, R., Hornskov, S. B., Larsen, J. and Mansfeldt, O.K. (2008) 'A dynamic framework of tourist experiences: Space-time and performances in the experience economy', *Scandinavian Journal of Hospitality and Tourism*, 8(2): 122–40.

Fast Company (2012) *Most innovative companies 2012. 19_Airbnb: For turning spare rooms into the world's hottest hotel chain*. Online. Available at: www.fastcompany.com/3017358/most-innovative-companies-2012/19airbnb (accessed 7 February 2012).

Fast Company (2013) *Most innovative companies 2013. 12_Airbnb: For upgrading itself into a five-star vacation destination.* Online. Available at: www.fastcompany.com/most-innovative-companies/2013/airbnb (accessed 11 February 2013).

Fast Company (2014a) *Inside Airbnb's grand hotel plans.* Online. Available at: www.fastcompany.com/3027107/punk-meet-rock-airbnb-brian-chesky-chip-conley (accessed 21 March 2014).

Fast Company (2014b) *Most innovative companies 2014. 6_Airbnb. For making the most of its hosts.* Online. Available at: www.fastcompany.com/most-innovative-companies/2014/airbnb (accessed 21 March 2014).

Feifer, M. (1985) *Going places,* London: Macmillan.

Gansky, L. (2010) *The Mesh: Why the Future of Business is Sharing,* New York: Portfolio/Penguin.

Guttentag, D. (2013) 'Airbnb: Disruptive innovation and the rise of an informal tourism accommodation sector', *Current Issues in Tourism.* Online. Available at: http://dx.doi.org/10.1080/13683500.2013.827159 (accessed 21 March 2014).

Hayllar, B., Griffin, T. and Edwards, D. (2008a) 'Urban tourism precincts: Engaging with the field', in B. Hayllar, T. Griffin and D. Edwards (eds) *City spaces – Tourist places: Urban tourism precincts,* Oxford: Butterworth-Heinemann.

Hayllar, B., Griffin, T. and Edwards, D. (2008b) 'City spaces – tourist places: A reprise', in B. Hayllar, T. Griffin and D. Edwards (eds) *City spaces – Tourist places: Urban tourism precincts,* Oxford: Butterworth-Heinemann.

Jakobsen, J.K.S. (2000) 'Anti-tourist attitudes', *Annals of Tourism Research,* 27(2): 284–300.

Judd, D.R. (1999) 'Constructing the tourist bubble', in D.R. Judd and S.S. Fainstein (eds) *The tourist city,* New Haven and London: Yale University Press.

Larsen, J. (2008) 'De-exoticizing tourist travel: Everyday life and sociality on the move', *Leisure Studies,* 27(1): 21–34.

Lorentzen, A. and Jeannerat, H. (2013) 'Urban and regional studies in the experience economy: What kind of turn?' *European Urban and Regional Studies,* 20(4): 363–9.

Löfgren, O. (2008) 'The secret lives of tourists: Delays, disappointments and daydreams', *Scandinavian Journal of Hospitality and Tourism,* 8(1): 46–58.

Luchs, M., Naylor, R.W., Rose, R.L., Catlin, J.R., Gau, R., Kapitan, S., Mish, J., Ozanne, L., Phipps, M., Simpson, B. and Weaver, T. (2011) 'Toward a sustainable marketplace: Expanding options and benefits for consumers', *Journal of Research for Consumers,* 19: 1–12.

MacCannell, D. (1999) *The Tourist: A new theory of the leisure class,* Berkeley and Los Angeles: University of California Press.

Maitland, R. (2008) 'Conviviality and everyday life: The appeal of new areas of London for visitors', *International Journal of Tourism Research,* 10(1): 15–25.

Maitland, R. (2010) 'Everyday life as a creative experience in cities', *International Journal of Culture, Tourism and Hospitality Research,* 4(3): 176–85.

Mansfeldt, O.K., Vestager, E.M. and Iversen, M.B. (2008) *Experience design in city tourism,* Nordic Innovation Centre and Wonderful Copenhagen. Online. Available at: www.nordicinnovation.org/Global/_Publications/Reports/2008/Experience%20Design%20in%20City%20Tourism.pdf (accessed 19 November 2013)

Pine, B.J. and Gilmore, J.H. (1999) *The experience economy: Work is theatre and every business a stage,* Boston: Harvard Business School Press.

Prahalad, C.K. and Ramaswamy, V. (2004) *The future of competition. Co-creating unique value with customers,* Boston: Harvard Business School Press.

Sundbo, J. and F. Sørensen (eds) (2013a) *Handbook on the experience economy*, Cheltenham: Edward Elgar.

Sundbo, J. and Sørensen F. (2013b) 'Introduction to the Experience Economy', in J. Sundbo and F. Sørensen (eds) *Handbook on the Experience Economy*, Cheltenham: Edward Elgar.

Svabo, C., Larsen J., Haldrup M. and Bærenholdt, J.O. (2013) 'Experiencing spatial design', in J. Sundbo and F. Sørensen (eds) *Handbook on the Experience Economy*, Cheltenham: Edward Elgar.

Urry, J. and Larsen, J. (2011) *The Tourist Gaze 3.0*, 3rd edn, London: SAGE Publications.

Yannopoulou, N., Moufahim, M. and Bian, X. (2013) 'User-generated brands and social media: Couchsurfing and AirBnb', *Contemporary Management Research*, 9(1): 85–90.

# Part IV
# Construction of stages and places in the experience economy

# 8 A comprehensive socio-economic model of the experience economy

## The territorial stage

*Delphine Guex and Olivier Crevoisier*

## Introduction

This chapter deals with the economic dimension of the experience economy (EE); that is to say, (1) with how economic value is created between customers and producers and (2) is articulated via monetary transactions. These transactions take spatial forms and steps in time that are typical of the EE.

'Work is theatre and every business is a stage'. We do not agree with this catchphrase of Pine and Gilmore (1999). Tourism resorts are good examples of the fact that value, in the experience economy, is not produced at the scale of a business (or only in some circumstances like Disneyland), but beyond companies. Monetary transactions, contrarily, operate at the scale of companies and customers. Value creation and monetary transactions, while being profoundly intertwined, are distinct phenomena. Therefore, the second metaphor of Pine and Gilmore, the admission fee to charge customers, does not solve the problem of how the created economic value is articulated with monetary charges either: experiential transactions do not occur in clubs – or only a few of them!

Consequently, what is the space–time entity which is relevant in order to capture, on the one hand, economic value creation for the customer and, on the other hand, the monetary transaction in favour of the producer in experiential economic transactions?

A second question deals with how the qualitative assessment of the value of a future experience made by the customer is articulated with the quantitative scale of the price proposed by producers. Value creation processes are largely described by the literature of tourism studies, for instance by examining the process of *enchantment of the world* (Réau and Poupeau 2007), but these works neglect the question of monetary exchanges in this enchantment or even consider them as incompatible – our position being that tourism is always an economic, monetized activity.

In order to deal with these questions, this chapter proposes a model of Territorial Economic Transactions (TETs), which displays the following features and aims to capture the following points:

- Space and time are not only the 'shape' generated by TETs. The space–time disjunction between, on the one hand, the concrete service and, on the other hand, the knowledge about it, is indispensable in order to sell meaning on the top of goods in a post-utilitarian economy. First, there is a time sequence between the customer, who develops an anticipated knowledge about the experience, and then possibly moves to the place where the experience is lived. Second, the mobility of customers and/or goods and services across space is also a fundamental component of value construction because places convey meaning for the customer that can be associated with goods and services.

•   Since Tarde (2006 [1901]) and Habermas (1997), social sciences have given an account of the development of the 'public space' as media where meanings are shared. This *symbolic scene* allows individuals to build their opinion about places, goods and services, initially partly independently of economic transactions. Innovation and value creation today consist precisely of exploiting customers' knowledge by selling associated concrete goods and services and by displaying the associated prices on this symbolic stage. Nevertheless, social sciences in general did not really focus on these transactions. In this chapter the *territorial stage* is made of a *symbolic stage* associated with *concrete stages* where concrete goods and services are delivered.

•   This model provides a general understanding of all the economic transactions that embody meanings and shows why time and space are at the heart of value creation and monetary transactions. In today's society, where knowledge about places is more and more shared thanks to new information and communication technologies, TETs are becoming a general model of economic transactions.

The first section is dedicated to the contextualization of this approach in the economic literature, in the literature about the EE and tourism studies. The second section is an extensive presentation of the model of the territorial stage and of TETs. Several examples based on research about the history of Swiss tourism resorts will be presented. Montreux will be used as an illustrative case of the functioning of the model.[1] In the third section the history of this Swiss resort is used in order to show how, through history, territorial transactions developed and became more and more diversified and complex. A typology of territorial transaction is presented, showing how such places create value and generate monetary flows thanks to meanings associated with the attraction of customers (tourists, excursionists, residents) or with the export of goods (water) and services (the Jazz Festival) conveying territorial value. Today, this place is a complex 'territorial stage' with high territorial value. On this basis, the conclusion suggests a broader validity of this model of territorial value. If tourist and experiential transactions matter more and more for territorial development, those 'presential' aspects should also be articulated, positively or negatively, with the more traditional production-based aspects.

## Economy, experience economy and tourism

Compared to the traditional understanding of mainstream economics, the EE requires a large number of additional elements in order to understand how value is constructed in transactions that go beyond the utility of goods. Nevertheless, the EE does not fully articulate those elements, especially the question of how time sequences and movements across spaces contribute to value creation. Tourism studies do not deal with economies, but with territorial practices and experiences. Tourism largely overlaps with the EE but cannot be assimilated to it. Here, again, issues about time and spatial mobility contribute to value creation.

## The economy and the experience

Mainstream economics theorize basic the economic transaction as the exchange of a good for a certain quantity of money. This vision implicitly postulates a certain number of things. First, all the properties contributing to the use-value for the customer are embodied in the good. Borrowing the terms of Orléan (Orléan and Diaz-Bone 2013), it is a 'substance value'. This essentially means that there is nothing like a 'meaning' contained in the good. The good and the knowledge about the good are a single thing. Second, all the income for the vendor is included in the price. Third, customers are passive players who match purchases with their preferences. EE transactions are usually much more complex. Experiences are embedded in the cultural knowledge of people. Therefore, customers actively contribute to value creation and to the shaping of their preferences.

Other traditions are marked by this archetypical transaction of a physical good which is exchanged via use of money. In the context of industrialization and industrial answers to basic needs, this probably used to make more sense than it does today. Fifty years ago, during the Fordist era, when industrial standardization and mass consumption were the engine of the economy and the society (Boyer and Saillard 2010), goods were not supposed to convey 'meanings'.

Several authors note that we are presently living in an intense *Erlebnisgesellschaft* (Dubet 1994; Schulze 2005). From an economic point of view, this contrasts sharply with a vision of the industrial society, up to the Fordist period, which would be dominated by the practical utility of main goods and services. The meanings of products, as well as the mind of a consumer, are related to abstract and symbolic frames of thought (Schulze 2005). To use (utilize) something is no longer the point; to 'experience' a product, a service or a place is what matters. The EE literature considers that most basic needs are satisfied and that a growing part of the income will be allocated to experiential goods and services. The EE is traditionally presented as an economy, which historically succeeds the traditional economy of goods and services (Sundbo and Sørensen 2013a). Here, the utility of a good or service is social and psychological. It concerns less the survival than the well-being: products are a substance which function as a cognitive 'stimulus' (Sundbo and Sørensen 2013b). There exists something which is not embodied in the product, but which exists as a distinct social and individual knowledge about the product.

Compared with value creation in the Fordist context of the 1960s, the value of experiential goods and services consequently exploits the time sequence, which starts with the meaning for the potential customer and his building of anticipation and expectations about goods, services and places before the actual transaction. The existence of this time lag plays a fundamental role because it allows the consumption of a good to become memorable, a fundamental element of the experience economy (Pine and Gilmore 1999). As Ek *et al.* (2008) point out for the case of the tourist experience, a 'performance and experience circle' has to be considered, with several phases: cognitive anticipation and planning before the experience; participation and enactment during it; travel tales, memory work and exhibitions; and people's feedback after the experience. Pine and Gilmore highlight the phenomena of authenticity: in business terms, authenticity is 'purchasing on the basis of conformance to self-image' (2013: 29). Value construction is therefore consubstantial with a time sequence with at least two distinct moments.

Regarding space, too, the value construction in the EE necessitates at least two 'places'. First, customers build their own opinion about a good and/or place thanks to the huge amount of information, knowledge and debates one can find in books, in media and on the Internet. Then, customers confront their opinions concretely. Value creation today consists of exploiting this difference between what customers expect, where they are and what other places supply. So the substance of the objects matters little up to here, but functions as 'external stimuli' (Sundbo and Sørensen 2013b), which corroborates or invalidates what was foreseen by the customer. Experiences can be positively or negatively memorable. This will have consequences in the long run. One experiential process in itself means enjoying (*Erlebnis*); the accumulation of it along time means learning (*Erfahrung*) (Sundbo and Sørensen 2013b). This learning can be considered as a lifelong socialization process (Mead and Morris 1967).

Regarding regional development, some places manage to accumulate more meaning in the mind of customers than others. Following Pine and Gilmore (2013), urbaneness can be staged (Pine and Gilmore 2013) to exploit the extra-substantial potential of a place to create value. Every place has the potential to be a 'creative hub' in the sense of Lash and Urry (1994). However, some places manage better than others to act on the knowledge of customers, which stimulates the latter to buy goods or services related to that place. 'Branding' or territorial marketing can be a much more rewarding practice than building an image of a place in the head of customers from nothing. It means exploiting and renewing the knowledge thanks to which customers participate in the regional process of value creation. In some European countries territorial marketing policies have dealt with experiences. Denmark developed innovative policies combining territorial marketing, place branding and experience policy (Lorentzen and van Heur 2012; Löfgren 2003). This has consisted in designing complex territorial stages. A regional development policy relies probably not so much on marketing alone, nor on branding (Therkelsen and Halkier 2008), but on territorial staging (Jeannerat 2015). The latter consists in shifting from a place-based production process to a place-based production and consumption process (Lorentzen 2009; Lorentzen and Jeannerat 2013; Manniche and Larsen 2013).

Up to here, we have seen how time and space lags generate new possibilities of combinations and consequently new value-creation sources, but nothing has been said about monetary transactions. However, pricing is a tricky question. Continuing on their metaphor about theatre and stages, Pine and Gilmore (1999) propose the admission fee as the main charging modality in the EE. Here, the metaphor is probably no longer satisfying and is likely misleading. In territorial systems, this system of payment encourages pricing packages for baskets of goods and services (Pecqueur 2001) instead of separated pricing practices. This also allows financing of the use of concrete processes (actual, physical; such as maintaining the landscape) and symbolic processes (meaning-making; such as the marketing of a destination), which customers cannot be directly charged for. However, most of the time, territorial economic systems do not function as pure 'clubs'. Tourism resorts are an example where admission fees cannot be considered as satisfactory.

## Tourism and experience economy

This section tries to clarify the relations between tourism and the EE. First, tourism is an emblematic, while very old, example of EE. Tourism is a part of the EE, but does not relate to all elements of it. Second, tourism has evolved considerably. Today one speaks of many kinds of tourism, from business to shopping tourism, and many others. 'Tourism' is probably too narrow a word to encompass all this. Several characteristics of tourism can help to understand the functioning of the EE, and especially its way to create value, as well as its way to charge customers.

The history of tourism shows that the premises of the EE go back to the very first hours of European industrialization. Was tourism from the beginning an experiential economic activity? This question would require more historical investigation, but tourism service producers probably did not become stagers (see below) in one day. Moreover, in traditional regions where some of the first resorts developed, few monetary exchanges occurred, and these were exclusively oriented towards basic goods and services like food and accommodation. The value of these products and services probably only grew dependent on symbolic dimensions with the growth of the flows of tourists and the specialization of tourism producers, creating more and more cultural content around tourism transactions. Hotelkeepers started selling landscapes, climate and meanings through payments for meals and beds; time and space matter and in this way substantial goods are transformed into experiential goods.

Tourism is a by-product of the industrial revolution (Tissot 1990, 2000). From its beginning, the diffusion of travel books and guides and narrations in newspapers widely constituted places and territories as symbolic and commodified entities. These symbolic spaces opened the possibilities to travel by creating symbolic links and hierarchies between places. This particular appropriation of space by tourists and tourism providers generated the cultural frame of specific places. From a territorial point of view, the accumulation process of symbolic and communicational knowledge is of major importance; the tourist capital

(Darbellay *et al.* 2011) of a territory is a peculiar result of the recycling of the knowledge stemming from the experiences of its hosts. This dynamic is particularly visible thanks to the Internet, where tourists rank the places visited, recommending certain places while stigmatizing others. Indeed, also in the past consumers who had a tourist experience used to speak about it, and not only in traditional media (guides, newspapers, etc.) but also simply by word of mouth.

Until recent times the conditions of mobility of people and the availability of information allowed only rare physical territorial experiences – in other words, tourism was quite elitist up to the 1960s. Today, territorial experiences can be found everywhere and everyday: commuters's migrations, day visits, local product consumption, business tourism, medical tourism, shopping tourism, special events, fiscal tourism, etc. The boundaries between here and somewhere else have become blurred. Geographers use the idea of 'after tourism' (Bourdeau *et al.* 2012) to deal with this issue. Other concepts like 'amenity migration' (Gosnell and Abrams 2011; Taylor 2001) provide an account of this generalization of value creation linked to the mobility of people, even in daily life. Tourism haunts the literature of the EE and up to now, while constantly mentioned in the most prominent examples of what the EE is, it has been poorly articulated in the conceptual framework of the EE.

Our reading leads to the suggestion that tourism is the archetype of the EE. Regarding the question of customization, for example, in tourism studies, as in sociology, the so-called pragmatic approach has developed rapidly since the 1990s. Before, the tourist was regarded for a long time as a socialized, gregarious, determined being (Knafou and Stock 2003). The notion of 'tourist gaze' qualifying the tourist experience completed this appreciation (Urry 1990): the visual, abstract experience mattered above all. With the 'performance turn' (Crouch 2003; Edensor 2001), the tourist is considered as being creative (Wearing and Wearing 1996). Physically, he acts and lives in the territory (Stock 2004) and participates in the creation of the tourist space (Mossberg 2007). The same evolution has been seen in the regional studies literature, where the co-creation idea exceeds the one of unidirectional customization (Jeannerat 2013). Customization occurs here not because the supplier offers a variety of goods and services, but because different individuals mobilize their own specific opinion in the experience. Now diversity and specialization are central in terms of economic growth: goods and services have to be customized (Pine and Gilmore 2013), but the value creation process is multi-directional – an unclear point in the original EE. In such a system, innovation no longer consists in inventing new products, or in discovering new substantial features, but in the suggestion of meanings and in the fulfilling of consumers's expectations in terms of experience. In staging terms, this means that collaboration (Bærenholdt 2004; Larsen *et al.* 2007) concerns two moments: collaboration to do tourism and to value it.

## The issue of money and the stage model

At the crossroads of these diverse academic traditions and empirical questions is the question of the pricing, and the way we can understand this process in the frame of the experience. Prematurely solved by the EE literature with the admission fee system, it nevertheless proves unsatisfactory in many cases. One of the points noticed by Schulze (2005) about the *Erlebnisgesellschaft* is that sociologists, but also a broad part of the population, develop disparaging discourses about the commercial and monetary dimension of this economy and probably tend to underestimate or to sideline the economic dimension of this experience society. Probably sociologists underestimate the role of monetary transactions and experiences in socialization. Nevertheless, since Marx or Polanyi, critiques about the commodification of everything are not new in social sciences (Bourdieu 2000; Rifkin 2005). This poses specific questions to the EE. If the commercial character of the transaction is too visible, it would compromise its authenticity value, the latter being defined by Pine and Gilmore as a purchase based on conformance to self-image.

Therefore, the value created would paradoxically benefit from a sidelining of its monetary dimension (Beckert and Aspers 2011). This is like in the 'magic world of tourism' (*enchantment of the tourist world*) from Réau and Poupeau (2007), where all the labour needed for the staging is hidden.

In the dynamic frame suggested in Figure 8.1, the monetary aspect (money box in Figure 8.1) is conceptually distinct from the substantive dimension of goods and services (substance box). Substance and money are not sufficient to realize an experience, or even any kind of transaction. This relies also on two

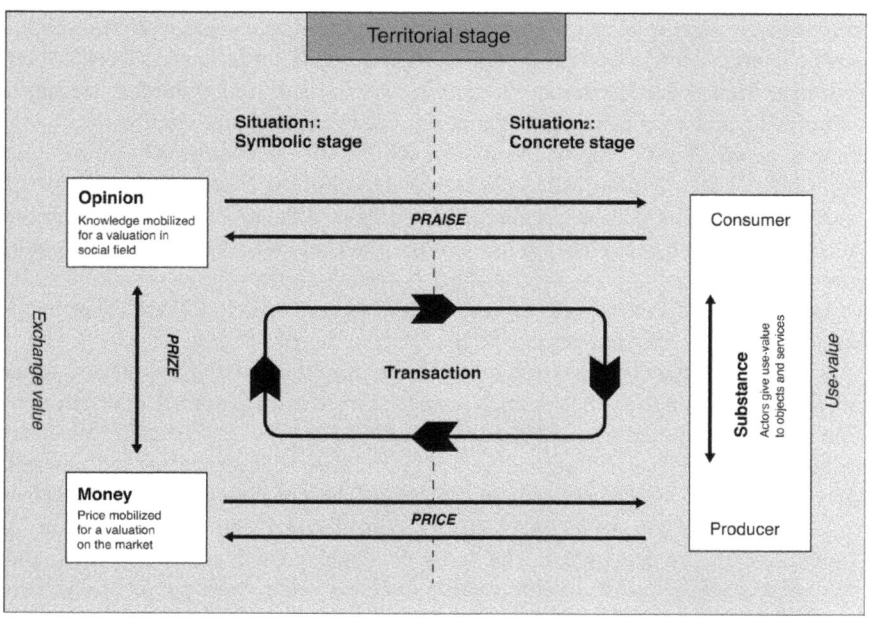

*Figure 8.1* The territorial economic transaction and the territorial stage (source: own elaboration).

kinds of symbols: qualitative and quantitative. The qualitative symbolic component is the cultural knowledge customers have about the object of transaction:
this is the 'opinion' value (Orléan and Diaz-Bone 2013) (opinion box). The
quantitative aspect is the monetary aspect, through the prices displayed on the
market. Economic value is a coin with two sides: it results from use as well as
exchange values, first perceptible on the concrete stage, and then evaluated
(opinion) and calculated (money) on the symbolic stage. These three dimensions
are interdependent. Together, they constitute the stage, on the one hand through
the concrete aspects (on the right in Figure 8.1), and on the other hand by the
symbolic ones (on the left in Figure 8.1): we speak of the concrete stage and the
symbolic stage, constituting the territorial stage together. Let's detail the elements of this model and its dynamic operation.

### Substance and knowledge building experience

Experience results from both substance and opinion dimensions, concrete and
symbolic aspects. Following the literature about the EE, experiences involve
people both 'physiologically' and 'mentally' (Sundbo and Sørensen 2013b), that
is to say in concrete and symbolic ways. The symbolic stage is a 'public space'
in the sense of Habermas (1997), an abstract space where individuals can exert
their rationality: an offer is launched on the market, an issue is set on the agenda,
and individuals start interacting in this space, building their 'opinions'. This
abstract interaction space has increased all through the nineteenth and twentieth
centuries as a complex and historically radical new social process. As pointed
out by Tarde (2006: 11 [1901]), 'there is no word, in Latin nor in Greek, which
answers what we understand by public', and '[But] the public is infinitely
stretchable, and, as it extends, its particular life becomes more intense, we cannot
deny it is the social group of the future' (2006: 15 – our translation). From our
point of view, sociologically, the advent of the experience society can be
explained by the explosion of shared knowledge. As the mobility and availability
of the information is increasing immensely, the range of possible enrichment of
goods and services is becoming infinite. If collective learning is crucial in order
to create the social symbolic context of the experience, individual learning is
valuable because customization is at the heart of the EE.

Today is indeed characterized by the huge importance of this symbolic space
of social coordination, considerably enlarged by the diffusion of new information and communication technologies. Tarde (2006 [1901]) expected this space
to be one 'social group' because he had in mind the 'audience' of the newspapers, which had been developing at that time. The opinions at play in experiential processes today have been shaped and fed by the huge diffusion of
knowledge in the audiences. The latter is today particularly easily available
thanks to the mobility of the information: a century ago, most people didn't care
about a special mineral water brand, for example,[2] because they didn't know
anything about it. But some people did: the leisure class (Veblen 1970 [1899]),
which for example knew Montreux as a thermal resort and as a mineral water

producer.[3] At different times in history, the opinion area (opinion box in Figure 8.1) in the market economy context is more or less complex; the more people have purchasing power for experiential goods, the more the social values concerned grow. This space acts today rather as an arena where these groups are constituted: for example a group of 'amateurs' (aficionado, loyal consumer, follower, etc.), or an Internet community where the experience of thermal resorts and/or water drinking is set as an issue, discussed and valued, or any social group in which particular consumptions are considered as valuable. The opinion of a community becomes the matrix which allows interpreting and valuing goods in an individual and collective way. The fact that agreeing on a particular *product* as being an issue to be discussed constitutes a remarkable social phenomenon.

After having acquired a 'symbolic use' of the product through its social valuation, the consumer may concretely (physiologically) use the product or service. Tourists staying in Montreux during the belle époque or at any particular time are present on the spot, with their sensory aptitudes: they are walking, eating, drinking, sleeping, etc. The substance and use-value of the experience mobilizes their physiological capacities. Here, the utility of the water they drink is clearly physiological, functional. Now, as we see, the drinker may not drink necessarily this thermal water in this place for its (almost standard) properties, but for everything else he or she can experience on this stage, which they know. This value of the water existed before it was drunk and independently of its nourishing properties, linked to the concrete stage in the moment.

## Monetary aspect to perform the experience economy

The monetary scale is an easy way to compare goods and services. Beyond hundreds of mineral water brands and social values associated with these, some are more expensive than others. Here (money box in Figure 8.1), the price is the quantitative symbol of the exchange value. This symbolic dimension of the market can be better understood by contrast to the self-production, self-consumption economy (Braudel 1979, 1985). For centuries, the latter used to be the dominant form of economic activity. In economic systems dominated by self-production and self-consumption, like a family, there is no need for an abstraction like a price because those systems are based exclusively on the use-value associated with cultural meaning. In such socio-economic organizations, there is no money, no clear distinction between producers and consumers and valuation processes take place in the frame of the community. A market economy requires more symbolic abstraction in order to allow the exchange value to emerge. The exchange value appears as the articulation between the cultural interpretative valuation and the quantitative calculation about an anticipated substance. Water for people of Montreux in the nineteenth century had no price, because it didn't exist on a market.

Amid other quantifiers (like weight and measures), money allows the coordination between heterogeneous, qualitative, subjective and inter-subjective valuations of quality and the price, that is to say the quantitative sign which institutionally designates the objectivized value of a good. Monetary exchange in the context of a market economy leads to the differentiation of producers and the multiplication of goods and services offered on the market. This leads to social and cultural learning in order to build meanings for those new activities which are largely dedicated to lifestyles in society.

To better understand this issue, we can relate the model to the valuation typology of Stark (2011). Following Dewey (1939), Stark distinguishes the valuation's triplicate of 'price', 'prize' and 'praise'. First, the 'praise' is relative to the fact that a substance connects the user to a world of imagination. In the model, this conceptually is the link between opinion and substance (on top in Figure 8.1). Then, 'prize' concerns the valuation through market pricing and 'praise' – the valuation through the social field. 'Price' and 'prize' are the actions conceptually linking money with, respectively, opinion and substance. While 'prize' (link on the left in Figure 8.1) refers to various cultural values like taste and health, 'price' (below link in Figure 8.1) is relative to market in the sense of the concurrent influences of policies, supply and demand, production costs, etc. The 'praise' is parallel to the 'price': the meaning of a substance in social space exists symbolically as well as the price of it on the market. In territorial transactions we found these three valuation processes.

### Territorial economic transaction: the archetype case of stay

Let's consider an example of the entire territorial transaction process with the same example. At first (Situation$_1$, the left side of Figure 8.1), consider somebody who is envisaging going to Montreux on holiday. The tourist is concretely standing in a place (for example, London), and wants to go to another one (Montreux). In this first place (London), cultural knowledge is available for the valuation by the potential customer of a good or a service: Montreux is at this moment on a symbolic stage were the individual is standing. Moreover, even if the tourist had never drunk mineral water nor been to Montreux before, she knows that they exist, she knows a little about their characteristics (the quality of water and the history and geography of the city, at least about Switzerland), she also knows if it is fashionable or not; in short, she has an opinion of it. This is the qualitative dimension of the anticipated exchange value, where the customer starts the experience process. Next to this are the prices displayed on the market by the suppliers. Out of this, the potential customer can make her calculation about the exchange value balanced against her own anticipated opinion about the experience she will have in the future. Seen from Situation$_1$, the experience performance approximates what Urry (1990) calls a 'hermeneutic cycle' for tourism, first considered as a visual experience – the striking visual aspect limiting itself here to a preliminary representation.

Later (Situation$_2$), the consumer is drinking water in Montreux. Here the use-value is realized and can be appreciated. Then, this experience gives rise to new knowledge by producers and customers. The exchange value was created on the symbolic stage both qualitatively (the opinion elaborated by the customer) and quantitatively (the prices displayed). It is now possible to confront the exchange value with the use-value created by the concrete side of the experience. This confrontation brings a new, adjusted opinion by the customer that she may now share with others (family, friends, Internet sites like Tripadvisor, for example) on the symbolic scene. Feedback on the symbolic stage is part of the process. In Situation$_2$, people are acting on the place: it's the 'performance turn' point of view. In Situation$_1$, interactions took place, but the players were not co-present. The interaction was 'real', but symbolic. Here, it is made concrete. On both stages there are increasing returns of adoption: the more people go, the more they talk about it; the more they go, the higher the territorial value rises. Consequently, the territorial value of a place is not only concretely shaped in the place, but relationally and also symbolically with other places.

Here the tourist experience is taken as an example of a territorial transaction. Because of the move from one place to another, we easily understand the anticipation phenomenon and the importance of both symbolic and concrete stages. This process is also valid for other kinds of transactions (see below); drinking Montreux water in London involves the entire territorial stage for economic value creation – immediately and in the long run. Nevertheless, presence on the spot has many implications.

All the consumptions are worth more than their substantial value. In the case of Montreux mineral water drunk at home by a British consumer, the symbolic stage of Montreux matters, probably in order to make himself distinct as an upper-class member. In the case of the water drunk on the spot by a tourist, Montreux as a territorial stage attracted her as a consumer on the spot – symbolic aspects relying on concrete infrastructures. In both cases, something occurred on a symbolic stage before drinking concretely and enjoying the water: this water already had a certain value – because of the expectations of the consumer, resulting from his previous experiences and other symbolic learning about quality. We talk in both cases of Territorial Economic Transaction (TETs), because the territory is involved in different ways in the economic value construction.

Regarding monetary transfers, the above example shows that the model of admission fees doesn't match, even if this case corresponds to the scope of the EE. The part of the EE which is related to a move into another concrete space is about presence, and presence is at the core of how these TETs are monetarily charged. We observe admission fees appearing under various forms: traditionally with entrance tickets, packages (e.g. all-inclusive stays), tourist taxes; but also under other forms such as parking taxes for one-day tourists, daily taxes for second-home residents, etc. In our example the tourist didn't pay an admission fee to walk on Geneva's lakeside, nor to drink free water at the village fountain, nor in the water bottle case. But in the case of staying, the free water drinking won't be the only action on the spot – all economic transactions count.

## Case study through TETs analytical grid

Transportation and information technologies have developed considerably, and accumulation processes produced specific places – resorts – which have built specific competences and infrastructures in the field of tourism. This growth has been exponential since the 1990s due to new information and communication technologies. This contraction of time and space had consequences for the value of all goods and services, not only for tourism. Because different articulations of time and space constitute the TETs, we suggest a typology (Figure 8.2) based on two criteria. The first one is the mobility in the transaction: do people move to goods and services or do goods and services move to people? The second criterion is the relation to the territory: how does the transaction involve the territory as a source of value? The idea suggested in these paragraphs is that we can speak of *presential* economy as a generalized form of all the economic activities that look like tourism while being much more diverse and pervasive today than tourism used to be in the nineteenth century. In contrast, non-presential economy would concern economic activities not involving the presence of the consumer on the spot, but as 'productive' territory from where products are exported. Nevertheless, a part of this concerns 'referential transactions', which involves territory in the economic value creation as well. From a value-creation point of view, all four territorial transactions depend on the territorial stage. From the territorial point of view (and especially planning), all kinds of transactions

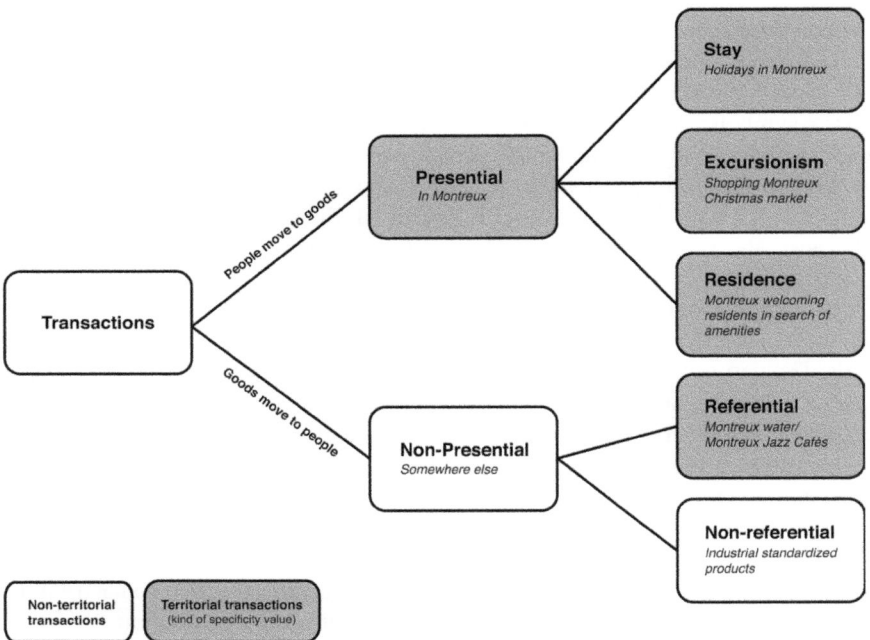

*Figure 8.2* A typology of territorial economic transactions (source: own elaboration).

depend on the territorial stage. They all directly or indirectly play a role in this stage as a part of its concrete and symbolic organization.

### Presential transactions

Presential goods and services combine real physical co-presence in a place. Transactions which depend on the mobility of consumers represent a growing part of the experiential market for two reasons. The mobility of people is easier and easier, and this is a historical trend. Second, as the EE literature stresses, it allows the creation of more value. Consequently, even companies that traditionally rely on the mobility of goods shift to exploiting people's mobility, like the oft-quoted examples from LEGO, Volkswagen, Disney, etc. This innovation feeds both the symbolic and the concrete stage of a company. It reinforces both their presential and non-presential businesses, the entire territorial stage. In the examples just given, companies are very large and are often part of the local identity: the territory depends more on these firms than the firm depends on the territory. Should one speak more of company stage than of a territorial stage? In many cases, like LEGO, companies made the reputation of the place. They invested in the territorial stage to increase the economic value of their products, the presential and non-presential economy contributing in theory to the increase of the value. Regarding decentralized territorial production systems, where many smaller players interact, places have tended to have a more visible reputation, sometimes more than companies on the symbolic scene. This is the case of the Swiss city of Montreux.

The term 'station' ('resort' – 'place where we settle') fits this city exactly because of the importance of *presential transactions*, which have taken place there thanks to the stays (see Figure 8.2) in its regional historic development. Consumers used to settle in this place for stays of several weeks or months. Montreux, with a present population of 25,000, was built for and by the presence of people spending money there from the 1830s onward. From 1850, the British clientele in particular sought the attributes of the Lake Geneva lakeside. The resort's golden age was between 1890 and 1914, when it totalled more than 7,000 beds in 100 hotels and 17,850 inhabitants.

In 1930, 47 per cent of persons with an economic activity in Montreux did so within the category 'trade, hotel business, transport'. The local economy is completely dependent on tourists, on consumers who gain their income somewhere else and come to spend it in Montreux. There are multiple attraction motives of this territory: the landscape remained attractive throughout this period; the climate, dry and gentle in winter, was significant until the interwar period; winter sports dominate between 1895 and 1945; the social life, nightlife, conferences and travel incentives[4] became important from the 1950s; music concerts were also important throughout (classics during the golden age, jazz from 1967). However, from the economic point of view these differences don't matter; the basic income comes from consumers having expected and planned to travel into this place which – for reasons of their own – is preferred to another place.

After the belle époque's euphoria, the situation of the territorial system degraded repeatedly during the First World War and the interwar period. The solutions envisaged for the territorial economic restart mainly focused on presential transactions (stays and excursions). The Tourist Information Office in particular developed diverse strategies to make people consume on the spot: conference participants and motor coach tourists in transit from northern to southern Europe. These efforts paid off and the situation again became gradually favourable in the 1960s and 1970s, until an upgrading of the local supply took place towards more affluent customers with the concomitant development of residential transactions (see below). Besides the tourists staying in hotels and second homes, the development of boutiques and events was assured by the excursionists. Many inhabitants of western Switzerland travel to Montreux for shopping, or to take part in events like the Jazz Festival.

Looking back on Montreux's trajectory as a whole, presential transactions played a major role in the development of the region. Actors built and exploited the territorial value, accumulating not only infrastructures, cultural activities and various service activities on the concrete stage, but above all, the actor's knowledge and the fame of the resort on the symbolic stage, thus raising the memorable value of the resort.

Next to the stay and excursionist experience, residential experience has been of great importance for the development of Montreux since the nineteenth century, when British tourists used to stay several months and often built their own houses there. During the last phase of its trajectory, Montreux has encountered a rapid growth in the residential phenomenon (main and second homes). Between 2000 and 2011, the share of the permanently occupied housing fell from 71 per cent to 40 per cent. In terms of flows of incomes, the holiday homes are doubtless important. From the 1980s, local tourism authorities developed an aggressive policy to attract affluent foreign residents. On top of the traditional residential charms of the region, this policy was based on a lump sum taxation regime inherited from the nineteenth century. With regard to the territorial value in general, this substitution has consequences. Residential transactions do not contribute to the renewal of the territorial value. It is based on routine everyday life experiences and no longer with intense service provision to tourists. Real estate development does not contribute in the same way to knowledge accumulation on the symbolic stage. In other words, the local residential transactions today exploit the territorial value inherited from former tourism activities, but they do not contribute to the renewal of this value.

### Non-presential transactions

Spatially speaking, in the non-presential TETs, the experience depends on the mobility of goods towards the consumer's home or nearby. The success of Starbucks was to propose a cosy design and a palette of coffees. By expanding all around the world, the company places, at the disposal of the consumers, a stage near them. A Starbucks distinguishes itself in a given place from local competitors, but all Starbucks are identical all around the world. With regard to what we can call the global experiential market, the experiences which depend on the mobility of goods and services have a specific importance. Non-presential goods and services represent a large part of TETs.

The economic value which is released by such transactions relies more on the time sequence dynamics than on the spatial dynamics: the memorable good or service is proposed to the consumers in their daily place of life. Regarding this aspect, it is basically a traditional productive organization. Nevertheless, there is some more complexity. In these non-presential transactions, goods or services can use a symbolic link between the concrete place of origin of the product and the place of consumption, as in the case of the Montreux bottle of water. This reference to a place distinguishes the latter from its competitors by mobilizing the element of territorial exclusivity. This kind of non-presential good or service is called referential (see Figure 8.2). The referential transaction deals with an expected territorial experience: the consumer is expecting to live an experience linked to a specific place and the producer can stage the symbolic territorial dimension; however the place is not involved concretely. It is steered by an experiential contract based on territorial value.

The producers mobilize the symbolic aspects of the territory, but they also indirectly have an impact on the place referred to. Producers based on the place of origin need to take care of the reputation of the territorial stage. For instance, if a mineral water producing region gets the reputation of being polluted, the value of its products would probably decrease. This is why producers of referential goods, who create more value thanks to territory, have to take care of the territorial stage (both symbolically and concretely): even if the customer is not directly in contact with the concrete stage, it contributes to the valuation of the good at home. In theory, this category includes any sorts of goods and services with a territorial value as the common cultural denominator (Pecqueur 2001); for example, all territorial references on food (for example AOC wines or cheeses) and on manufactured goods (for example the *Swissmade* 'label' for watches).

An example of a referential transaction in Montreux is the catering school of Glion.[5] Indeed, this company was originally part of an expansion plan within tourism in the 1960s. Rather than providing a trained labour force for the local system, the school itself rapidly became an important part of the territorial stage due to: (1) affluent students in residence (who are subjected to the tourist tax during their studies); (2) their relatives who come to visit; and (3) finally, by former students, who later visit their place of training and eventually invest in this company. As a consequence of such an acquisition by former alumni, a restructuring, and due to land availability issues, the catering school of Glion relocated part of its activities to a nearby little city. Afterwards it opened a new campus in London. We speak about referential transactions, because the value in this case clearly depends on the 'label' Glion-Montreux.

The same phenomenon happens with the Jazz Festival, which exploits its knowledge accumulated over time. First, the festival was literally divided into halves abroad – in the USA in the 1990s, in Japan until now. Second, it signed contracts to play its recordings on board Swissair planes thanks to an exclusive partnership. Finally, today Montreux Jazz Festival opens café-restaurants in European train stations and airports in partnership with a catering company. The concept relies on the broadcasting of the archives; the offer's specificity compared with standardized competitors (like Starbucks, for example) in places of passage is the reference to Montreux. With regard to the functional and standardized competitors, the entertainment legitimated by the territorial reference participates in value creation by suggesting a memorable experience.

Presential transactions differ from referential transactions because in the first case consumers move to the place, whereas in the second case goods move to consumers. Nevertheless, both types are based on territorial value and both mobilize the territorial stage. Those two types, when successful, reinforce each other because they both act on the territorial value to create economic value. This latter point is crucial to understanding the necessity also for traditional productive industrial regions to take care of their stage: with the Internet and the exponential availability of information and knowledge about places, the value of their traditional production depends more and more on this. Of course, shifting from an industrial tradition to presential competences is not that easy. Many food-producing regions have managed to do it, like the wine-producing ones, but also other industrial regions producing watches, chocolate, cars, etc. In both cases some regions started to do it by transforming their industrial tradition into heritage following cultural motivations, but this is not yet a 'stage': one needs more devices to capture more monetary income.

### *Territorial transactions*

TETs involve the territory in value creation. They can concern tourism (stay) as well as export referential industry. Indeed, a TET puts territory in play, but in two different ways, depending on whether it is a presential or referential transaction. In both cases, the link with the territory is not the geographic demarcation of a price to be paid, but the meaning of the territory for the consumer; stagers have to manage these meaning (the various insertions at different scales: Montreux,[6] but also the Canton de Vaud, the Alps, Switzerland). In both cases, the territorial stage matters, in the short run for value creation or in the long run for the territorial value. Here again, the development of transport and information technologies have drastically changed the present way of operating TETs. The territorial shape of today's experiential activities is a complex network of interactions, involving intensively the Internet sphere and the physical circulation of goods, people and capital.

### Conclusion

This chapter suggests that the complementarity of presential and referential transactions and the link between TETs and usual industry opens new ways to think about territorial development in a time when the mobility of people and information increases continuously and consequently when sociocultural value becomes an increasing component of economic value. Through the micro issue of the complex economic value creation process explained here via the model of the territorial transaction and territorial stage, the issue for regional development is to take into account both the symbolic and concrete dimensions of the territory. The typology of TETs presented above helps to conceptualize the presential and productive dimensions. To distinguish these two stages positions the stream of thought of the EE better at the conjunction between the literatures of sociology, economy and tourism studies.

Once upon a time, territories like Montreux acted on their symbolic stage by using territorial advertising. Yet, in successful tourism resorts, the complexity of the goods, the services and the regional organization did not stop growing. Today, most regions have to stage their territory. This change is obviously easier in regions traditionally concerned with tourism, like resorts or metropolises, because they have been sensitive to the experiential potential in economic value creation for a long time. They would, for example, be the first subjects of 'event-ification' (Jakob 2013). In other words, they are used to acting on the symbolic and concrete stage together, contrarily to industrial areas where economic development was always based on the substantive value of exported goods and services, provoking dissociation between the competitiveness of the exported goods and the quality of local living conditions.

In summary, today's development of the EE is the result of a double movement of 'touristification'. First, the mobility of people has increased and opens infinite possibilities to develop presential transactions. Second, traditional goods are more and more transformed into referential goods, that is to say, goods enriched by symbolic territorial meanings. In spite of the specific properties of tourism, the literature on innovation and on regional development once treated tourism in the same way as other traditional productive sectors, that is to say stressing the generation of economies of scale and of innovation systems, and even talking about tourism 'clusters' (Hjalager 2010). This transposition of the cluster concept (Hall 2005) shows well that the main concern here is to maintain competitiveness and sustainability of the tourism resort by focusing solely on the productive side. The point highlighted in this chapter is that innovation in the EE consists in reducing the complexity of goods and services either by improving the mobility of the information (by constituting territorial knowledge by people thanks to guides, Internet sites, etc.) or by improving the mobility (by facilitating the presence on a place, by developing the production of referential goods and services). These improvements occur through a double logic of inter- and intra-territorial connections. This setting is far more complex than the cluster model as it includes the symbolic stage – and consequently the knowledge of potential consumers – as a central resource of value creation. The value-creation process of TETs appears as an increase of the territorial value in a local–global dynamic. These kinds of presential and referential innovations, based on the staging of the territory, only started recently for industrial regions, but are much more ancient for tourism resorts, as well as wine-producing regions and metropolises.

## Notes

1 This frame and results come from qualitative historical research (analysis of archival documents, press and interviews), a thesis carried out under the Swiss National Science Foundation project 'Between Abyss and Metamorphosis: An Interdisciplinary Approach to the Development of Tourist Resorts' (subsidy No. CR11I1_135390, principal applicant Prof. Mathis Stock).
2 We take here an example from our case study, but the famous Pine and Gilmore's coffee on St Mark's Square would match too. See below for other similarities between these examples.
3 In 1899, for example, three mineral water plants in Montreux exported 300,000 bottles a year to France and Great Britain. This industry did not survive after the First World War.
4 Travel incentives are shapes of reward, incentives to the commitment of the employees (or regular customers), which had developed in an important way in the USA during the 1960s.
5 *Glion Institute for Higher Education*. Glion is a hamlet in the municipality of Montreux.
6 Here in the case of Montreux the geographic scale of municipality.

## References

Bærenholdt, J.O. (2004) *Performing tourist places*, Farnham: Ashgate.
Beckert, J. and Aspers, P. (eds) (2011) *The worth of goods. Valuation and pricing in the economy*, New York: Oxford University Press.
Bourdeau, P., Daller, J.-F. and Martin, N. (2012) *Les migrations d'agrément: du tourisme à l'habiter*, Paris: L'Harmattan.
Bourdieu, P. (2000) *Les structures sociales de l'économie*, Paris: Seuil.
Boyer, R. and Saillard, Y. (2010) *Théorie de la régulation, l'état des savoirs*, Paris: La Découverte.
Braudel, F. (1979) *Civilisation matérielle, économie et capitalisme*, Paris: Armand Collin.
Braudel, F. (1985) *La dynamique du capitalisme*, Paris: Flammarion.
Crouch, D. (2003) 'Spacing, performing, and becoming: tangles in the mundane', *Environment and Planning A*, 35(11), 1945–60.
Darbellay, F., Clivaz, C., Nahrath, S. and Stock, M. (2011) 'Approche interdisciplinaire du développement des stations touristiques. Le capital touristique comme concept opératoire', *Mondes du tourisme*, 4: 36–48.
Dewey, J. (1939) *Theory of valuation*, Chicago: University of Chicago Press.
Dubet, F. (1994) *Sociologie de l'expérience*, Paris: Seuil.
Edensor, T. (2001) 'Performing tourism, staging tourism: (Re)producing tourist space and practice' *Tourist studies*, 1(1): 59–81.
Ek, R., Larsen, J., Hornskov, S.B. and Mansfeldt, O.K. (2008) 'A dynamic framework of tourist experiences: Space-time and performances in the Experience Economy', *Scandinavian Journal of Hospitality and Tourism*, 8(2): 122–40.
Gosnell, H. and Abrams, J. (2011) 'Amenity migration: Diverse conceptualizations of drivers, socioeconomic dimensions, and emerging challenges', *GeoJournal*, 76(4): 303–22.
Habermas, J. (1997) *L'espace public: archéologie de la publicité comme dimension constitutive de la société bourgeoise*, Paris: Payot.

Hall, C.M. (2005) 'Rural wine and food tourism cluster and network development', in D. Hall, I. Kirkpatrick and M. Mitchell (eds) *Rural tourism and sustainable business*, Bristol: Channel View Publications.

Hjalager, A.-M. (2010) 'A review of innovation research in tourism', *Tourism management*, 31(1): 1–12.

Jakob, D. (2013) 'The eventification of place: Urban development and experience consumption in Berlin and New York City', *European urban and regional studies*, 20(4): 447–59.

Jeannerat, H. (2013) 'Staging experience, valuing authenticity: Towards a market perspective on territorial development', *European urban and regional studies*, 20: 370–84.

Jeannerat, H. (2015) 'Towards a staging system approach to territorial innovation', in A. Lorentzen, K.T. Larsen and L. Schrøder (eds) *Spatial Dynamics in the Experience Economy*, Abingdon: Routledge.

Knafou, R. and Stock, M. (2003) 'Tourisme', in J. Lévy and M. Lussault (eds) *Dictionnaire de la géographie et de l'espace des sociétés*, Paris: Belin.

Larsen, J., Urry, J. and Axhausen, K.W. (2007) 'Networks and tourism: Mobile social life', *Annals of Tourism Research*, 34(1): 244–62.

Lash, S. and Urry, J. (1994) *Economies of signs and spaces*, London: Sage.

Löfgren, O. (2003) 'The new economy: a cultural history', *Global Networks*, 3(3): 239–54.

Lorentzen, A. (2009) 'Cities in the experience economy', *European Planning Studies*, 17(6), 829–45.

Lorentzen, A. and Jeannerat, H. (2013) 'Urban and regional studies in the experience economy: What kind of turn?', *European urban and regional studies*, 20(4): 363–9.

Lorentzen, A. and van Heur, B. (eds) (2012) *Cultural political economy of small cities*, vol. 49, Abingdon: Routledge.

Manniche, J. and Larsen, K.T. (2013) 'Experience staging and symbolic knowledge: The case of Bornholm culinary products', *European urban and regional studies*, 20(4): 401–16.

Mead, G.H. (1934) 'Mind, self, and society: From the standpoint of a social behaviorist', reprinted in C.W. Morris (ed.) (1967) *Works Of George Herbert Mead*, vol. 1, Chicago: University of Chicago Press.

Mossberg, L. (2007) 'A marketing approach to the tourist experience', *Scandinavian Journal of Hospitality and Tourism*, 7(1): 59–74.

Orléan, A. and Diaz-Bone, R. (2013) 'Entretien avec André Orléan', *Revue de la régulation. Capitalisme, institutions, pouvoirs*, 14.

Pecqueur, B. (2001) 'Qualité et développement territorial: l'hypothèse du panier de bien et des services territorialisés', *Economie Rurale*, 261: 37–49.

Pine, B.J. and Gilmore, J.H. (1999) *The experience economy: Work is theatre and every business a stage*, Boston: Harvard Business School Press.

Pine, B.J. and Gilmore, J.H. (2013) 'The experience economy: past, present and future', in J. Sundbo and F. Sørensen (eds) *Handbook on the Experience Economy*, Cheltenham: Edward Elgar.

Réau, B. and Poupeau, F. (2007) 'L'enchantement du monde touristique', *Actes de la recherche en sciences sociales*, 170: 5–15.

Rifkin, J. (2005) *L'âge de l'accès*, Paris: La Découverte Poche.

Schulze, G. (2005) *Die Erlebnisgesellschaft: Kultursoziologie der Gegenwart*, Frankfurt: Campus Verlag.

Stark, D. (2011) 'What's valuable?', in J. Beckert and P. Aspers (eds) *The Worth of Goods: Valuation and Pricing in the Economy*, Oxford: Oxford University Press.

Stock, M. (2004) *L'habiter comme pratique des lieux géographiques*. Online. Available at: www.espacestemps.net/en/articles/lrsquohabiter-comme-pratique-des-lieux-geographiques-en/#reference.html (accessed 1 June 2014).

Sundbo, J. and Sørensen, F. (eds) (2013a) *Handbook on the experience economy*, Cheltenham: Edward Elgar.

Sundbo, J. and Sørensen, F. (2013b) 'Introduction to the Experience Economy', in J. Sundbo and F. Sørensen (eds) *Handbook on the Experience Economy*, Cheltenham: Edward Elgar.

Tarde, G. [1901] (2006) *L'opinion et la foule*, Paris: Editions du Sandre (F. Alcan).

Taylor, J. (2001) 'Authenticity and sincerity in tourism', *Annals of Tourism Research*, 28: (7–26).

Tissot, L. (1990) 'La Conquête de la Suisse: les agences de voyage et l'industrialisation du tourisme (1840–1900)', *Société Suisse d'Histoire Economique et Sociale*, vol. 8.

Tissot, L. (2000) *Naissance d'une industrie touristique. Les Anglais et la Suisse au XIXe siècle*, Lausanne: Payot.

Therkelsen, A. and Halkier, H. (2008) 'Contemplating place branding umbrellas. The case of coordinated national tourism and business promotion in Denmark', *Scandinavian Journal of Hospitality and Tourism*, 8(2): 159–75.

Urry, J. (1990) *The tourist gaze: Leisure and travel in contemporary societies*, London: Sage.

Veblen, T. [1899] (1970) *Théorie de la classe de loisir*, Paris: Gallimard.

Wearing, B. and Wearing, S. (1996) 'Refocussing the tourist experience: The flaneur and the choraster', *Leisure Studies*, 15(4): 229–43.

# 9 Val d'Europe

## An experience economy landscape tamed by affect

*Anne-Marie d'Hauteserre*

## Introduction

The changing global economy influences urban forms and determines the hierarchy of world cities that compete in it. Paris is not immune to this increasing competitivity so the French state responded by supporting a major investment by the Walt Disney Company in the last sector of one of its new towns. The development of Val d'Europe illustrates this turn to the 'culturalization of economic goods' and the commodification of cultural goods (Pratt 2011: 324). Is Val d'Europe an extreme project of experience planning that might be a mirror to utopian desire, a sort of crossroads of magic and positivism introduced by the Walt Disney Company? Could its consumers be aware that the paradise offered is an illusion considering that re-territorializing for the pursuit of hedonism often means that boredom and monotony soon invade? Such questions arise when global cities like Paris plan to maintain or possibly improve their rank and standing to ensure their visibility, their visitability and their positionality on the global stage.

This chapter will discuss how affect can develop in aestheticized urban spaces and transform them into neighbourhoods. It seeks to deconstruct how space takes form in different physical, social and emotional dimensions. Space has not become irrelevant; it is being re-territorialized, resulting in the reapportionment of space. In Val d'Europe, the Walt Disney Company (hereafter: the Company) did not, contrarily to all the affirmations of the critics of the French state, manage to bend the French planning apparatus. The urban spaces constructed by the Company and its contractors have been recomposed and reapportioned but layout and design principles imposed by the French state ensure(d) that the urbanization of Val d'Europe is at least minimally readable to future residents so they can maintain a unique sense of place rather than struggle with a myth of identity as unreal as the hyper-world of the Magic Kingdoms®. The partners involved in the development of Val d'Europe have made the effort, through sometimes very contentious discussions, to provide the means for affect to develop among the residents and other actors/actants living and operating in that space. The Company thus had to contend with how such interactions transform(ed) the area into a French place.

I have used a qualitative methodology to focus on meanings and on the interests that have socially constructed the landscape of Val d'Europe and to reveal the tension and contradictions in the implementation there of 'experience planning'. Rather than examining buildings and urban structures themselves, I have studied the in-between spaces of urban life, the places where people have met, interacted, lived and performed since 1992. The turn to experience planning in this large project combined what appeared to be hegemonic state policies and corporate neo-liberal approaches, which, for many observers, had little chance of translating into a 'competitive but livable' urban environment. Arguments in the chapter are based on my critical cultural and social analysis of texts (published by academics, the French state and the Walt Disney Company), interviews that I carried out over three sabbaticals, and narratives of local officials and residents (some of these last recorded officially in state documents) and members of Euro Disney SCA, combined with (participant) observation. The chapter starts with how space was transformed to enable the birth of Val d'Europe within greater Paris. It then defines the experience economy and planning as implemented in Val d'Europe. The third section introduces affect theory. How it has been integrated in the experience economy of Val d'Europe is demonstrated in the fourth section, while the results of this collaboration between the state and the Company are discussed in the fifth section.

## Val d'Europe and Greater Paris

Val d'Europe, the name of sector IV of the new town of Marne-La-Vallée (see Figure 9.1), was to secure the place of Paris on the world stage thanks to the construction of theme parks by the Walt Disney Company but the state also wanted to develop an urban neighbourhood. Greater Paris is faced with increasing global competition as a tourist destination even if (or because) for close to 30

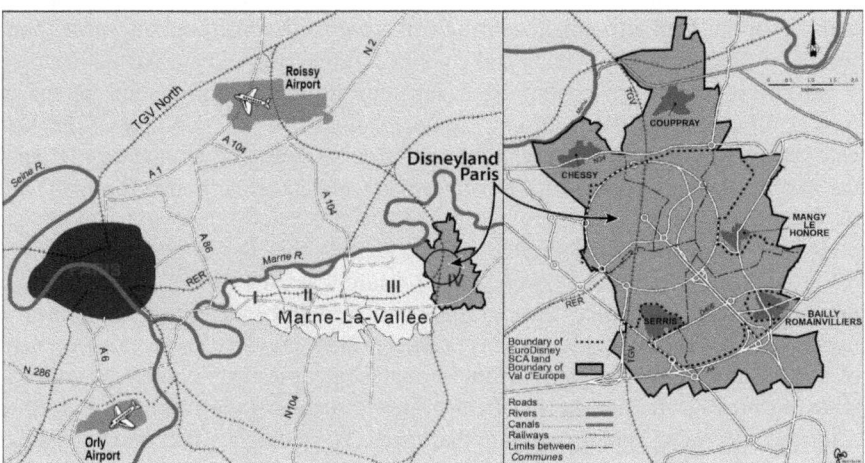

*Figure 9.1* Location map of Marne-La-Vallée, Val d'Europe and the SAN townships (map © Anne-Marie d'Hauteserre 2014).

years it was the main tourism destination for congresses in the world. In order to compete on the world stage it has had to reconsider its 'attractiveness'. The state has thus turned from top-down planning to supporting urban projects which are easier to negotiate with local authorities (Bouinot 2002; Roncayolo 2003; Ingallina 2004). Competitivity includes greater 'liveability' through better services and facilities. Policies are implemented through a variety of instruments such as a Schéma de Cohérence Territoriale (SCOT: planning for regional level integration), a Plan Local d'Urbanisme (PLU: planning at the local level) and the Projet d'Aménagement et de Développement Durable (PADD: planning for sustainability as required by the Grenelle agreement). A Schéma directeur régional d'Île de France (SDRIF: planning for the integrated development of the Paris Basin, also called Île de France) was drawn up in 2006 for the region. Planning is still an important activity in France even if the state has retreated from direct involvement.

The state has always distrusted Paris as a city: that is why, to this day, its extent has been maintained to its 1860 boundaries, except for the annexation of the fortifications area in 1921 (Veltz 2012). It is part of a constant strategy of containment that included the choice of the location of the Disney parks. The state has historically muzzled the development of the city of Paris. Politics of land use in and around Paris explicitly sought to reduce the role of Paris within France. It is ironic when one considers Napoleon's vision for the capital:

> My dreams included making Paris the true capital of Europe. Sometimes I wanted her to become a city of two, three, four million inhabitants, something fabulous, colossal, totally unknown until now.
>
> (Bonaparte 1991: 146)

The experience that encourages consumption (by tourists) or occupation (by residents) remains a 'situated' process: it occupies space, and is sometimes place based. Although producers and the places where production occurs as well as consumers need not exist at the same location, they have to engage each other for a consumer's experience to occur. Consumption also links individual daily practices to the urban environment: visits to the parks or other leisure sites in the Paris Basin, for example. State policy has supported the development of spaces of 'experience' in partnership with the Walt Disney Company in Val d'Europe: they have a specific location. The results have local, regional, national and international resonance (Figure 9.2). The parks, built by an international company, attract international visitors as well regional and local ones; the shopping centre is a local and regional magnet, occasionally an international one. The residents are national citizens who might also come from nearby (local area or close regions).

Space has gained different meanings and attributes. People live in multiple diverse social circles and spaces are articulated by each participant in very different ways (Territoires 2040 2011). New towns (like Marne-la-Vallée) contribute to the spreading and to the restructuring of outer urban spaces as they relay the

*Figure 9.2* Haussmannian architecture near the commercial centre of Val d'Europe and Place d'Ariane (photo © Anne-Marie d'Hauteserre 2014).

influence of the centre. Planning by the French government was to offer greater liveability to those migrating to the Paris area through a more coherent use of land. On the other hand, in the experience economy, the consumption of products and space is turned into an event, a happening that entices people to consume more: 'It is a competitive and market-oriented planning strategy that subtly re-legitimizes regressive social redistributions within the city' (Peck 2007: 8). Such a strategy normalizes experiences of urban and social fragmentation and segregation and increases the public's ability to tolerate or even accept splintering forms of development. Val d'Europe is one of the few areas urbanized under the new experience economy regime in France but it seems to have attracted residents of different income levels without causing polarization between the various groups.

## Defining the experience economy and planning

Many cities, or at least portions of the larger ones, have transformed themselves into landscapes of simulation, i.e. they have become stages for consumption (Roost 2000; Baudrillard 1996) but the city of Paris has avoided much of such aestheticization due to developments in Val d'Europe and the rest of the new

towns that surround it. Experience economy, experience planning and their physical, spatial manifestations have meant a shift of production to a stage that inte-
grates productive resources and consumer engagement. Or should we speak of
'totalizing' capitalism which attempts to impose its values throughout social life
in ways that deflect any contestation and reduce opportunities for participation,
except as a consumer? Human relations and interaction seem governed by a
system of prescribed syntactical forms. The Company speaks of a harmonious
urban development but the source of the desire for such harmony may well be a
normative value dictated by an exclusive (neo-liberal) world view that leaves
nothing undefined, as was demonstrated in Celebration, Florida, the ultimate
gated, privatized, urban development totally controlled by its promoters, free of
public scrutiny and regulation (Archer 1996; Ross 1999).

Already in the 1960s, in France, the situationists sought to encourage the
staging of everyday life but they stimulated it for the benefit of residents
through proper architecture and urban policy. The situationists were French
intellectuals (e.g. Constant, Debord or Lefebvre) who in the 1950s and 1960s
decried people's alienation from work and life because they were forced to live
in architecturally deplorable high-rise cement barracks. They believed the
everyday had to be reinvented. Today, planners follow or apply the 'experience turn' to tourism and urban economic development as they plan to satisfy
the quest for pleasure and for living well together as illustrated in the following quote:

> *competitive* places that thrive economically and facilitate *creativity* and
> *innovation*; *liveable* places that provide a choice of housing, work and *life-
> style* options; *environmentally* responsible places that manage all aspects of
> the environment *sustainably*; inclusive places; distinctive places; well-
> governed places.
> (Draft New Zealand Urban Design Protocol 2004: 5, emphasis added)

Improving the quality of places is the way to influence the direction of flows of
people, of investment, of communication and creativity. Leisure or pleasure
experiences are seen as key drivers. History, authenticity, local culture and
leisure offerings or a vibrant retail sector are considered assets in local development also outside of the big cities. Conditions have changed as the local influences more and more the global. Even remote provincial towns and new cities play
a major role in world affairs today (Brugmann 2010). The worldwide connected
system of cities are re-engineering global economics, politics and ecology,
accelerating local conditions into global trends.

The new urban models, however, are just fantasies for pedestrians (Benjamin
1983). Main Street USA sets the tone and pace of Disneyland: it is a place for
strolling (De Roos 1994), a rare practice in the USA where walking raises suspi-
cions of criminal intent. Casinos and shopping malls are dedicated to walkers,
but strolling is only a pretext to encourage spending by visitors. They are closer
to the shops whose windows they can peer into and that entice them to enter. In

large commercial centres, walking itineraries are scripted, like a movie scenario. Control leads to efficiency, calculability and predictability (Ritzer 1996), catering to fabricated needs in order to provide the ultimate desirable experience: it exacerbates desire. Authors assert that though staged, these experiences are real, not in any way artificial (Pine and Gilmore 1999: 30–6; Sundbo and Sørensen 2013). The new commercial centre of Val d'Europe, inspired by the architecture and atmosphere of the Baltard passages in Paris, illustrates this new organization of urban space (see Figure 9.3 and Figure 9.4).

Cultural and creative industries have gained great economic and social importance in the experience economy as well as tourism attractions. Cultural activities are defined as more than tourist attractions based on heritage and cultural assets (which are most readily visible in regenerating inner city neighbourhoods) but they all have some relation with culture since they produce cultural goods and services. Baumont and Boiteux-Orain (2006: 233) and Scott (2000) confirm that in France, too, reliance on cultural activities had increased. They show that employment in the French cultural sector had increased faster (11 per cent) than total employment (3 per cent) reaching 18.1 per cent of jobs in 2011 (INSEE 2014) and that the sector continued to be concentrated in Île de France (45 per cent of jobs in the sector) and in the South (Rhône-Alpes and Provence regions). Since they are characterized by innovation, creativity and skilled labour, these activities tend to choose urban locations or places that are attractive to workers in that field (Scott 2010). An experience product like the Disney parks, which was accepted by the French state as part of this turn to the 'culturalization of economic goods' (Pratt 2011: 324) on the other hand needed wide spaces, not available within Paris but abundant in the far sector of the new town of Marne-La-Vallée thanks to planning decisions made in the 1960s. This space is yet still accessible to Paris and to the majority of the European market.

*Figure 9.3* Entrance to and images of two other Baltard passages in Paris (photo © Anne-Marie d'Hauteserre 2014).

*Figure 9.4* Entrance from Place d'Ariane to the commercial centre and one of its corridors of shops (photo © Anne-Marie d'Hauteserre 2014).

## Affect and the experience economy

Urbanism emphasizes the city as a place of mobility, flow and everyday practices: transitivity, daily rhythms and footprint effects. Rhythm, defined as 'localized time' and 'temporalized place' (Lefebvre 1996: 227), registers the daily tempo of the city. It is then necessary to recognize everydayness (daily praxis) as an immanent force in how the city or how urban space evolves. 'Space' expresses fluidity or contingency; space is the framework but it is not static. 'Place', on the other hand, implies interaction between individuals and space, the physical location. Social spaces are always emergent, responding, for example, to everyday practices of their residents/occupiers (procedures of everyday creativity or 'ways of operating' – de Certeau 1984: xiv). They do not engage just with what architects and builders, planners and government policies have imposed. Interaction between them all, however indirect, does occur. Latour (2005a: 179) shifts attention to the labour that goes into the fabrication of places and times: 'we never encounter time and space but a multiplicity of interactions with actants having their own timing, spacing, goals, means and ends' (2005a: 181).

For Latour (2005b) the social is the arena of associative connections and ties. The social field is considered to be temporary and hybrid, composed of strings of association, an arena of enactment involving varied human and non-human inputs. As performers in the experience economy weave temporary social relations, and use and occupy space, they are conjointly engaged both in its co-construction and in the creation of place. They might, however, unwittingly participate in the totalization of the landscapes they perform in, guided by an anonymously and globally established set of standards and normative expectations. This seems to happen especially in those spaces where urban tourism has been used as a spur to regeneration (Judd and Fainstein 1999; Zukin 1991).

Latour or de Certeau, however, never explained how residents communicated with each other and their surroundings. They did not show how the collective experiences of bodies, matter and technology fused to create place. Affect theory is used here to complement their contribution, to explain how new residents can form bonds in new spaces to create real neighbourhoods. Affect determines how links develop between travelling bodies and their environments. Affect can be forged beyond face-to-face encounters and spatial proximity as place-making is also technologically induced between all varieties of actants especially since individuals are perpetually moving between the various spaces they use. All of this demands flexibility to adjust or to accommodate through repetitive action: 'the interaction of bodies is simultaneously a process of ordering and disruption ... which condition social action in powerful ways' (Amin 2008: 10).

Social bonding then results from affect relations and experiential connections that determine the intensity of belonging to place. Authors (Deleuze 1995; Greene 1999; Ettlinger 2006) have confirmed affect as a relational force: affect is what circulates to link humans into social bodies. It can describe a relation to the physical, to the other people present, or even to the self. As individuals we all seek recognition, even validation of our existence by others. Though recent, such attention is not new as demonstrated in the work of Spinoza (1997 [1678]) who took pains to show how affect is a form of social bond. He reconceptualized relations between individuals, fluctuating between acting and being acted upon. Aristotle had already exclaimed that if there are no relations, there can be no social life. Social relationality implies affect.

Geographers have focused their interest in emotions and affect as composite relations of meanings shared through space: 'emotion adheres to and shapes selves differently in certain times and contexts' (Thrift 2008: 188) (see also Clough 2010; McCormack 2003). Böhme (2006) insists on the spatiality of atmospheres created by affect. Affect thus plays a major role in how our social imaginaries are constituted, also because of the interactions that occur between space, identity and values (Davidson and Milligan 2004; Davidson *et al.* 2008). Affect occurs in all spaces occupied by bodies. As bodies weave temporary social relations and use and occupy spaces, they also create places. Places in and of themselves can evoke certain emotions, engender familiarity and belonging or repulse. Duff (2010: 884) confirms that the 'affective experience of place making' does enrich places and augments the feeling of belonging. It is not just a minor academic matter. Certain settings are more prone to produce specific kinds of emotions than others: as a result of particular configurations of social scripts, the performance of the actors present, and the staging of that space (Irvine 2007).

Affect can provide for a deepened experience of place. Affect as an integral component of experience actively constitutes place (Anderson 2009) because place may provide the resources that can be engaged with (Figure 9.5). The absence of resources can lead to non-memorable uniform homogeneity and refusal to engage with a space, as was the case until the late 1980s for the French middle class relative to the eastern side of Paris or of the Paris Basin. According

*Figure 9.5* Renovation in Coupray Village, the town hall (photo © Anne-Marie d'Hauteserre 2014).

to McGrawth *et al.* (2008: 58), 'experience is equally affective, spatial, embodied, material, technological, and so on'. As space is transformed into place, by the praxes of its users, their experiences impact on the place created and in turn on the first changes recorded since places in turn are shaped by the multitude of practices and encounters experienced there (Thrift 2008). Experience qualities can be connected to urban design, where particular designs stimulate citizens' learning and activity in the urban space. They can also be connected to more tourist-related large-scale projects of experiential mass consumption as in the case of the Disney parks.

## Planning with the experience economy to enable the spread of affect

In Val d'Europe, both the state through its Établissements Publics d'Aménagement (EPAs) and in this case through EPAFrance (Établissement especially created to handle the Walt Disney Company's participation in developing Val d'Europe), and the Company had recognized the need to offer a framework for the development of a positive ambiance in Val d'Europe, through building quality of life. Residential development has centred more directly on the future residents to favour the development of social mixing rather than attempting to produce it, following Harvey's dictates: 'We should not aim to obliterate differences, homogenize according to some conception of bourgeois or Disneyfied social order' (2003: 103). Such a policy required creating an attractive urbane atmosphere for people of varied social origins. Improving the quality of places is the way to influence flows: a variety of residents is more likely move to the area, and its quality will anchor them by enabling them to generate positive affect. Residential neighbourhoods need to privilege diversity rather than to stimulate autarchic social homogeneity, in order to reduce individual retreat from civic society.

Housing construction and architecture have been programmed in great detail in order to generate the desired social variety through the five communes that make up the Syndicat d'Agglomérations Nouvelles (SAN – townships within the new towns are encouraged to regroup themselves) of Val d'Europe. The SAN too, however, is bound by the original plan or Projet d'Intérêt Général (Project of General Interest), which was drawn up in the 1980s between the state and the Company and signed as a contract between the two parties in 1987 (d'Hauteserre 2013). This has raised problems of logistics between the various areas that make up this sector IV that the construction of the park has split apart. This has translated into instructions for each specific development, almost right down to each building put up in Val d'Europe.

This has raised problems of logistics between the various areas that make up this sector IV that the construction of the park has split apart. This has translated into instructions for each specific development. Since 1997, about 4,000 housing units have been built in Chessy, Serris and Bailly-Romainvilliers (Figure 9.1). For every 300 to 500 units, 30 to 40 per cent are to be rental units that should include the 20 per cent of social housing demanded by the Loi sur la Solidarité et le Renouvellement Urbain (SRU – law voted on 13 December 2000 that is directly concerned with social solidarity); this percentage has been reached in all three communes named above. However, no project should offer more than 50 per cent of units of the same size (Figure 9.6). The new Projet d'Intérêt Général signed in 2010 by all parties (decree No. 2010–1081 of 15 September) has made these policies compulsory. These regulations have also allowed for the sale of expensive housing within these same areas.

Safety within its neighborhoods is considered the basis for social cohesion and quality of life in Val d'Europe. Parties responsible for the development of Val d'Europe agreed on a number of policies to create this 'safe ambiance'. Some concern the planning stage, to avoid accumulating risk factors within a given neighbourhood and to locate early on the equipment necessary to monitor safety and to protect private and public property without being obtrusive. Others were turned towards education: about responsibility and about rights and how to monitor the success (or not) of these policies. A committee manages public spaces and is in charge of mitigating all forms of disorderly conduct and cleaning problems within 15 days, its costs covered by the SAN. Public spaces in Val d'Europe are generally as clean as those within the Disney parks and indicate the high level of the quality of life in the sector.

Both the French state and the Walt Disney Company have very definite views as to what is required to maintain the value of their investments. Discussions between the state and the Company centred on different conceptions of this urbanity: Americans favour stacked parking lots above ground; the French prefer to

*Figure 9.6* Mixed forms of residential development: individual houses close to apartment buildings (photo © Anne-Marie d'Hauteserre 2014).

build them underground. Americans choose segregated land use with larger buildings and roads, and broad open spaces. Europeans prefer denser and more diversified city blocks. The French state has always insisted on a classic form of urban development: typically French urban landscapes of streets that separate groups of buildings, with small public parks and urban squares. The streets and parks are to be lined with and contain trees, hedges and other vegetation of local species. The urban squares are to offer commercial activities and services at ground level. The role of EPAFrance has been to maintain the objectives and the constraints of the urban characteristics of the project: an appropriate density of land use to give it/retain its urban character, the integration of the many elements which are being built over a 30-year period, into the final project and its high degree of functionality.

The Company's priority has always been the coherence of the project. It defines coherence as the perfect articulation of all concepts used, their logical sequencing, their consistent functionality as well as their manifest aesthetics all organized in harmony so the end product seems to have always existed. This is particularly true for its parks, but has been systematically adopted in its urban projects. Colour schemes have been determined in consultation with elected officials of the SAN townships, the French state and the Walt Disney Company. All must adhere, including subcontractors, to the scheme established and published officially in 1992. The same 'neo' architecture (e.g. Haussmannian pastiche) is imposed on all residential construction, whatever its value so it is impossible from passing by to determine the monetary value of any housing project. Specific instructions for roofs or decorations help identify the commune they are built in.

Attention to detail and to the finish was essential to the Company, which kept hovering over every detail of the construction of the parks and remains extremely vigilant over what others do in its name as they develop economic activities and housing in Val d'Europe (Architecture Intérieure 2002). One of its requirements included the ability to ensure perfect harmonization of urban projects that the state might envision in the surrounding area. The Company seeks to maintain its magic (or at least that it not shrink) even outside the parks. The Company pays particular care to the landscaping of its projects, right down to its backstage areas, especially since they will become visible to the occupants of newly urbanized plots. For example, the backside of the parks along the circular boulevard must not mar the view of future developments on the other side of the boulevard. When the Walt Disney Company agreed to preserve a small wood stand at the very edge of Disneyland Paris, it was neither just an effort by Disney to look green, nor a token demand on the part of the French state.

The Company is concerned with exchange values and profits from its real estate deals, while the present and future inhabitants are concerned with use-values, such as the quality of the housing they have invested in. Many take the quality of life of their neighbourhoods as part and parcel of that investment: the affect they have developed is not questioned. The situation became confrontational when poor workmanship and unfinished lodgings threatened their affect for the area. The recourse of the affected residents to obtain repairs, so use-value and affect would be restored, was by putting up big ugly posters on the front lawns (*L'Humanité* 1999: 41). Such confrontation illustrates 'the complex articulation between symbolic universes of meaning, capital accumulation and space' (Gottdiener 1985: 155). Some of the French subcontractors (the builders of the houses and of the apartments that were shoddy) were not always as dedicated to quality as the Company, but they quickly learned to assume their responsibilities. The Company is very vigilant about conditions that will enable affect to develop and transform its urban projects into vibrant places.

## How affect transforms neo-liberal experience planning in Val d'Europe

Val d'Europe is a project embedded in the new town vision, 'the result of public action in which the will of the state remains exceptionally strong' (Béhar 2004: 31), translated by heavy investments, in particular in facilitating access to lodgings by all members of French society and to ownership (Fouchier 1999). Val d'Europe has remained a territorialized space because it has been closely monitored by the French state and lower levels of elected government (d'Hauteserre 2013). The Company was unable to create its own fully controlling, 'imagineered' urban reality. Since 1995, local governments and residents have participated in negotiating the emerging landscape. Place identity is dynamically produced and performed since it is embodied and becomes translated into a specific cultural landscape (Dovey *et al.* 2008). Many residents of Marne-La-Vallée were not new to that territory; they had lived or been raised in the area but they remained within the perimeter of the new town, having developed strong affect prior to its implementation (Imbert 2004). New residents appreciate the affective links they have developed in the new town since they too tend to remain in the new town, moving to another part rather than leaving the new town if they have to change lodgings (Programme Interministériel 2005: 131–44). Residents of Val d'Europe denied any lack of sociability that critics felt were inherent to new developments (IAURIF 2006).

Individuals do have the power to re-territorialize their local landscapes as Hastrup asserts: 'individuals' meaningful action is always partly based on a sense of the plot in which one participates' (2004: 223). Those who settle in Val d'Europe respond to an anticipated cultural reality even though it comes into being only as they act on it. These new residents also bring their mythical and cosmic imaginary from elsewhere to create the landscapes they will move into. Since most buyers are French and the project exists within France, the country still provides the context for enforcing dominant cultural idea(l)s within Val d'Europe. Moving to virgin urban territory, newcomers to Val d'Europe could/ can construct through their affect a different type of spatialized experience. People's 'ways of operating' constitute the means by which they can appropriate their place (de Certeau 1997). Val d'Europe has remained a recognizably everyday experience, a reality that can be lived by those who are consuming it as residents. The majority of them are of the middle class, not wealthy cosmopolitans in search of global symbolic capital.

Residents themselves, through their praxis and the affect that derives from it, will determine what will become of Val d'Europe. Val d'Europe is located within the new town of Marne-La-Vallée (Figure 9.1). The geographic extent of Marne-La-Vallée and its now rather long history (started in the early 1960s), militate against affective relations by many of its residents. Residents feel they belong to specific parts of the new town rather than to the whole area. One resident, for example, asserted that 'I wouldn't say I live in Marne-La-Vallée. I live in Val d'Europe. It is more convenient for me. That is where I live, in fact. For me, Marne-La-Vallée is this huge area' (in Brevet 2011: 237). Although most residents of Marne-La-Vallée have not developed allegiance to the new town generally (nine out of ten (IAURIF 2005)), they move within that broad perimeter as they work, shop and socialize over more than just their residential area. They recognize that their affective community or neighbourhood exists within the ambit of Marne-La-Vallée and they recognize that it expresses their geographic location, if not the place of their affect (Figure 9.7).

Most elected officials consider that Marne-La-Vallée is just a legal entity. The officials of each sector seek to go their own way, against the directives of the EPAs and some even publish regular newsletters to keep their electorate informed: Val Maubuée SAN (sector II) and Val d'Europe SAN (sector IV) in particular. The situation led Stutter (1992: 48–9) to declare that 'political conflicts in the new town make it impossible to identify with the whole territory'. Political conflicts have been ongoing. The situation has not prevented residents from

*Figure 9.7* A square near Serris town hall and Place Toscane, at the other end of the Val d'Europe commercial centre (photo © Anne-Marie d'Hauteserre 2014).

identifying with their local commune (township – 46 per cent), the neighborhood (18 per cent) or more generally with Île de France (13 per cent) (IAURIF 2005). This identification with Île de France could be a distinguishing feature of Marne-La-Vallée: more of its residents were born in the region than residents in any other part of the Paris Basin (Brevet 2011).

People in France use space in two main ways, according to Ascher (1998), depending on whether the referent is their residence or the urban area. The residence means roots through everyday existential living, in the more traditional communal way of life that was supposed to ensure continuing urban cultural values in the face of change. The size of urban areas today requires mobility which has become an integral part of modern ways of living even in France: the moving body with all of its senses alert is at the heart of the affective turn. The local landscape no longer reflects faithfully localized ways of life as new kinds of community are formed because lives are governed by mobility rather than sedentarism (Amin and Thrift 2002). In turn, mobility determines urban socio-spatial organization. Walking and the opportunities for face-to-face meeting are no longer an option in the periphery of Paris and its new towns, except within a few defined centres or through commercial places, but a well-planned landscape will still enable the diffusion of affect. The area residents move through is determined by the location of their employment, of services and of access routes (provided by the urban area) as well as by social and affective ties (linked to their residence).

This mobility remains anchored in the location of their residence and affect enables this residential anchoring even as people change jobs. It then determines their life 'catchment area'. Levy and Lussault (2003: 912) define these territories as 'providing the material and symbolic resources for individuals or social groups to structure their daily life and to construct their identity'. These practices of mobility and their intersections in space enable new imaginaries and differing landscapes to interrupt the city planned by architects and administrators. These movements weave patterns of spatial and social appropriation that enable residents to develop affect with the different destinations they visit or to maintain affective links with other parts of Marne-La-Vallée that they had previously lived in or that they have discovered since they moved there. These movements, though, remain limited even within Marne-La-Vallée, so the radius of affect hardly spreads further than the sector of residence rather than to the whole of the new town. Of residents of sectors III and IV (includes Val d'Europe), 39 per cent have their jobs, 55 per cent do their studies, 58 per cent practise their leisure and 52 per cent their cultural activities there. Seventy-six per cent belong to local associations and 86 per cent use the local commercial centres. Only 20 per cent or fewer use facilities in sectors I and II (IAURIF 2005).

## Conclusion

Planning in the face of the crisis of modernist urbanism need not signify a retreat from dreaming utopian alternatives, although it has often been accused of authoritarian production of spaces that deny differences. Bernard Ousset (the vice director of EPAFrance) confirms that in Val d'Europe, the challenge was not just to create a tourist destination. We also had to integrate that project into the Schéma de Développement et d'Aménagement Urbain (SDAU plan, Planning for urban land use development) for the new town to develop an urban centre at that location.

(quoted in Belmessous 2002: 23)

Urban competitivity today requires going beyond planning for the development of a space in need of enhancement. To transform such space into a significant area for economic and residential investment and development and not just for economic returns through specialization required recognition of the role of affect. Affect is unconscious, but it dictates whether people and activities will remain anchored in a space and transform it into place. Economies today rely on cooperation and flows of people and ideas but mobility need not mean outmigration: neighbourhoods that provide an ambiance where residents and businesses can deploy affect will more securely anchor even very mobile participants.

This chapter has demonstrated how both the French state and the Company understood the importance of providing an extraordinary landscape in the eastern section of Marne-La-Vallée to anchor people and investments through affect in a part of the Paris Basin that had been until then ignored. It has enabled Val d'Europe to act as the intended urban pole for the area. The chapter has underlined the role of affect in transforming space into place. The Walt Disney Company's requirements led it to a strategic compromise with the state, the local governments and the residents to implement its expertise in the experience economy. The high quality of the projects resulting from the contentious decisions made through the partnership (French state and the Company) has enabled all entities to receive a handsome return on their investments while it provided improved well-being equitably. The dynamic relations set in motion within the urbanizing area have encouraged positive affect (a notion until now rarely used) for Val d'Europe, which has ensured the continued success of Val d'Europe's development.

Any change has the potential to transform a place; change is not synonymous with positive development but it can be guided to ensure integrity and vitality. The collaboration of the French state and the Walt Disney Company in Val d'Europe can be viewed as a positive pioneering implementation of the 'experience turn' in the French economy. The expertise, investment and attractivity of the Company were welcome, but unbridled speculative gains were not. Urban and economic development in Val d'Europe occurred within an institutional and regulatory context that eased social and political inequalities by enabling local residents and businesses to get involved in its growth and to develop affect for the place they helped transform. The result has been a compromise with an emphasis on liveability.

## References

Amin, A. (2008) 'Collective culture and urban public space', *City*, 12(1): 5–24.
Amin, A. and Thrift, N. (2002) *Cities: Re-imagining the Urban*, Cambridge: Polity Press.

Anderson, B. (2009) 'Affective atmospheres', *Emotion, Space and Society*, 2: 77–81.

Archer, K. (1996) 'The limits to the imagineered city: Socio-spatial polarization in Orlando', *Economic Geography*, 18: 322–36.

Architecture Intérieure (2002) 'That fun … Mickey, grand urbaniste', *Architecture Intérieure*, April: 99–120.

Ascher, F. (1998) *La République contre la ville. Essai sur la modernité de la France urbaine*, Paris: L'Aube.

Baudrillard, J. (1996) 'Disneyworld Company', *Libération*, March 4: 16.

Baumont, C. and Boiteux-Orain, C. (2006) 'La culture en Ile de France: toujours une histoire de centralité urbaine', in A. Larceneux and C. Boiteux-Orain (eds) *Paris et ses franges: étalement urbain et polycentrisme*, Dijon: Editions Universitaires.

Béhar, D. (2004) 'Les villes nouvelles en Ile de France ou la fortune d'un malentendu', *Pouvoirs Locaux*, 60: 31–5.

Belmessous, H. (2002) 'Disney à Val d'Europe: la ville rêvée des anges', *Urbanisme*, 323: 18–25.

Benjamin, W. (1983) *Der Flâneur, Das Passagen – Werk, 2 Bde*, Frankfurt: Suhrkamp.

Böhme, G. (2006) 'Atmosphere as the fundamental concept of a new aesthetics', *Thesis Eleven*, 36: 113–26.

Bonaparte, N. (1991) 'Mémorial de Sainte Helene', cited in C. Bailhe *Villes d'autrefois et de toujours*, Paris: Edition Milan.

Bouinot, J. (2002) *La ville intelligente*, Paris: LGDJ.

Brevet, N. (2011) *Le(s) bassin(s) de vie de Marne-La-Vallée*, Paris: L'Harmattan.

Brugmann, J. (2010) *Welcome to the Urban Revolution: How Cities are Changing the World*, New York: Bloomsbury Publishing.

Clough, P. (2010) 'Afterword: The future of affect studies', *Body and Society*, 16: 222–30.

D'Hauteserre, A.-M. (2013) 'Constructing alterity in Ile de France?', *Urban Geography*, 34(6): 864–86. Online. Available at: http://dx.doi.org/10.1080/02723638.2013.784079 (accessed 4 June 2014).

Davidson, J. and Milligan, C. (2004) 'Embodying emotion sensing space: Introducing emotional geographies', *Social and Cultural Geography*, 5(4): 523–32.

Davidson, J., Smith, M., Bondi, L. and Probyn, E. (2008) 'Emotion, space and society: Editorial introduction', *Emotion, Space and Society*, 1(1): 1–3.

De Certeau, M. (1984) *The practice of everyday life*, Berkeley and Los Angeles: University of California Press.

De Certeau, M. (1997) *Culture in the plural*, translated by Tom Conley, Minneapolis: University of Minnesota Press. Luce Giard, editor.

Deleuze, G. (1995) *Negotiations, 1972–1990*, New York: Columbia University Press.

De Roos R. (1994) 'The magic worlds of Walt Disney', in E. Smoodin (ed.) *Disney Discourse*, New York: Routledge.

Dovey, K., Wood, S. and Woodcock, I. (2008) 'Senses of urban character', in F. Vanclay, M. Higgins and A. Blackshaw (eds) *Making Sense of Place*, Canberra: National Museum of Australia Press.

*Draft New Zealand Urban Design Protocol* (2004), Auckland: Government Printing.

Duff, C. (2010) 'On the role of affect and practice in the production of place', *Environment and Planning D: Society and Space*, 28: 881–95.

Ettlinger, B. (2006) *The matrixial borderspace (Theory out of bounds)*, Minneapolis: University of Minnesota Press.

Fouchier, V. (1999) 'Le polycentrisme: du concept au concret', *Urbanisme*, 301: 53–9.

Gottdiener, M. (1985) *The social production of urban space*, Austin, TX: University of Texas Press.

Greene, A. [1973] (1999) *The fabric of affect in psychoanalytic discourse*, translated by A. Sheridan, London: Routledge.

Harvey, D. (2003) 'The right to the city', *International Journal of Urban and Regional Research*, 27(4): 939–41.

Hastrup, K. (2004) 'The imaginative texture of social spaces', *Space and Culture*, 7: 223–36.

*L'Humanité* (1999) Société nouvelle du journal L'Humanité, Saint-Denis, 9 September.

IAURIF – Institut d'Aménagement et d'Urbanisme de la Région d'Ile de France – (2005) *Enquête modes de vie en ville nouvelle*, Paris: Iaurif.

IAURIF (2006) *Modes de vie en villes nouvelles: le point de vue des habitants*, Paris: Iaurif.

Imbert, C. (2004) 'Proximités familiales et géographiques en Ile de France', *Bulletin de l'Association des Géographes Français*, 1: 17–30.

Ingallina, P. (2004) *Il progetto urbano*, Milan: Feltrinelli.

INSEE (2014) *Répartition par grande branche de l'emploi des services marchands*, Institut National de la Statistique et des Études Économiques. Online. Available at: www.insee.fr/fr/themes/series-longues.asp?indicateur=emploi-composantes-services-marchands (accessed 4 June 2014).

Irvine, J.M. (2007) 'Transient feelings: sex panics and the politics of emotions', *GLQ, A Journal of Lesbian and Gay Studies*, 14(1): 1–40.

Judd, D. and Fainstein, S. (1999) *The tourist city*, New Haven: Yale University Press.

Latour, B. (2005a) 'Trains of thought: the fifth dimension of time and its fabrication', in P.A. Perret-Clémont (ed.) *Thinking through Time: A Multi-Disciplinary Perspective on Time*, Cambridge, MA: Hogrefe and Huber.

Latour, B. (2005b) *Reassembling the Social: An Introduction to Actor-Network-Theory*, Oxford: Oxford University Press.

Lefebvre, H. (1996) *Writings on Cities*, translated by E. Kofman and E. Lebas (eds), Oxford: Blackwell.

Levy, J. and Lussault, M. (eds) (2003) *Dictionnaire de la géographie et de l'espace des sociétés*, Paris: Belin.

McCormack, D.P. (2003) 'An event of geographical ethics in spaces of affect', *Transactions of the Institute of British Geographers*, 28: 488–587.

McGrawth, L., Reavey, P. and Brown, S.D. (2008) 'The scenes and spaces of anxiety: Embodied expressions of distress in public and private fora', *Emotion, Space and Society*, 1: 56–64.

Peck, J. (2007) 'The creativity fix', *Fronesis*, 24: 1–12 (or *Eurozine*).

Pine, B.J. and Gilmore, J.H. (1999) *The experience economy: Work is theatre and every business a stage*, Boston: Harvard Business School Press.

Pratt, A.C. (2011) 'An economic geography of the cultural industries', in A. Leyshon, R. Lee, L. McDowell and P. Sunley (eds) *The Sage Handbook of Economic Geography*, London: Sage.

Programme Interministériel (2005) 'Villes nouvelles françaises: rapport final', Paris: Ministère des transports, de l'équipement, du tourisme et de la mer.

Ritzer, G. (1996) 'The McDonaldization Thesis: Is expansion inevitable?', *International Sociology*, 11(3): 291–308.

Roncayolo, M. (2003) *La ville et ses territoires*, Paris: Gallimard.

Roost, F. (2000) 'Die Disneyfisierung des Städte' [Disneyfication of cities], *Grossprojekte des Entertainmentindustrie am Beispiel des New Yorker Times Square und der Siedlung Celebration in Florida*, Opladen, Germany: Stadt Raum Gesellschaft, vol. 13.

Ross A. (1999) *Celebration Chronicles: Values in Disney's New Town*, New York: Ballantine Books.

Scott, A.J. (2000) 'The cultural economy of Paris', *International Journal of Urban and Regional Research*, 24: 567–82.

Scott, A.J. (2010) 'Cultural economy and the creative field of the city', *Geografiska Annaler: Series B, Human Geography*, 92(2): 115–30.

Spinoza, B. de. [1678] (1997) *Ethics Part III*, Gutenberg project. Online. Available at: www.gutenberg.org/cache/epub/948/pg948.html (accessed 20 March 2013).

Stutter, N. (1992) *Marne-La-Vallée, identité territoriale et concertation d'acteurs*, Paris: DESS.

Sundbo, J. and Sørensen, F. (2013) *Handbook on the experience economy*, Cheltenham: Edward Elgar.

Territoires 2040 (2011) *Territoires 2040 N°3: Des systèmes spatiaux en perspective*, Paris: La Documentation Française.

Thrift, N. (2008) *Non-representational Theory: Space, Politics, Affect*, London: Routledge.

Veltz, P. (2012) *Paris, France, Monde*, Paris: L'Aube.

Viard, J. (2009) 'La ville nuage', *Revue Futuribles*, juillet.

Zukin S. (1991) *Landscapes of power: From Detroit to Disneyworld*, Berkeley and Los Angeles: University of California Press.

# 10 Bollywood-in-the-Alps

## Popular culture place-making in tourism

*Szilvia Gyimóthy*

## Introduction

This chapter studies the character and impact of popular cultural place-making. Regions are increasingly bringing books and screen productions into play in order to position themselves on the global market. Pop-cultural phenomena like *The Lord of the Rings*, *The Da Vinci Code* and *Dracula* have remarkably stimulated tourism flows to specific destinations in New Zealand, Scotland and Romania and inspired a new generation of promotional campaigns based on fictive narratives (Buchmann 2010; Huebner 2011; Light 2007; Månsson 2011; Reijnders 2011). This study addresses the spatial consequences of mediatized tourism in Switzerland and demonstrates how pop-cultural representations in Indian cinema trigger new entrepreneurial initiatives and relationships transcending local trajectories. Based on illustrative cases of Alpine destinations pandering to Bollywood, the chapter explores how popular culture transforms place-making imageries and practices in established tourist destinations.

### Context: mountain of India (Mount Titlis, Engelberg)

Similar to any other cable-car-connected mountain tops in Switzerland, the Glacier Station on Mount Titlis (3,239 m) is jam-packed with international tourists on any random summer day. They enjoy the breathtaking views from the rotating gondola, frolic around in the snow and flick their cameras and smartphones to document their visit. Some peep through the cardboard cut-out of a faceless snowboarder and get photographed as sportive adventurers – imitating light-heartedly proud Alpinist traditions dating back to the eighteenth century. Such tourism practices and sportive props are typical for an Alpine location. But the sun terrace of Mt Titlis features a cultural anomaly setting it apart from any other destination. Alongside the cardboard snowboarder, there is a life-size poster of two Bollywood superstars, Shah Rukh Khan and Kajol, triggering amused Indian tourists to make bhangra poses (a fusion between Punjabi folk dance and Western dance styles). And it does not stop here. Down in the valley, it is not unusual to see honeymoon couples from India striking poses at the church of Montbovon, on the bridge in Saanen or dancing with souvenir cowbells at the railway station of Zweisimmen. There are signposts and information boards in Hindi giving directions. What's more, Engelberg, the town where the Titlisbahn departs from, almost transforms into an Indian village in late spring and September. The elegant Terrace Hotel has specialized in accommodating Indian tour groups and one can easily spot the mobile food van serving samosas, hot desi snacks and masala chai around the town. But what draws Indians to Titlis and Engelberg of all places when visiting Europe? What makes people like Vishal and Jagruti from Mumbai travel across half the globe to pose in colourful saris and kurtas in front of quite ordinary sights of no particular historical interest? Apart from sparse media coverage and traveller blogs making amused comments on this phenomenon, there is no research focusing on the implications of Bollywood films and Indian popular culture on European destinations.

## *Research background and objectives*

Pop-cultural tourism, defined as travel induced by films, TV series, music and screen adaptations of books, is a growing leisure phenomenon worldwide (Mintel 2003; Lundberg *et al.* 2011), and screen tourism in particular has been recognized as a significant economic contributor to regions hosting blockbuster productions (Roesch 2009; Young and Young 2008; Månsson and Eskilsson 2013). However, the majority of film tourism case studies are concerned with Hollywood productions and their implications for Western travellers. Consequently, we know very little about how Bollywood films[1] are changing the travel behaviour of millions of long-haul Indian travellers or how local tourism development is affected by the numerous Bollywood productions which were made in European destinations in the past decades. In particular, the Alps became a significant part of the occidental imageries, and are one of the most important destination preferences among emergent Asian travellers. Bollywood imageries may provide new symbolic ammunition for place-making strategies deployed by tourism marketers and destination management organizations (DMOs) and, as demonstrated above, change the touristic landscape of Engelberg and its surroundings.

The objective of this chapter is to explore how Indian popular culture transforms place-making strategies in established tourist destinations in Europe. More specifically, it traces the history and contemporary character of place-making campaigns and practices of Alpine destinations opting to fit their traditional imaginary with Bollywood-inspired themes. This exploratory objective is framed along the following questions:

- How did Switzerland arise, develop and consolidate as a Bollywood shooting location and which particular Alpine destinations are affected by Bollywood tourism?
- Who are the key actors involved in new initiatives pertaining to pop-cultural place-making?
- How have global–local relationships between Indian film-makers and local entrepreneurs contributed to the transformation of specific locations into a Bollywood destination?

- What are the consequences of new pop-cultural imageries as well as multiple and possibly contested place meanings?

## *Methodology and intended contribution*

The present study on Bollywood's impact on reputable Alpine destinations acknowledges the dialectic, networked and multi-scalar character of place-making and is thus grounded in a theoretical intersection of media studies, human geography, as well as cultural (experience) economy. The empirical illustrations are derived from various data sources from an ongoing ethnographic study exploring 'Bollywood-in-the-Alps' in multiple locations (Interlaken and Engelberg in Switzerland, Tyrol in Austria as well as Val D'Aosta, Trentino and Sudtirol in Italy). Swiss and Austrian travel trade statistics and film tourism promotional leaflets were acquired to capture the scope of the emerging Indian incoming market. The author interviewed representatives of local tourism boards, regional film commissions, incoming agents and tourism providers. The locations and informants were selected based on suggestions from the tourism boards or based on their appearance in a SRF documentary (2000), *Bollywood im Alpenrausch*. Tourism perceptions and performances were captured by on-location observations at Mount Titlis/Engelberg as well as through online (Tripadvisor) reviews and newspaper travelogues.

## *Structure of the chapter*

The theoretical sections below provide a cross-disciplinary literature review of the conceptualization of place-making, mediatized culture, and pop-culture-induced tourism. The findings are organized according to research objectives stated above, offering a historical account of Bollywood-induced tourism in Switzerland, a review of key place-making agents as well as controversies arising from new, oriental pop-culture imageries. The chapter concludes with a reflection on likely challenges and conflicts that may emerge from catering for tourist segments yearning for fundamentally different Alpine experiences.

## Theoretical departures

The phenomenon of pop-cultural place-making has been partially addressed in a number of human geography, media studies as well as tourism. This section gives an overview of discussions of the 'cultural turn' and 'experience economy' in these theoretical fields and points at potential synergies.

## *Place-making in the experience economy*

'Place-making' is a term coined by cultural economists (McCann 2002), referring to a variety of commodification processes along which local (cultural, social and economic) resources are mobilized, refined and packaged (or valorized) for contemporary experience consumption (Jeannerat 2013). In this process, marketers draw on and enhance established imageries to fabricate appealing lifestyle associations connected to a place, for example through provenance tags of premium local products or through pop-cultural narratives. Hence, tourism place-making strategies aim at increasing a locality's 'symbolic capital' and to transform it into a destination worth visiting. Place-making is not solely a discursive practice, nor is it a centralized marketing campaign led by tourism boards alone. Rather, it is brought about by a wide range of actors (local entrepreneurs, regional developers, national trade organizations, global travel intermediaries and media) and hence transcends multiple geographical scales. It is materially and spatially manifested through luxury fashion items, gastronomic offerings or innovative tourism experiences.

Confronting the conceptual compartmentalization of market demand and supply, both critical human geographers (Thrift 1996) and pragmatic experience economists (Pine and Gilmore 1999; Boswijk *et al.* 2005) call for reconciliation between dichotomous notions of production (economy) and consumption (culture). Globalization, mediatization and consumer mobility have greatly contributed to the new cultural landscapes. These are conceived along experience economic development processes where traditionally non-related resources are creatively configured into marketable experiences to satisfy conspicuous consumption needs. Prahalad and Ramaswamy (2004) suggest that the market has become an interaction platform where value is interactively co-created between firms and customers, while Pine and Gilmore (1999) offer theatrical metaphors to depict experiences as performances, staged along dramaturgical, scenographic and narrative techniques.

However, as Boswijk *et al.* (2005) remark, consumers are not passive audiences of staged performances, but personally and collectively engaged in creating their own memorable experiences. Consumers (visitors, tourists, audiences, communities) are assigned an active role in the commodification of places, history and culture. Leisure and tourism are typical contexts for such experiential market valuation (Jeannerat 2013), and even more importantly, they have the ability to connect spatially and culturally distant local economies and global consumer cultures. The co-location of experience production and consumption can be thus seen as territorial staging system (Jeannerat and Crevoisier 2010), which identifies the mobility and preferences of consumers central to the valorization of local creative processes. This framework offers a fundamentally new way to depict complex interdependencies between places and socio-economic value creation processes.

In a similar vein, Ateljevic (2002) suggests that tourism production and consumption systems are interconnected through reproduction and their dialectics can be studied simultaneously through Gold's notion of negotiation (Gold 1994: 377):

> The circuits [of tourism] rest upon the crucial point of negotiation between interests, infrastructure and social relations of production, and consumption forces of changing class, gender, race, locality and culture distinctions of motivation and taste within the potential population of visitors.

Negotiation refers to sense-making processes along which promotional expressions and individual experiences are attuned into a wider ideological framework. In Ateljevic's perspective, tourism is a nexus of production-consumption place-making circuits, where producers and consumers 'feed off each other in endless cycles of place creation, imagination, perception and experiences' (Ateljevic 2000: 372). While the infinite and non-linear characters of interpretive processes linking the production/consumption of tourism spaces and places are acknowledged by both frameworks (territorial staging system and the circuits of tourism), the conceptualization of these remains vague. What are the drivers of territorial staging and experiential value creation? What are the elements and stages of negotiated reproduction of place?

### Mediatized culture and pop-culture-induced tourism

A valuable way forward may be to consider the notions of mediatized culture and mediatized tourism. Scholars adhering to the spatial turn in media and communication studies (Couldry and McCarthy 2004; Hjarvard 2008; Falkheimer and Jansson 2006) regard tourism and mobility as mediatized practice, suggesting that interactions are affected by blurred mediatized boundaries between physical and imaginary places. New analytical terms are coined, for instance Jensen and Waade (2009) propose the concept of hypermediatization, referring to an intricate process of communication and sense-making. Media consumption changes and amplifies (augments) the tourist experience, manifesting itself in media-driven ritualized tourism performances. By engaging with stories appearing on multiple media platforms, for instance screen adaptations of books, people tend to build strong emotional bonds with the characters and the landscapes portrayed, and develop a primary travel preference (Beeton 2005; Connell 2012). This implies that pop-cultural phenomena inspire new forms of daydreaming and novel ways of personalizing the spaces we visit as tourists (Lundberg and Lexhagen 2012).

Furthermore it may also change the landscape of local experience economies. The pop-cultural narrative, the technical portrayal or the story behind the film provides a place with an additional narrative layer. For instance, the recent wave of 'Nordic noir' (crime novels adapted to the big screen) envelops the Scandinavian countryside with a gloomy, foggy and scary atmosphere; a scenographic template for crime scenes. The mixing of both fictitious and authentic foundations lead to new regional narratives and identities (Frost 2009), which become performed along discursively added hyper-real layers (e.g. New Zealand is now marketed as the 'Home of Middle Earth and Hobbits'). Place-branding campaigns based on blockbuster successes are subsequently implemented across new experience offerings and thematized niche products like 'murder walks' (thematic guided tours in the footsteps of crime novels or films) or vampire experiences are conceived (Lexhagen *et al.* 2013). The novelty of these kinds of place-making processes lies in the fact that the pop-cultural tourism experiences are often grounded in fictive narratives, which do not (necessarily) originate from local image resources, and hence no authenticity claims can be made. For instance, bhangra dance moves and samosas have nothing to do with Swiss cultural history or traditions; still they have become an integral part of Engelberg's experience-scape.

An important driver of pop-cultural tourism is media convergence (Jenkins 2004, 2006), which is when topical stories are recirculated and adapted to multiple media platforms. Media convergence also marks the establishment of synergies across the creative industries resulting in a wide portfolio of entertainment products related to the same pop-culture phenomenon. Media convergence augments the exposure frequency of pop-culture phenomena and may likely strengthen the bonding between the consumer and the narrative and its characters. However, media convergence is not solely commercially driven. Maria Månsson (2011) applied the convergence approach to visitor narratives about Rosslyn Chapel on social media networks and found how tourists actively contributed to *Da Vinci Code*-induced place-making by adding their own personal experiences on social media. Contemporary mediatized tourist practices and sense-making processes highlight the collective capacity of consumer communities in influencing and altering pop-cultural narratives (Brown 2007; Gyimóthy *et al.* 2014).

In sum, advances in various theoretical traditions provide useful departure points to study and conceptualize pop-cultural place-making phenomena. Human geographers, experience economists and media theorists enunciate how culture and economy intertwines through the dialectics of production and consumption systems. In experiential market valuation, consumers actively contribute to creative processes of experience creation and hence to negotiated reproduction of space. The notions of hyper-mediation and media convergence as well as the tentative model of territorial staging systems enables researchers to address contested and multilayered place identities, cultural translation of global consumer tastes and lifestyle values or material, spatial and cultural transformations.

In the remainder, pop-cultural place-making will be illustrated through the analysis of Bollywood-in-the-Alps. After a brief historical overview, several examples of experiential market valuation are given, analysing producer–tourist interactions in value co-creation processes. Finally, the negotiated reproduction of Engelberg as a Bollywood tourism destination is discussed, highlighting contested spatial imageries.

## *The rise of the Alps as a Bollywood location*

India's Hindi-language film industry, Bollywood, began its fascination with Switzerland as a movie location in the 1960s, when military tension in the Kashmir region forced film crews to look elsewhere for exotic backcloths in romantic productions. Allegedly it was the instructor Raj Kapoor who first discovered this small Alpine country to shoot his film *Sangam* (Confluence) (1964). Soon, Switzerland became 'the upgraded, offshore version of Kashmir' (Ali, as quoted in Letzing 2013), offering snow-capped mountains, lush Alpine meadows, blooming villages and picturesque lakes to shoot the compulsory song and dance scenes. These dreamlike musical interludes, where lovers croon in each other's arms, are sometimes totally disconnected from the storyline, and therefore referred to as the 'Cut to Switzerland' motif. Without any significant commissioning activity, Switzerland has become Indian cinema's A-list destination, now featuring over 200 Indian film productions, of which *Chandni* (Moonlight) (1989) and the Hindi romantic cinematic blockbuster of all times, *Dilwale Dulhaniya Le Jayenge*, also referred to as *DDLJ* (The Bravehearted Will Take the Bride) (1995) still enjoy an unprecedented popularity. The film used picturesque locations in the Obwalden region (Montbovon, Titlis, Saanen and Engelberg) setting the scene for key dialogues and songs. Soundtracks can be bought several weeks up to the premiere in India, and if they become a hit, it is most likely that the film itself will be a blockbuster. This was the case with *Dilwale Dulhaniya Le Jayenge* and the more recent *Bachna Ae Hasseno* (*BAH*) (Watch Out Girls) from 2008, which made several intertextual references to *DDLJ*. For instance, *BAH* reused several cult locations from *DDLJ* and since then these have become sites of pop-cultural pilgrimage for Indian travellers. As Sonja Nazareth so aptly remarks; 'This sacred mountain ... Titlis became more than just recommended; it was thronged, adored, turned into the hajj[2] of the Bollywood lover' (Nazareth 2012). Indeed, the 'Indianization' of Engelberg follows the cultural logic of media convergence (Jenkins 2004) and mediatization (Couldry and McCarthy 2004), claiming that stories encapsulated in pop-cultural representations (films, songs) enable readers to identify or engage emotionally with the narrative. The ultimate form of this engagement entails visiting iconic scenes from these productions.

Although being the most legendary Bollywood production, *DDLJ* is far from the only one shot in Switzerland. Over 200 Indian films have been produced here (the majority around Interlaken), raising the awareness of this small Alpine country among the Indian public. Going to movies to watch a two to three-hour-long musical film is a central aspect of contemporary Indian culture. As instructor Mukesh Bhatt explains (Bhatt as quoted in SRF 2000), the cinema is the second home of many Indians, many of whom would gladly skip one meal a day to afford a ticket.

Film-makers are thus central players in the territorial staging system (Jeannerat 2013). The widescreen of the movie theatre opens a direct window between a spatially distant market and the Alps. They have created a tremendous appeal for the Alpine romantic getaways and honeymoon tourism for generations of middle-class Indians, who are now affluent enough to travel here in search of their dreams. For many years, it has been a status symbol in India to visit the Alps at least once in a lifetime. As one guide notes: 'if you have visited Switzerland, you belong to high society. Coming to Switzerland is reaching out to the ultimate ... yes ... we have come to Paradise'.

However, the cultural distance carries important implication for how these Swiss mountains are interpreted (with Gold's (1994) term, negotiated) by potential Indian customers. Green pastures, cowbells and creviced snowy peaks mirrored in pristine lakes are admittedly far from mundane realities of Indian metropols. 'This is a great place … a gift of God', said one elderly tourist from Mumbai, adding: 'no noise, no pollution, no crowds'. As such, Bollywood productions function as shortcuts between Switzerland and the Indian travel market, showcasing the country as a romantic land of dreams much before the Swiss Tourism Board started its first campaign on the subcontinent. This phenomenon is reminiscent of Sheppard's (2002) notion of positionality and 'wormholes', capturing random and asymmetric interdependencies of places connected in the global economy:

> Like networks, wormholes leapfrog across space, creating topological connections that reduce the separation between distant places and reshape their positionality. The presence and frequency of wormholes is then a measure of the degree to which positionality stretches selectively across geographic space.
>
> (Sheppard 2002: 324)

A concrete evidence of these wormholes can be detected along the travel choices and behaviour of some of the 12 million Indian outbound tourists heading for international destinations. Accordingly, the effect of Indian cinema on Swiss incoming tourism is demonstrated in the next section.

## The impact of Indian cinema on Alpine tourism

The effects of Bollywood are palpable through visitor statistics. Over the past decades, more than 200 Bollywood films have been shot in Switzerland and 80 in Tyrol, which have resulted in a great increase in Asian visitors, in particular from India. According to Swiss Tourism Statistics (FSO 2013), the number of overnight stays of Indian tourists increased almost sevenfold from 71,000 to 475,000 between 1993 and 2012, with annual growth rates of 3–4 per cent. Also the Austrian department of Tyrol has experienced a massive growth in visitor numbers from the subcontinent, which increased fourfold in the period 1990–2012 (Cine Tirol 2013). Considering that Indian visitors spend almost twice as much as an average international tourist (245 vs 145 euros per day), Alpine tourism promoters consider India as one of the new markets to target. The director of emerging markets and special projects at Switzerland Tourism (2012) explains the link between destination placement in Bollywood movies and tourism arrivals, as follows:

> Ten to 20 years ago the average Indian was going to the cinema two, three times a week, and if he or she was captivated by the love story and discovered that Switzerland was where their favourite actor shot the movie, then they wanted to visit the same place. For us that was an excellent promotion.
>
> (Stevens 2012)

For several decades, Switzerland did not have to put any effort in capitalizing on Bollywood. It was the only European mountain destination Indian travellers had been exposed to, and pop-cultural representations (as organic image sources) work better than large-scale promotion campaigns. Today, the volume of Indian incoming traffic grows steadily; however, the interest of Indian film-makers in Switzerland has recently dwindled in favour of other destinations. Compared to a dozen film shoots per year in the 1990s, these last years only two to three productions are carried out in Switzerland per year. Some location scouts claim that Indian audiences are getting tired of the cliché of serenades under Switzerland's snowy peaks and look for more realistic or novel settings. Another factor is an intensified competition among aspiring film locations. Currently, quite a few other destinations have realized the branding potential of Bollywood and have started opening their doors to Indian film-makers, using professional commissioning strategies. Film commissions and national tourism boards in England or Spain offer financial incentives and budget-friendly packages to international crews, while Cine Tirol (Austria) provides exclusive location services and production support. The new competitors have forced the Swiss Tourism Board to innovate and reinvent the country's appeal in order to maintain its position on the Indian market. STB organizes regular famtrips (familiarization trips) and travel-markets, but also engages in annual roadshows to India with relevant Swiss partners and tour operators visiting metropolitan centres as well as tier II and III cities every year. The next section identifies key actors and enterprises engaged in these innovative initiatives.

## Dream tourism: capitalizing on mediatized romance scenes

The breathtaking honeymoon setting scenery is not the sole asset accountable for the enduring romance between the Swiss Alps and visitors from India. Behind the scenes, an intricate territorial staging system has emerged (Jeannerat 2013), turning mediatized imageries into palpable offerings and production–consumption synergies. Having recognized the commercial opportunities residing in Bollywood's dreams, several actors are now involved in staging experiences specifically designed for the Indian market. Market valuation processes are implemented through new relationships among various institutional actors (public authorities and tourism boards), tour operators and film production houses, local hospitality services and, of course, tourists. These relational dyads and networks are presented and analysed below:

### Indian film-makers – Swiss authorities

Production houses from the south, like Yash Raj Films and Govinda, are particularly active in filming in the Alps, but it is arguably the late director Yash Chopra (also known as the *King of Romance* in Bollywood) who contributed most to promoting Switzerland as a romantic destination for the Indian audience. As the story goes, he got so impressed by the beauty of the country during his honeymoon that he decided to integrate a Swiss sequence in each of his movies. For these achievements, the Embassy of Switzerland awarded him with the honorary Swiss Ambassador title. Today, both a lake in Obwalden (featured in many of his films) and a train carriage at Jungfrau Railways bears his name, exemplifying Jensen and Waade's (2009) notion on hyper-mediatization.

Having acknowledged the impact of Bollywood on incoming tourism, the Swiss authorities are eager to assist with travel arrangements, speedy visa processes for tourists and film crews alike. Over the past 20 years, a whole business infrastructure has emerged, entailing firms specialized in location scouting, equipment rentals and logistics. And despite Switzerland being known as infamously expensive, film crews may shoot free in most public spaces, unlike in some cities. Mehul Kumar, the director of *Mrityudaata*, explains: 'It's a no-problem country. Once you secure permission, you can shoot where you want. No archaic laws, no greasing palms, no delays, no running round in circles'. Pamela Chopra agrees in another interview: 'Switzerland is my favourite place; people are so honest, pleasant and straightforward. You come here and you shoot'. The reduction of administrative entry barriers for film crews and productions is similar to Jeannerat's (2013) notion on technical market valuation.

### Indian film-makers – Swiss logistic services

An entrepreneur accountable for the increase in Swiss shoots was the late Jakob Tritten, the man first to provide a wide range of services to film-makers since the early 1980s. Activities of his 'mum-and-dad' business: *Tritten Filmlogistik* entailed (among others) organizing buses, vans, helicopters, police escorts, mobile kitchens, supplying generators and lighting equipment as well as occasionally acting as stuntman. Throughout two decades, he managed to fulfil increasingly unusual wishes from Indian crews – coordinating last-minute changes and the logistics of several crews simultaneously from his garage. He had developed close personal relationships with several Bollywood directors and visited them occasionally in Mumbai. Today, there are several highly diversified logistic operators available in and around Interlaken, although their strong market ties and interdependencies with the Indian film industry are probably accountable to a random meeting (using Sheppard's term, 'positioning') between one single Swiss entrepreneur and Yash Chopra.

### Indian film-makers – Swiss tour operators

The negotiated reproduction of Switzerland, enhanced by Bollywood representations, also entails tourist packages to 'experience the magic' of these colourful movies. The production of these is enabled by an innovative partnership between Yash Raj Films and the Indian affiliate of Kuoni Travel. Their all-inclusive, customized Movie Fan package, offered since 2010 (entitled *Yashraj Films Enchanted Journeys*), exemplifies a system staging nostalgic Bollywood experiences connected to specific locations. While travelling from site to site, groups are entertained by singalong Bollywood soundtracks and DVDs or related trivia quizzes; enhancing the emotional bonding with their film heart-throbs as well as with the Alpine scenery. 'This is the way Switzerland is positioned in our minds; it was the place for romance and natural beauty', claims one of the guides on Enchanted Journeys. Another moonstruck female visitor adds: 'Switzerland is our second home. We have seen these wonderful landscapes in the Bollywood films and our dream destination is always the Alps, never mind the weather!' If shared on social media, such insights will further add to the experiential value creation of the country.

### Indian backpackers – online tourist community

Furthermore, private backpacker blog posts, like that of *Switzerland and Romantic Songs of Indian Movies*, lists detailed descriptions and screenshots of must-visit scenes from the most popular productions. This is an example of the circuit of representation in tourism and of hyper-mediatization – in the sense that both refer to Swiss destination placement in Indian productions as well as to increased tourist flows and ritualized practices (where to buy the cowbells made popular by Kajol). Albeit this individual is driven by his passion for Bollywood, rather than monetary interests, his contribution to the virtual tourism community will subsequently affect strategic adaptations and commercial experience concepts.

### Local and migrant entrepreneurs – Indian tourists

Other actors are also cashing in on the economic opportunities of this emerging segment. The city of Thun organized its first Bollywood festival in 2012, and there is a Restaurant Bollywood at the top of the Jungfraujoch. The 1905-built Terrace Hotel in Engelberg offers Indian gourmet weeks, romantic wedding packages and Bollywood dance evenings to their guests. The Luzern-based catering firm *Gourmindia Services* supplies the Terrace Hotel and the Panorama Restaurant at Mt Titlis with fresh Indian specialities suitable for vegetarians and those with religious dietary requirements, such as Gujarati, Marwari, Kutchi or Jain. As such, the hotel is transformed from being a supporting stage (accommodation, catering) for other, more memorable, activities into an experience in itself. However, by catering primarily to the needs of Indian tourists, it may risk losing some of its appeal as a traditional and authentic Swiss palace hotel.

Trickle-down effects are obvious, even for smaller tourism actors. During its 20 years of operations in this niche market, Gourmindia has partnered a number of hotels, tourist attractions and tour operators, and developed the mobile catering concept *Indian Kitchen Caravans* as well as production catering for Indian film crews. Homiyar Antalia, the entrepreneur behind the concept, claims that pampering to a homesick appetite is crucial for the satisfaction of the Asian guests, adding that even though being in the most magnificent surroundings, 'the guest is unhappy if the belly is unhappy'. Such gastronomic diversification exemplifies how the preferences of new mobile consumer groups and the knowledge resources of migrant entrepreneurs intertwine to valorize local commodities in new and innovative ways.

## Contested performances

However, not everyone shares the Swiss entrepreneurial dream of Bollywood. A recent article in the *ZüricherTages-Anzeiger* interviewed some luxury hotel managers reluctant to take Indian guests in their establishments. They complained about guests cooking curry dishes on camping stoves in their rooms, using bath oils that blacken tubs; or guests booking one double room for a family of 12. According to a staff member of the tourist office, there are villages in Obwalden where Indian film crews are no longer welcome – or obliged to pay a deposit of CHF 2,000 per day in order to get permission to shoot. Also, some European tourists yearning to encounter a Swiss pastoral idyll are unsettled and feel overwhelmed by large Asian groups dominating Engelberg hotels. As one reviewer on Tripadvisor laments:

> In all fairness, this is a nice hotel.... However if you are expecting to soak up Swiss culture and use the German you've been studying, this is definitely NOT the place, at least not in September. You would be better off studying Japanese or Indian before you arrive, because the clientele is overwhelmingly from those countries. Don't get me wrong. India and Japan are two great countries and their people are good people. But when a hotel is completely taken over by huge tours of one or two ethnic groups, individual tourists from other countries tend to get lost in the shuffle. A great part of traveling is the people you meet. The tour people, however, are very involved with each other and do very little mingling with outsiders. (Few, if any, speak German or English.) They eat together, socialize together and, yes, sing together into the night. My wife and I and a German family were the only ones at the hotel who were not part of these tours and we all felt kind of isolated. The restaurant, the bar, the sitting area, the outdoor children's area were all taken over by the hundreds of people (yes hundreds) from the tours. Even the funicular which takes hotel clients up and down the hill to the village below was over-run with tour people, sometimes causing long waits to get up or down.

> (Posted 21 September 2006)

This example excellently illustrates a conflict in the negotiated reproduction of place, as traditional imageries of Switzerland are challenged by new tourism practices and altered interactions. The Indian traveller contributes with new symbolic and cultural capital that may be potentially detrimental to established value co-creation constellations and platforms. Oriental spatial imageries may not only boost or reposition, but also tamper with the historical past of a destination and thus challenge the traditional Alpine imagery sought after by Western tourists for centuries.

## Discussion

The co-presence of local economies and global consumer cultures bring about new ties between market actors leading to increased connectivity and knowledge flow opportunities between spatially and culturally distant places. This study shows that Alpine locations featured in motion pictures gained increased awareness in distant markets, which has consequently affected tourist flows to Switzerland and Tyrol. Drawing on Sheppard's notion of positionality, it can be argued that the first Bollywood films can be considered random 'wormholes', through which Swiss villages became connected with Indian popular culture producers and consumers. *DDLJ* and subsequent productions reduced the separation between Mumbai and Engelberg and opened it up for transnational commercial relationships.

The 'Indianization of Switzerland' and the emergence of 'Tirollywood' are novel place-making mechanisms driven by pop-cultural expressions, where local (symbolic and cultural) resources are reinterpreted and configured with those of Asian consumers and film-makers. Pop-cultural place-making entails mediatized practices, rationales and interactions within complex stakeholder ecologies. Locations like Mount Titlis are staged, enacted and marketed on several levels (as 'Mountain of India'), where the place of pop-cultural imagination becomes an intermediary, negotiable platform for film-makers, fans, visitors, tourism professionals and regional planners. This co-created valorization process brings in both fictive and authentic elements that contribute to the reimagination of the Swiss Alps as well as to experience economy innovations.

In order to expand the insights put forward by the territorial staging system approach (Jeannerat and Crevoisier 2010), this study suggests combining it with Ateljevic's notion of the tourism (Ateljevic 2000). The pop-cultural place-making loop (Figure 10.1) takes note of both frameworks' notion of co-constructed and

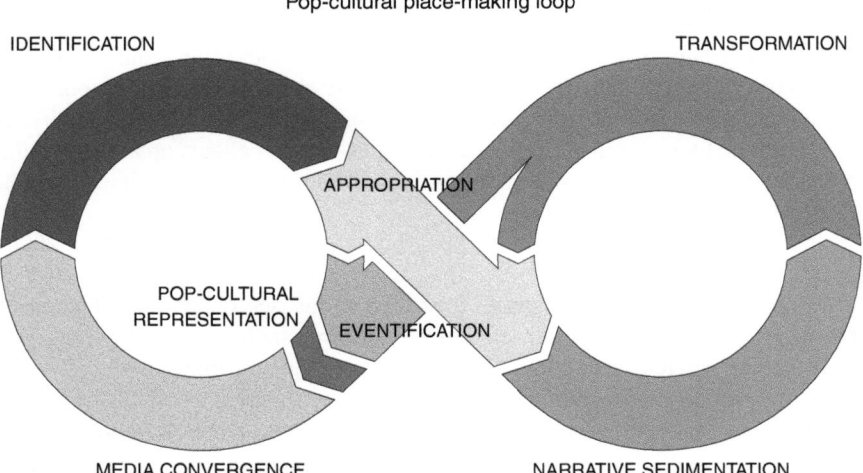

Pop-cultural place-making loop

IDENTIFICATION                                               TRANSFORMATION

APPROPRIATION

POP-CULTURAL
REPRESENTATION        EVENTIFICATION

MEDIA CONVERGENCE                          NARRATIVE SEDIMENTATION

*Figure 10.1* Pop-cultural place-making loop.

co-consumed tourism spaces. Furthermore it addresses aforementioned short-comings by refining the phases of negotiated place reproduction processes. The loop entails seven phases, interlinking consumption-related features (left loop) with place-production processes (right loop) through the notion of mediatization.

Stories encapsulated in pop-cultural representations may *converge* across different media platforms (e.g. books, films, games), providing viewers/readers with an opportunity to *identify* or engage intellectually and emotionally with the narrative. Audiences (who potentially double as tourists, marketers, local entrepreneurs or global travel bloggers) employ cultural resources and interpretative skills to make sense of these narratives, which also entail appropriating parts and elements conveying a particular identity message. Illustrative examples of *appropriation* practices may be following in the footsteps of stars or emulating the habits of fictive characters or re-enacting popular film scenes in a concrete physical location. In doing so, tourists or other actors (re)produce the iconography of landscape, adding a new *narrative layer* (sediment) on top of the imagined space. Ultimately, culturally constructed, circulated and altered place meanings trigger material *transformations* in a locality. The public space of popular film destinations is today densely populated with signposts and physical props related to the fictive narrative, while commercial operators develop marketable experience offerings to tap into fan needs. Finally, these initiatives may be coordinated along *eventification* strategies (cf. Jakob 2013), denoting development policies prioritizing pop-culture-based activities.

## Conclusions

Pop-cultural tourism may contribute significantly to regional development dynamics, transform the landscape of regional competitiveness, and reposition established destinations. The sudden emergence and fading of popular cultural destinations are not random trends, but determined by the convergence of narratives simultaneously appearing on a variety of media platforms which are today strategically exploited by destination marketers, regional planners and tourism organizations. Consequently, pop-cultural place-making is inherently collective, as fans actively contribute to narratives by personal engagement and enactment of featured stories. Seen from a regional planning perspective, pop-cultural place-making marks the dawn of new commodification strategies, which may be at odds with the development interests of the local community or the preferences of traditional guest segments. Managing the balance between different sources of imaginary attributes may present vast challenges for destinations embarking on pop-culture-induced tourism trajectories, which must be addressed in future research projects.

## Notes

1 Bollywood houses over 4,000 production houses and produces over 800 films annually (three times more than Hollywood).

2  Hajj ('pilgrimage' in Arabic) denotes the religious duty of Muslims visiting Mecca at least once in their lifetime.

## References

Ateljevic, I. (2000) 'Circuits of tourism: Stepping beyond the "production/consumption" dichotomy', *Tourism Geographies*, 2(4): 369–88.

Ateljevic, I. (2002) 'Small Tourism Firms: Owners, Environment and Management Practices in the Centre Stage of New Zealand', unpublished PhD thesis, Victoria, University of Wellington.

Beeton, S. (2005) *Film-induced tourism*, Clevedon, NY: Channel View.

Boswijk, A., Thijssen, J.P.T. and Peelen, E. (2005) *A new perspective on the Experience Economy: Meaningful Experiences*, Bilthoven, the Netherlands: The European Centre for the Experience Economy.

Brown, S. (2007) 'Harry Potter and the Fandom Menace', in B. Cova, R.V. Kozinets and A. Shankar (eds) *Consumer Tribes*, Oxford and Burlington, MA: Butterworth-Heinemann.

Buchmann, A. (2010) 'Planning and development of film tourism: Insights into the experience of Lord of the Rings film guide', *Tourism and Hospitality Planning & Development*, 7(1): 77–84.

Cine Tirol (2013) *Welcome to Tirol*, Innsbruck: Tirol Werbung.

Connell, J. (2012) 'Film tourism: Evolution, progress and prospects', *Tourism Management*, 33: 1007–29.

Couldry, N. and McCarthy, A. (2004) *Mediaspace: Place, scale and culture in a media age*, London: Routledge.

Falkheimer, J. and Jansson, A. (2006) *Geographies of Communication: The spatial turn in media studies*, Gothenburg: Nordicom.

Federal Statistical Office, FSO (2013) *Swiss Tourism Statistics 2012*, Neuchâtel, Switzerland: FSO.

Frost, W. (2009) 'From backcloth to runaway production: Exploring location and authenticity in film-induced tourism', *Tourism Review International* 13(2): 85–92.

Gold, J.R. (1994) 'Locating the message: Place promotion as image communication', in J.R. Gold and S.V. Ward (eds) *Place Promotion: The Use of Publicity and Marketing to Sell Towns and Regions*, Chichester: Wiley.

Gyimóthy, S., Lundberg, C., Lindström, K., Lexhagen, M. and Larson, M. (2014) 'Pop-culture Tourism: A research manifesto', in D. Chambers (ed.) *Tourism Social Science Series Tourism Research Frontiers* (in review, forthcoming).

Hjarvard, S. (2008) *En verden af medier*, Copenhagen: Samfundslitteratur.

Huebner, A. (2011) 'Who came first – Dracula or the tourist? New Perspectives on Dracula Tourism at Bran Castle', *European Journal of Tourism Research*, 4(1): 55–65.

Jakob, D. (2013) 'The eventification of place: Urban development and experience consumption in Berlin and New York', *European Urban and Regional Studies*, 20(4): 460–72.

Jeannerat, H. (2013) 'Staging experience, valuing authenticity: Towards a market perspective on territorial development', *European Urban and Regional Studies*, 20: 370–84.

Jeannerat, H. and Crevoisier, O. (2010) 'Experiential turn and territorial staging system: What new research challenges?', paper presented at Regional Studies Association Workshop on the experience turn in local development and planning, Aalborg University, Aalborg, September 2010: 16–17.

Jenkins, H. (2004) 'The cultural logic of media convergence', *International Journal of Cultural Studies*, 7(1): 33–43.

Jenkins, H. (2006) *Convergence culture: Where old and new media collide*, New York: New York University Press.

Jensen, J.L. and Waade, A.M. (2009) *Medier og turisme*, Århus, Denmark: Academica.

Letzing, J. (2013) 'Bollywood's big-screen love affair with Switzerland fades to black', *The Wall Street Journal Online* 21 July. Online. Available at: www.wsj.com/articles/S B10001424127887324348504578610282715525770 (accessed 12 July 2013).

Lexhagen, M., Larson, M. and Lundberg, C. (2013) 'The Fan(g) community: Social media and pop culture tourism', in S. Gyimóthy and A.M. Munar (eds) *Tourism Social Media: Transformations in Identity, Community and Culture, Tourism social science series 18*, Bingley: Elsevier Science.

Light, D. (2007) 'Dracula tourism in Romania: Cultural identity and the state', *Annals of Tourism Research*, 34(3): 746–65.

Lundberg, C. and Lexhagen, M. (2012) 'Bitten by the Twilight Saga: From pop culture consumer to pop culture tourist', in R. Sharpley and P.R. Stone (eds) *The Contemporary Tourist Experience: Concepts and Consequences*, Abingdon: Routledge.

Lundberg, C., Lexhagen, M. and Mattsson, S. (2011) *I populärkulturturismens spår: Twilight + Vacation = Twication©*, Östersund, Sweden: Jengel Förlag.

McCann, E.J. (2002) 'The cultural politics of local economic development: Meaning-making, place-making, and the urban policy process', *Geoforum*, 33(3): 385–98.

Mintel (2003) *Film Tourism – International*, London: Mintel International Group.

Månsson, M. (2011) 'Mediatized tourism', *Annals of Tourism Research*, 38(4): 1634–52.

Månsson, M. and Eskilsson, L. (2013) *The attraction of screen destinations*, Report commissioned by Film London and the Euroscreen Partnership, Rzeczow, Poland.

Nazareth, S. (2012) 'Slopes of snow, rooms of ice', *The Hindu Sunday Magazine* 2 December. Online. Available at: www.thehindu.com/todays-paper/tp-features/tp-sundaymagazine/ slopes-of-snow-rooms-of-ice/article4155307.ece (accessed 2 December 2012).

Pine, B.J. and Gilmore, J.H. (1999) *The experience economy: Work is theatre and every business a stage*, Boston: Harvard Business School Press.

Prahalad, C.K. and Ramaswamy, V. (2004) 'Co-creation experiences: The next practice in value creation', *Journal of Interactive Marketing*, 18(3): 5–14.

Reijnders, S. (2011) 'Stalking the Count: Dracula, fandom and tourism', *Annals of Tourism Research*, 38(1): 231–48.

Roesch, S. (2009) *The experiences of film location tourists*, Bristol: Channel View Publications.

Sheppard, E. (2002) 'The spaces and times of globalization: Place, scale, networks, and positionality', *Economic Geography*, 78(3): 307–30.

SRF, Schweizer Radio und Fernsehen (2000) *Bollywood im Alpenrausch – Indische Filmemacher erobern die Schweiz* [Bollywood Conquers the Alps], Documentary by Christian Frei.

Stevens, T. (2012) 'Giving Swiss film locations some direction'. Online. Available at: www.swissinfo.ch/eng/giving-swiss-film-locations-some-direction-/32071506/ (accessed 24 February 2012).

Switzerland Tourism (2012) *Switzerland for movie stars*, Lucerne: Schweiz Turismus.

Thrift, N. (1996) *Spatial formations*, Thousand Oaks, CA: Sage.

Young, A.F. and Young, R. (2008) 'Measuring the effects of film and television on tourism to screen locations: A theoretical and empirical perspective', *Journal of Travel & Tourism Marketing*, 24(2): 195–212.

# 11 The spatial and experiential dimensions of coastal zone tourism in Denmark

*Lene Feldthus Andersen*

## Introduction

Coastal tourism has been a significant type of tourism since the rise of mass tourism. In Denmark, however, this type of tourism has stagnated or even declined in the past few years, with overnight stays down by as much as 10–15 per cent from 2007 to 2011 (Erhvervs- og Vækstministeriet 2014; Hedetoft and Marcussen 2012). Consequently, the redevelopment of coastal tourism has achieved political focus on national and local levels. Coastal tourism development initiatives have hitherto mostly focused on the production side. Especially improved cooperation at destination level has been seen as a means to increase the joint promotion of the destination and its existing offer (Halkier 2013). In this context, innovation has hardly been an issue, and it has not been considered how tourists, among themselves or in interaction with producers, may contribute to tourism development and innovation (Sundbo and Sørensen 2013).

The role of consumers in innovation is considered in theories on the experience economy. These theories have influenced tourism research and practice in recent years in three main ways (Manniche *et al.* 2014). First, at the level of the firm, where the focus is on experience innovation, and the question of whether and how it differs from service innovation (Sundbo *et al.* 2013; Sundbo and Jensen 2009; Fuglsang *et al.* 2011). This includes experience design, the way businesses organize and facilitate valuable experiences for particular segments (Eide and Mossberg 2013; Bærenholdt and Haldrup 2010). Second, experience economy concepts have influenced research on the tourist as a consumer, particularly within consumer culture theory. In this consumer perspective, physical products as well as immaterial experiences are understood as resources being bought and consumed as part of the social and cultural positioning of the consumer (Gyimóthy 2009a, 2009b). Moreover, the sharing of experiences gives meaning to and constructs the tourist experience for other tourists. Lastly, the experience economy has influenced local and regional tourism planning. With the experience economy has followed the realization that regional competitiveness is not only based on the competitiveness and mobility of goods and knowledge, but also on the competitiveness of regions to consumers as tourists (Lorentzen and Jeannerat 2013). Accordingly, local and regional authorities increasingly focus on enhancing the attractiveness of places (Lorentzen 2009, 2013), to the point where some places emerge as 'experiencescapes' (O'Dell and Billing 2005).

Holiday home tourism and attraction tourism are the two most important types of tourism outside of metropolitan Denmark in terms of volume, share of Danish tourism overall, and economic importance for the host regions. It is also these two types of tourism that are most challenged (Hedetoft and Marcussen 2012).

The overall aim of the chapter is to investigate the experiential and spatial dimensions of these two types of tourism. Can these two types of tourism be seen as forming two distinct experience production and consumption systems, characterized by different experience demands and geographical configurations? The chapter will discuss how value is created in the two types of tourism in the interaction between production, consumption and place, and discuss its implications for tourism and destination development policies. The hypothesis is that each type of tourism is dominated by different production and consumption systems which in turn produce two different types of tourism experiences.

The chapter is organized in three main sections. First, its theoretical basis is discussed. The concepts of experiences and experiencing at the individual and organizational level are introduced, followed by a discussion of how the tourist destination may be perceived based on consumer experience demands. The section also briefly touches on what insights the emerging theorizing on territorial staging systems may bring to understanding the concept of the destination. The following section is empirical and starts with a description of the geographical distribution of tourism outside of metropolitan Denmark. This is followed by identification and analysis of the main value-creating economic activities in the two main types of tourism, holiday home and attraction tourism. Finally, the tourist experiences of each type are identified and analysed. The chapter closes with a discussion of the findings and their implications for the conceptualization of production and consumption systems in the experience economy as well as for tourism and destination development policies.

## Methodological approach

The purpose of the chapter is, as mentioned earlier, to investigate the experiential and spatial dimensions of the two types of tourism, holiday home tourism and attraction tourism. The investigation entails a deconstruction of each type of tourism into four empirical dimensions. Altogether they characterize the core tourism activity, defining the destination as experienced by the tourist. The four empirical dimensions are based on existing data and studies:

1   The first empirical dimension is a geographical distribution analysis, where different types of tourism are found to be associated with different parts of Denmark. This dimension is described by mapping different tourism 'typologies', based on a variety of statistics on the scale, resources and performance of tourism outside of metropolitan Denmark (Hedetoft and Marcussen 2012).

2   The second empirical dimension is the pattern of production expressed through the distribution of tourism spending. The analysis identifies the main value creation, and thus economic activity, in each of the two types of tourism. This dimension is described through use of data on the distribution of tourism spending from the tourism satellite accounts of Denmark (Visit-Denmark 2012).

3   The third empirical dimension is a segmentation of the tourist demand into experience segments and their correlation with accommodation demand. This empirical dimension is described using the results from a quantitative study of accommodation as an experience product based on a survey among visitors to the island of Bornholm. The survey applied the four experience realms of Pine and Gilmore in the design of the questionnaire (Feldthus 2007). The purpose of the study was to link accommodation preferences to experience preferences and to segment the visitors into experience segments.

4   The fourth empirical dimension attempts to differentiate the segmented tourist experience at the individual level. This level is identified and descri-bed with the help of the work of Larsen (2013) through a qualitative study of the family holiday home experience in Northern Jutland. The study addresses the place, as well as the individual and social perspectives of the intra-family experience dynamics at the holiday home destination.

## Conceptualizing organizations and individuals in the experience economy

In the literature on the experience economy, the processes related to experiences are described at two different levels: an organizational level and an individual level. At the organizational level, focus is on the interaction of the different ele-ments that together create an experience and an economic activity and may be environment-, encounter- or effect-centred (Snel 2013). At the individual level, experience is understood as a psychological process, as the act of human experi-encing (Jantzen and Vetner 2007). At the organizational level, the focus is on how to do business in the experience economy. The organizational approach is, however, not able to grasp the important subjectivity of experiences (Snel 2013). The individual approach, on the other hand, is preoccupied with the psychology of experiences from the biological to the cognitive level of the individual.

Pine and Gilmore (1999: 30) suggested four realms of experiences along the two dimensions, passive–active and immersion–absorption. These dimensions frame four experience realms. These are Entertainment (passive absorption), Edu-cation (active absorption), Aestheticism (passive immersion) and Escapism (active immersion). This approach is organizational, like many approaches in the business and marketing literature that perceive the firm as able to determine and manage the experience and the effects the individual should experience (Snel 2013). Jantzen (2013) in turn outlines the psychological structure of experiences with three basic processes: that of the physiological response to stimuli, followed by that of the emotional evaluation of those responses, and lastly that of the cognitive insertion of those evaluations into the framework of past experiences, forming habits and social practices. Applying Apter's theory on reversal (Apter 1989), according to which we oscillate between high and low levels of arousal, searching for a state of pleasure, both Jantzen (2013) and Larsen (2013) describe experiencing as unfolding on two continua. These are anxiety–relaxation, where we seek to avoid anxiety, and boredom–excitement, where we seek excitement. The optimal experience is found at the right level of pleasure and arousal somewhere along these continua.

These ways of understanding experiences and experiencing will be applied in the analysis of the experience consumption patterns of the two types of tourism. The concepts of experiencing on the individual level oscillating between high and low levels of arousal, reaching an ideal state of excitement, then processed, forming habits and social practices, will be used to examine how the individual process of experiencing may influence the overall observed patterns of experience consumption and reveal differences within travel groups. The concepts of the organizational level approach, with the two dimensions of passive–active and immersion–absorption forming four distinct experience realms, will be used to identify and analyse the overall demand characterizing each of the two types of tourism. Can the experience production and consumption patterns of the two types of tourism be understood from just one perspective? Or will important aspects of experience consumption patterns be overlooked, if both approaches are not applied?

## Conceptualizing the tourist destination in the experience economy

As mentioned earlier, the purpose of the chapter is to explore the spatial dimensions of the two different types of tourism and their experiential consumption and production patterns. To do so, we are in need of concepts that may help understand the interactions between production, consumption, experiences and place and how they can be spatially assigned. The destination could be one such concept.

The concept of the tourist destination is widely used in tourism studies (Cooper *et al.* 1998: 98; Cooper and Hall 2008: 112) and prevalent in tourism policy as well as in applied research. It serves as a unit of analysis as well as of action and is infused with notions of location, geography, space and place. It is, however, understood very differently among researchers and across disciplines as shown by Framke (2002), who has reviewed the theoretical constructions of the concept. The concept of the destination is an abstraction or construction and in spite of its wide use, it is not easily made operational. This does not stop researchers, businesses and planners from trying. They focus on the actors and their networks, organizations and cooperation at the level of the tourist 'destination'. An example is Fussing Jensen's resource-based approach of the 'Dynamic Destination' with attractions, facilities and demand as resource bases (Framke

2002: 98; Jensen 2001: 6). Similarly, borrowing from the concepts of clusters and industrial districts, tourist destinations are also regarded as regional production systems (Hjalager 2000). In a literature-based comparison of tourist destinations with industrial districts, Hjalager, however, found that tourist destinations represent very few of the features characteristic of industrial districts (Hjalager 2000). A dependency on multinationals, free-riding behaviour of firms and a lack of stabilized collaborative structures drive tourism destinations to merely become delivery regions. This means that they as collective are not able to learn and thus be innovative.

If it is not fruitful to regard a tourist destination as a cluster or industrial district with businesses, facilities and a resource base in a composite structure, it could alternatively be regarded as a result of social practice, where every activity is localized and therefore forms the place (Framke 2002). The destination is a process, in which the place is reshaped by the interaction and interpretation of the actors (Framke 2002). In this view, the tourist is an important actor among several. If other social actors – tourist businesses and marketers – had not put meaning into the historical, cultural or natural elements of an area, the tourist might not have chosen to visit. This means that a destination is not a physical agglomeration of facilities and businesses, but a process which at any specific moment reshapes the place as seen through the eyes of the actors participating in this process. This implies that the term 'destination' is hardly used in the static sense of the word and places come instead to have several different identities with a variety of activities taking place and many different people passing through on different routes (Framke 2002). Framke concludes that as all these perspectives fail to specify the destination geographically, the concept should only be applied to marketing, as the mediation of a place called the destination.

In a more constructive stance, Ren (2009) suggests accepting the destination in an all-inclusive way by the use of Actor–Network Theory (ANT). Ren understands the destination as a heterogeneous network of people and things that is being constructed. In this way, the physical space is integrated in a broader definition. The construction of the destination is the process of connecting, stabilizing and disseminating relations between a tourism network and its actors where – in accordance with ANT – not just humans but also non-humans act and participate. A destination has many expressions, each of which results from the continuous performance of actors in a network.

This discussion of the concept of the destination shows that it does not help us to geographically bind the combined production and consumption systems of tourism nor to bridge the economic and sociocultural dimensions of destinations. The destination concept is useful for understanding the marketplace of tourism as where industry creates an economic space for the tourist; or how the tourist through social practices and interactions with other actors – human and non-human alike – constructs the destination. The approach of Ren captures the socio-material dimensions with its all-inclusive perspective of ANT, but does not offer an analytical framework for understanding the economic or business processes of value creation in the constructed destination. Thus we still lack an approach that can integrate economic and socio-material perspectives, while also recognizing the territorial aspects of tourism. The territorial staging system may be one such approach.

## The territorial staging system approach

The territorial staging system was originally proposed by Jeannerat and Crevoisier (2010) in an effort to model the relations between the production and consumption sides of experience markets and to describe territorially embedded economic systems for creation, commercialization, validation and consumption of experiences. The territorial staging system has as its centre the stage where the 'stage setting' by the producer and the 'experiential engagement' of the consumer meet and drive value creation and innovation. The stage is not a place or space as often understood in tourism, but a network of relations between and among producers and consumers. Based on production resources such as the natural, historical or cultural assets of a territory, the producers transform these assets into products that are brought to the market through stage setting. On the consumption side, the economic, social and cultural capital of the consumer is transformed into experiential engagement, which in turn influences the 'stage setting' of the producer and so on (Manniche and Larsen 2013).

The analytical model of the territorial staging system may inspire an understanding of how the destination, as well as the tourist experience, is constructed in a process in which tourists interact with the various tourism resources of a particular territory (Jeannerat 2013; see also Guex 2013). As we have seen earlier, the social processes can be encompassed by the destination concept, but not in a fully satisfactory combination with business systems and processes. The territorial staging system approach may bring this aspect to destination concepts.

## The structure and geography of Danish tourism

Different types of tourism outside of metropolitan Denmark were identified in a quantitative study on the geographical distribution of tourism (Hedetoft and Marcussen 2012). There are four main types of tourism outside of the large cities in Denmark: 'Holiday home tourism', 'attraction or amusement tourism', 'second home tourism' and 'urban or cultural and business tourism' (Hedetoft and Marcussen 2012).[1] Each type is distinctly concentrated in different geographical areas of Denmark:

- 'Holiday home tourism' is mainly related to the commercial letting of second homes to domestic and foreign visitors. This type of tourism is concentrated along the west coast of Denmark.
- 'Attraction or amusement tourism' is based on man-made attractions and is found in Billund municipality as well as in Northern and Eastern Jutland.
- 'Second home tourism' is based on private owners' own use of their second homes with low commercial letting frequencies. This type is concentrated in the northern and western parts of Zealand.

- 'Urban or cultural and business tourism' has a large hotel and restaurant sector as well as a high concentration of business travellers. This type is concentrated in city municipalities such as Vejle, Esbjerg and Kolding (Hedetoft and Marcussen 2012).

Holiday home tourism and attraction tourism are the two most dominant and important types of tourism outside metropolitan areas.

More than half of tourism outside Danish metropolitan areas (measured as overnight stays), takes place in just 12 out of the 78 municipalities with tourism activities. If we focus on foreign overnight stays alone, more than half take place in only seven municipalities. Moreover, holiday home overnights dominate in most of these seven municipalities where as much as 70 per cent of registered (i.e. commercial) overnight stays take place in holiday homes. The dominant form of tourism in coastal zone Denmark is thus a stay in a holiday home. Not surprisingly, these areas also have the largest natural attractiveness, measured as the concentration of specific types of natural areas. Lastly, they are also the areas that have the lowest commercial experience content, measured as man-made attractions, dining and shopping opportunities. In Western Jutland, the Ringkøbing-Skjern and Varde municipalities together form the largest centre for this type of tourism in Denmark, accounting for approximately 2.5 billion DKK in tourism turnover. However, in terms of performance, most of these areas are characterized by stagnation or even decline in tourism.

Attraction tourism, on the other hand, takes place in areas with a much higher concentration of commercial experience offerings. These areas are at the same time characterized by a more varied composition of accommodation types, and hotels and holiday centres play a significant role with a share of up to 67 per cent in Billund and 28 per cent in Northern Jutland, which is significantly above the national average outside of metropolitan areas. Camping is, however, a prominent accommodation sector in a number of areas in this category. Some of the attraction tourism areas have experienced economic growth and can in this respect be distinguished from holiday home tourism areas.

## Production and co-production perspectives

In this section, the two dominant tourism types mentioned above are considered and it is analysed where value mainly is created in each type. By examining the value creation in the two systems, we may be able to establish where and how the production and co-production of the two types of tourism differ. To do this, the tourism satellite account figures for the tourism consumption and production of respectively Danish holiday home tourists and Danish hotel tourists are used (VisitDenmark 2012).[2] The tourism satellite account method ensures a correspondence between consumption and production, by aligning the tourism demand based on tourist spending with the tourism supply from the national accounts. In consequence, the distribution of tourist spending is also a measure of the distribution of production among different products. The primary activities of value creation on location in tourism are distributed among the following products in three categories:

- Tourism products, covering local transportation, accommodation, restaurants, travel services and attractions;
- Tourism-related products, covering retail;
- Non-tourism products covering all other products.

The total spending at national level for tourists in hotels is more than double that of holiday home tourists (VisitDenmark 2012). Spending is distributed very differently in the two types of tourism (see Table 11.1).

The major differences that emerge by comparing the two different tourism spending patterns are the following:

1   While the amount spent per night per travel group on accommodation is not so different, accommodation spending accounts for a significantly larger share of total spending for holiday home tourists (53 per cent) than for those staying in hotels (22 per cent).
2   The share of the travel budget spent on eating out by hotel tourists is three times the share of the travel budget of holiday home tourists. Holiday home tourists, on the other hand, spend much more on food and beverages bought in shops.
3   Hotel tourists spend about twice the share of their travel budget on local transportation and fuel than holiday home tourists do.
4   Similarly, hotel tourists spend twice the share of the travel budget on shopping for non-food products than holiday home tourists do.

*Table 11.1* The distribution of daily tourism spending and production per travel group for Danish leisure tourists staying in holiday homes or hotels (VisitDenmark 2012)

| Component | Holiday home tourists | | Hotel tourists | |
|---|---|---|---|---|
| | *In DKK* | *In %* | *In DKK* | *In %* |
| Local transport/fuel | 115 | 9 | 470 | 18 |
| Accommodation 1[1] | 205 | 16 | 575 | 22 |
| Accommodation 2[1] | 478 | 37 | NA | NA |
| Travel service | 0 | 0 | 287 | 11 |
| Eating – in | 167 | 13 | 105 | 4 |
| Eating – out | 90 | 7 | 575 | 22 |
| Events/attraction | 26 | 2 | 78 | 3 |
| Shopping | 90 | 7 | 340 | 13 |
| Other products | 115 | 9 | 183 | 7 |
| Total | 1,286 | 100 | 2,613 | 100 |

Note
1  In the tourism satellite accounting, VisitDenmark uses the general rule of distributing the rent paid by holiday home tourists of 30% to the rental agency and 70% to the owner. Accommodation 1 is the rental agency share while Accommodation 2 is the share of the owner.

5　The amount spent on attractions and events is about three times larger for hotel tourists than it is for holiday home tourists, even if the share of such expenses is as low as 3 and 2 per cent.

Does this imply that holiday home and hotel tourists have different patterns of experience consumption, resulting in different experience production patterns as well? Based on these figures, it can be suggested that the greatest value creation for the tourists staying in hotels lies in accommodation, eating out, shopping and sightseeing. For holiday home tourists, the greatest value creation is simply in the holiday home itself. Moreover, as the holiday home tourists are not particularly mobile nor spend very much on attractions and events, it is likely that the holiday home is the base for their experiential engagement. This would mean that the holiday home and its environment are important resources and locations for experiencing in holiday home tourism. The holiday home is not just a place to sleep and eat, but is an intricate aspect of what is experienced. The total tourist experience is produced and consumed in the holiday home and its nearby environment – and by the tourists themselves. The rent paid for the holiday home may even be considered as the 'entrance fee' paid by the tourists to experiencing, and in this way, the stay is turned into economic value (Jeannerat 2013).

For the other type of tourist, the attraction tourist, the experiential engagement is more likely to unfold outside and away from the place of stay, opposite to what is the case for the holiday home tourist. One can also describe the difference between these two types of tourism as more or less commoditized tourist experiences, where attraction tourism is more commoditized. Spending is not only larger, but also more varied. Holiday home tourists spend less in total and much less on commoditized tourist experiences. The holiday home experience can be seen as a co-developed experience in which the consumer develops the experience (Larsen 2012). In contrast, the experiences of the attraction tourists may be planned or arranged experiences developed by producers (Carù and Cova 2007).

## Consumption perspectives – the tourist experiences

The idea of two different ways of experiencing is supported by research on the Danish island of Bornholm, which has shown that the demand for accommodation is related to experience demand. The research was based on a study of accommodation as an experience product, through a survey among visitors to the island of Bornholm. The survey was conducted after the tourists' visit and applied the four experience realms of Pine and Gilmore in the design of the questionnaire (Feldthus 2007). The purpose of the study was to link accommodation demand to experience demand, to segment the visitors into experience segments and to explore the influence of characteristics such as nationality, travel group and price consciousness on experience preferences.

It was found that tourists chose the holiday home as accommodation because it brought them close to nature, gave them the opportunity to spend time together, relax and do things together in the immediate environment of the holiday home. Holiday home tourists preferred to spend most of their time just being 'at home'. Among the factors which influence the choice of accommodation, they rated 'close to nature', 'by the sea', 'atmosphere' and 'price' as most important. At the same time, they rated factors such as 'proximity to attractions', 'the food', 'service' and 'possibility of being together with other guests' as least important.

The tourists who had chosen a hotel as accommodation sought a feeling of indulging themselves, wanting to experience comfort and a high level of service, though there were also hotel guests who favoured this type of accommodation simply because it was practical and offered good value. Among all guests, hotel guests rated the place of accommodation as 'just a place to stay' and 'spend most of my time' least important, implying a higher degree of mobility as also seen in the overall consumption pattern. Among the factors influencing the choice of accommodation, the hotel tourists rated as most important 'value for money', 'the service', 'atmosphere' and 'food' in that order. While they rated factors such as 'common facilities', 'possibility of being together with other guests', 'the hosts' and 'child-friendly' as least important.

Tourists seek different types of experiences that can be grouped into experience realms. Statements of experience preferences that could be associated with each of the four experience realms were presented to the respondents, asking them to rate their importance. Cluster analysis[3] applied to the responses regarding experience preferences generated four different experience segments. The first is accommodation as place of community formation and instigator of shared activity. The second is accommodation as site of experiences based on access to nature, rest and relaxation. The third is accommodation as site of entertainment, culture and wellness, while the fourth is a functional approach to accommodation, i.e. as a place to sleep. It is the second and third of these experience segments that are relevant for the focus in this analysis on holiday home tourists and attraction tourists, respectively.

The tourist segment which prefers accommodation as site of experiences based on access to nature, a relaxed atmosphere and place of rest, corresponds well with the types of experiences sought by holiday home tourists. This type is constituted by a combination of the following preferences: 'a place where I spend most of my holiday time', 'a place where I can relax and enjoy the immediate environment', 'a place that brings me close to nature' and 'a place that makes me feel I am on Bornholm because of its character and atmosphere'.

The tourist segment which prefers accommodation as site of entertainment, culture and wellness corresponds well with the spending pattern seen for hotel tourists. This type is based on a combination of the preferences 'a place that is an experience because of the architecture', 'a place with entertainment and social interaction in the evenings' and 'a place where I can be pampered in nice surroundings with good food and/or wellness and good service'.

In Figure 11.1, these two segments are placed into the four experience realms by Pine and Gilmore (1999: 30) indicated as holiday home and hotel tourist

*Figure 11.1* Experience segments and tourist types placed into the experience realms of Pine and Gilmore (1999: 30).

segments. Hotel tourists are absorbed by entertainment or education and balance between passive entertainment and active learning. Holiday home tourists, on the other hand, are immersed into the experience of the holiday home where they oscillate between aesthetic enjoyment and active creation of experiences.

In summary, the study on Bornholm of experience preferences related to accommodation demonstrates that accommodation can be considered as experience product. Holiday home and hotel tourists have different experience preferences and can as a consequence be said to belong to different experience realms. It is also possible to divide the tourists into experience segments, which moreover are related to the experience realms of Pine and Gilmore.

The findings from Bornholm are supported by studies in Northern Jutland on holiday home tourists and their experiences from a place perspective, at both the individual and social levels (Larsen and Therkelsen 2011; Larsen 2013). In this study, where all respondents were members of family groups, the holiday home offered a break from everyday life, an opportunity to be together as a family and to relax without having to worry about the tedious chores of everyday life. Just being together and being able to relax were central motives. The interviewed families spent a lot of their time in the holiday home. They also described the holiday home as a practical holiday environment providing everything needed, and as a base for play and other shared activities. The parents emphasized the holiday home as a private sphere, safe and secluded. The holiday home is closely connected to the surrounding environment where the beach and the house are key elements of the holiday product. The holiday home tourists did not wander far from the holiday home in search of activities and experiences. All together, this places the family holiday home experience in the realm of aestheticism. The study, however, revealed underlying experience dynamics in the social interactions of the family. Experiencing turned out to be ultimately individual, but influenced by family interactions. The study applied reversal theory, described earlier in the chapter, as a process generating experiences of pleasure, when reaching an optimal level of arousal through excitement seeking and anxiety avoidance. It helped explain the dynamics of experiences and differences at the individual level. The children tend to seek excitement while the parents, particularly the mothers, tend to avoid anxiety. Applying experience realms, the children's experience preferences when seeking excitement could equally be in the realms of escapism, education or entertainment. The parents' experience preferences when avoiding anxiety are rather found in the realm of aestheticism. In other words, if experiencing is considered at the individual level, the holiday home tourism experience is a composite of experiences in all realms.

## Summary and discussion

The overall purpose of the chapter was to investigate the experiential and spatial dimensions of the two types of tourism, holiday home tourism and attraction tourism. Can these two types of tourism be seen as forming two distinct experience production and consumption systems, characterized by different experience demands and geographical configurations? Based on the empirical analysis, the conclusions about the main characteristics of the two types of tourism are summarized in Table 11.2.

The analysis of the main value creation and economic activities of each type of tourism revealed two different consumption and production patterns. On the one hand, the very localized and homogenous spending patterns, centred on the holiday home and its close (beach) environment. On the other hand, the more mobile, dispersed and varied spending patterns of attraction tourism with geographically spread attractions, restaurants and shops. As demonstrated by both

*Table 11.2* Main characteristics of the two types of tourism

|  | *Holiday home tourism* | *Attraction tourism* |
|---|---|---|
| Experience spaces and places | The holiday home<br>The beach | Hotels and holiday centres<br>Man-made attractions<br>Restaurants and shops |
| Main production resources | The coastal environment<br>Privately owned holiday homes | Physical and economic capital<br>Culture and history |
| Experiential engagement | Self- and co-developed<br>Aestheticism | Planned and arranged<br>Entertainment |
| Mobility | Low | High |
| Main economic transaction | Rent for holiday home | Entrance fees |

the study on Bornholm and in Northern Jutland, the differences in consumption patterns reflect differences in the experience preferences and the experiential engagement of consumers. In holiday home tourism, the tourists' experience preferences are in the realm of aestheticism, while in attraction tourism, the experience preferences are in the realm of entertainment. The holiday home tourists socio-materially engage with the holiday home and its immediate environment and become co-developers of experiences as they bring and invest emotions, family social practices and perceptions of the holiday home as 'home away from home'. In contrast, the hotel-based attraction tourists buy commoditized tourism experiences through shopping, eating out or visiting attractions and sights. Thus, their experiential engagement and role as co-producers are quite material and indirect and mainly consist in consuming commodities and 'taking in' various material cultural, historical or natural manifestations of the place. The holiday home tourists identify the holiday home as the main location for their holiday experience, while the attraction tourists staying in hotels declare themselves least likely to spend their holiday time in the place of accommodation and are more mobile. The main economic transaction of the co-developed experience of the holiday home tourist is rent for the holiday home. For the attraction tourist the main economic activity is in the form of shopping or entrance fees.

All together, the two types of tourism exhibit different production, co-production and consumption characteristics and have different spatial implications. The experience spaces and places of holiday home tourism are the holiday home and its environment, particularly the beach, and are mainly located on the west coast of Denmark. The experience spaces and places of attraction tourism are not to the same degree tied to the accommodation site, but relate to commoditized experience products and services which are supplied and consumed within a broader geographical area, though concentrated in particular parts of Denmark, e.g. East Jutland and Billund/Legoland.

The chapter has shown how accommodation can be considered an experience product and has argued that tourists' choice of type of accommodation is driven by experiential preferences. The experiential preferences of the tourist are important to understand for innovation and development within tourism. Specifically, an understanding of the heterogeneity of tourist experiences in groups such as families and the role of the place of the holiday home is needed for developing the holiday home tourist product. Discussions on tourism innovation in research and policy have primarily been dealt with from production and supply side. Innovative potentials of consumers as co-producers have been more or less absent. This chapter has shown how an understanding of the experiential engagement of the tourists as they meet the production resources in an experience space can be useful in developing experiences that also meet the demand of the tourists. Providing the full picture of such dynamic processes, however, will require the analytical inclusion of both the psychology of experiencing of individuals and the organizational aspects of planning and executing the provision of experiences as economic offerings.

These empirical findings illustrate the social construction of destinations, continuously shaped and reshaped through tourists interactions with material resources, narratives, local people, etc., and resonate with the socio-material understandings of the tourist destination of, among others, Ren (2009). As argued by Framke (2002), places come to have several different identities with a variety of activities taking place and many different people passing through on different routes. Thus, it is hardly meaningful to define tourist destinations as geographically bounded territories, fixed in content or shape. Rather, destinations could be considered vessels of opportunities for tourist experiences, where the exact geography is shaped by the tourists' choices that in turn are driven by their experience preferences.

Notwithstanding the advantages of this interpretation of the tourist destination, it does not entail any conceptualization of the specific types of economic and social dynamics that characterize experience markets, including the co-producing role of consumers at systems level. The notion of the territorial staging system (TSS) may be more useful in this respect due to four features. First, it opens the perspective for the understanding of how products and economic value are created not only by producers but by the engagement of tourists and consumption resources as well. Second, interactions and practices of producers and consumers are considered not only in economic but also in social terms. Third, the territorial staging system deals with territorially embedded experiential resources and processes, appropriate for tourism studies, while space and place are not conceptualized as bounded territories. Fourth, it involves temporal and spatial dynamics, offering analytical sensitivity to processes of innovation and value creation. The notion of territorial staging system thus may be able to analytically integrate the territorial embedded dynamics of tourism businesses, their experience products, and the people consuming them. By considering 'territory' as relational and continuously constructed by actors, the notion of territorial staging system may also be helpful in identifying how specific experience production and consumption systems connect to and interact with other staging systems elsewhere.

The author would like to thank Anne Lorentzen and the team of editors for much needed advice, suggestions and editing along the way, as well as colleague Jesper Manniche who helped by cutting to the core and into the essence of the chapter.

## Notes

1 'Holiday home' and 'second home' are here understood according to the defining glossary of Larsen (Larsen 2012: 60) where 'second home' is an 'umbrella term for *non-commercial* and recreational use referring to ownership (primary) or other recurrent use, such as loan, of a property (secondary) while 'holiday home' denotes '*Commercial* use in the form of short lease rental of someone else's second home for holiday purposes'.
2 Danish holiday home tourists and Danish hotel leisure tourists have been chosen as indicator tourists for respectively holiday home tourism and attraction tourism as there

are only detailed data on spending distribution available for this nationality. All other nationalities are pooled together. Moreover, they are prevalent tourists in areas dominated by holiday home tourism as well as attraction tourism. The spending distribution also exhibits roughly, though with some minor variations, the same pattern as the composite spending of foreign leisure tourists.

3 Cluster analysis or clustering is the task of grouping a set of objects in such a way that objects in the same group (called a cluster) are more similar (in some sense or another) to each other than to those in other groups (clusters). It is a main task of exploratory data mining and a common technique for statistical data analysis.

## References

Apter, M.J. (1989) *Reversal theory: Motivation, emotion and personality*, London: Routledge.

Bærenholdt, J.O. and Haldrup, M. (2010) 'Tourist experience design', in J. Simonsen, J.O. Bærenholdt, M. Büscher and J.D. Scheuer (eds) *Design Research: Synergies from Interdisciplinary Perspectives*, London: Routledge.

Carù, A. and Cova, B. (2007) 'Consuming experiences: An introduction', in A. Carù and B. Cova (eds) *Consuming experience*, London: Routledge.

Cooper, C. and Hall, C.M. (2008) *Contemporary Tourism*, Oxford: Elsevier.

Cooper, C., Fletcher, J., Gilbert, D., Shepherd, R. and Wanhill, S. (1998) *Tourism: Principles and Practice*, Essex: Prentice Hall.

Eide, D. and Mossberg, L. (2013) 'Towards more intertwined innovation types: Innovation through experience design focusing on customer interactions', in J. Sundbo and F. Sørensen (eds) *Handbook on the Experience Economy*, Cheltenham: Edward Elgar.

Erhvervs- og Vækstministeriet (2014) *Danmark i arbejde – Vækstplan for dansk turisme*, 2013/14: 10, Copenhagen: Erhvervs- og Vækstministeriet. Online. Available at: www.evm.dk/~/media/oem/pdf/2014/2014-publikationer/20-01-14-vaekstplan-for-dansk-turisme/vaekstplan-for-dansk-turisme-20-01-14.ashx (accessed 3 February 2015).

Feldthus, L.F. (2007) *Bornholms overnatningskapacitet – er den fremtidssikret?*, Nexø, Denmark: Center for Regional and Tourism Research.

Framke, W. (2002) 'The Destination as a concept: A discussion of the business-related perspective versus the socio-cultural approach in tourism theory', *Scandinavian Journal of Hospitality and Tourism*, 2(2): 92–108.

Fuglsang, L., Sundbo, J. and Sørensen, F. (2011) 'Dynamics of experience service innovation: Innovation as a guided activity', *The Service Industries Journal*, 31(5): 661–77.

Guex, D. (2013) 'La circulation des connaissances: Convention touristique alpine et mises en scène des heritage alpins dynamiques socio-economiques territorial dans l'historie de la station de Montreux', Working Paper 10–2013, MAPS – Maison d'analyse des processus sociaux.

Gyimóthy, S. (2009a) 'Casual observers, connoisseurs and experimentalists: A conceptual exploration of Niche Festival Visitors', *Scandinavian Journal of Hospitality and Tourism*, 9(2–3): 177–205.

Gyimóthy, S. (2009b) 'Thrillscapes: Wilderness mediated as playground', in B. Knudsen and A.M. Waade (eds) *Re-investing Authenticity: Tourism, Place, Emotions, Tourism and Cultural Change Book Series*, Bristol: Channel View Publications.

Halkier, H. (2013) 'Innovation and destination governance in Denmark: Tourism, Policy Networks and Spatial Development', *European Planning Studies*, 22(8): 1659–70.

Hedetoft, A. and Marcussen, C.H. (2012) *Kystturismen i Danmark,* Hvidesande, Denmark: Videncenter for Kystturisme.

Hjalager, A.M. (2000) 'Tourism destinations and the concept of industrial districts', *Tourism and Hospitality Research,* 2(3): 199–213.

Jantzen, C. (2013) 'Experiencing and experiences: A psychological framework', in J. Sundbo and F. Sørensen (eds) *Handbook on the Experience Economy,* Cheltenham: Edward Elgar.

Jantzen, C., and Vetner, M. (2007) 'Oplevelsens psykologiske struktur', in J.O. Bærenholdt and J. Sundbo (eds) *Oplevelsesøkonomi. produktion, forbrug, kultur,* Frederiksberg, Denmark: Samfundslitteratur.

Jeannerat, H. (2013) 'Staging experiences, valuing authenticity: Towards a market perspective on territorial development', *European Urban and Regional Studies,* 20: 375–84.

Jeannerat, H. and Crevoisier, O. (2010) 'Experiential turn and territorial staging system: What new research challenges?', paper presented at Regional Studies Association Workshop on the experience turn in local development and planning, Aalborg University, Aalborg, September 2010.

Jensen, C.F. (2001) 'Den innovative adfærd i oplevelsesintensive virksomheder. Et strategisk perspektiv i turisme', Forskningsrapport 01: 2, Center for Servicestudier, Roskilde Universitet.

Larsen, J.R.K. (2012) 'Family holiday homescapes – Place, individual and social perspectives on the intra-family experience dynamics at the holiday home destination', unpublished PhD thesis, Department of Culture and Global Studies, SPIRIT, Aalborg University.

Larsen, J.R.K. (2013) 'Family flow: The pleasures of "being together" in a holiday home', *Scandinavian Journal of Hospitality and Tourism,* 13(3): 153–74.

Larsen, J.R.K. and Therkelsen, A. (2011) 'Udviklingspotentialer i det danske feriehusprodukt:. Et efterspørgselsperspektiv på samspillet mellem feriehus, feriehusområde og attraktioner', *Økonomi & Politik,* 84(4): 40–55.

Lorentzen, A. (2009) 'Cities in the experience economy', *European Planning Studies,* 17(6): 829–45.

Lorentzen, A. (2013) 'The experience turn of the Danish periphery: The downscaling of new spatial strategies', *European Urban and Regional Studies,* 20(4): 460–72.

Lorentzen, A. and Jeannerat, H. (2013) 'Urban and regional studies in the experience economy: What kind of turn?', European Urban and Regional Studies. 20(4): 363–9.

Manniche, J. and Larsen, K.T. (2013) 'Experience staging and symbolic knowledge: The case of Bornholm culinary products', *European Urban and Regional Studies,* 20(4): 401–16.

Manniche, J., Marcussen, C.H. and Rømer, L. (2014) *Kortlægning af kystturismeforskning og samspil mellem forskning og turismeerhverv i Danmark,* Nexø, Denmark: Centre for Regional and Tourism Research. Online. Available at: http://ufm.dk/publikationer/2014/filer-2014/kortlaegning-af-kystturismeforskning-2014.pdf (accessed 28 October 2014).

O'Dell, T. and Billing, P. (2005) *Experiencescapes. Tourism, culture and economy,* Copenhagen: Copenhagen Business School Press.

Pine, B.J. and Gilmore, J.H. (1999) *The experience economy: Work is theatre and every business a stage,* Boston: Harvard Business School Press.

Ren, C. (2009) 'Constructing the tourist destination. A socio-material description', unpublished PhD thesis, Centre for Tourism, Innovation and Culture, University of Southern Denmark.

Snel, A. (2013) 'Experience as the DNA of a changed relationship between firms and institutions and individuals', in J. Sundbo and F. Sørensen (eds) *Handbook on the Experience Economy*, Cheltenham: Edward Elgar.

Sundbo, J. and Jensen, J.F. (2009) 'Værdikædeinnovation. Innovation af oplevelser og service', Forskningsrapport 09:1 fra Center for Servicestudier, RUC, Roskilde.

Sundbo, J. and Sørensen, F. (2013) 'Introduction to the experience economy', in J. Sundbo and F. Sørensen (eds) *Handbook on the Experience Economy*, Cheltenham: Edward Elgar.

Sundbo, J., Sørensen, F. and Fuglsang, L. (2013) 'Innovation in the experience economy', in J. Sundbo and F. Sørensen (eds) *Handbook on the Experience Economy*, Cheltenham: Edward Elgar.

VisitDenmark (2012) *Turismens økonomiske betydning i Danmark 2011*, Copenhagen: VisitDenmark.

# Part V
# Governance in the experience economy

# 12 Pursuing happiness in planning?

## The experience economy as planning approach

*Anne Lorentzen*

## Introduction

The trigger for this chapter was a small article by Grant (2010) on experiential planning based on a series of interviews with a well-known urban planner, Larry Beasley, from Vancouver. Grant quoted him for saying that:

> what we were doing in Vancouver – but we hadn't put a name to it – was to try to create for people the experience that they aspire to in their day-to-day lives in the city that houses and accommodates that day-to-day life.... I have dubbed it experiential planning, because it is a planning approach based on the experiential expectation of the users of that environment.
>
> (Grant 2010: 364)

This planning approach seemed to differ quite considerably from the global experiential flagship approach practised today by cities and regions striving to enhance their position in the urban hierarchy (Friedman 2010: 150). Today Vancouver unites high density with proximity to natural beauty, public transportation and bicycle lanes, nightlife and shopping, architectural quality and experimentation (Berelowitz 2005; see also Punter 2003), and it serves as showcase of a liveable city for planners and architects around the world. The purpose of this chapter is to investigate and develop the notion of experiential planning as a theoretical construct and as planning practice. Theoretically the chapter takes its point of departure in the classical concept of the experience economy, in which actors are united in experiential staging processes (Pine and Gilmore 1999). It is suggested that city planners act as stagers of urban development. The second section of the chapter unfolds the case of experiential planning in Vancouver, in which planners act as stagers of complex and participatory planning processes. The concluding section summarizes the lessons for urban planning and questions the difficult balance between liveability and economic development.

## The aims of economic activity

Already in 1921 Veblen (quoted in Lebergott 1993: 26) wrote that about 'half of actual output is consumed in wasteful superfluities'. Lebergott exemplifies superfluities as health expenditure, transport and recreation. Andersson and Andersson (2006: 34–57) show an increase in recreation consumption in a number of industrialized countries between 1870 and 1979. Lebergott considers the increase in superfluous consumption as an increase in 'happiness' and suggests that economic activity does not aim for output. Rather it aims at experiences via consumption (Lebergott 1993: 3). Toffler (1970) suggests that the aim of superfluous consumption is 'psychic gratification' and prophesizes the emergence of a separate production system of luxury (meaning superfluous) demand and supply. Consumption is thus the aim of production, and consumers increasingly want emotional rather than functional values.

## The experience economy and the role of the customer

The pursuit of non-functional values by consumers is the starting point for Pine and Gilmore in their writings on the experience economy (Pine and Gilmore 1998, 1999, 2011). Rather than seeing experience offerings as a separate production system, they see the most important potential for value creation in the integration of experiences in mundane products and services. The ultimate aim of experience-based innovation is to increase customer satisfaction and loyalty, and thereby sales. The products are valued in the market by (higher) prices and by praise (Jeannerat 2015). 'Work is a theatre and every business is a stage' was the subtitle of the first book by Pine and Gilmore (1999). The subtitle alludes to the idea that experiences need to be staged. Stages, props and actors are used as resources that can be utilized to arouse the feelings of the customers. Therefore staging is part of the job in which employees act as in a theatre play. In this scenario consumers participate as audience, as object.

Better staging and consumer engagement can be achieved in different ways. One is by theming according to, for example, seasons, places or history (Pine and Gilmore 1999: 49); another is to engage the five senses of the customers to enrich their experience (Pine and Gilmore 1999: 59).

The intensity of the experience can also be graduated by differentiating the relationship between the customer and the experience offering. Consumers may be absorbed by the experience or they may be immersed in the experience by becoming part of its production as audience or participant. In both cases, their participation may vary between active participation and passive watching (Pine and Gilmore 1999: 30).

In this approach, customers do not have an independent role but they are needed as sources of knowledge for firms. Learning about the customers is part of the job to engineer experience offerings. Their knowledge is dug out by different techniques ranging from direct conversation through to covert observation (Pine and Gilmore 1999: 94; Pine and Gilmore 2011: 142). Engagement and knowledge-mining techniques share the aim of creating loyal customers. Accordingly, Chapter 9 in their book is called: 'The customer is the product' (Pine and Gilmore 1999: 163ff.).

However, a more independent role for customers seems to evolve in theory as well as in practice. Not only do customers as expert users contribute with knowledge which may enhance the functional quality of products as well as their experiential value (Hauge and Power 2012), it has also been suggested that customers have become tired of being manipulated. Therefore, customers create arenas for unfiltered exchange among themselves, where they articulate and develop demands to the products as well as to companies that produce them (Agger 2013: 3). In this way they not only represent an important source of knowledge for innovation beyond what the market signals provide, they can even be seen as resourceful innovators in their own right (see also Bogers *et al.* 2010).

## Experience economic planning

A parallel broadening of values and tasks, and a change of focus, can be found in urban planning during the last three to four decades. First, there has been a move away from planning understood as an exclusively technical exercise towards planning as a whole-of-society process involving holistic spatial visions and strategies at the urban or regional levels. Second, planning is becoming an activity much more focused on mediation of societal decision processes. Finally, planners' roles have become entrepreneurial, rather than just advisory (Hall and Hubbard 1997; Friedman 2008: 254; Albrechts *et al.* 2003; Healey 2007). The changes have taken place in a context of rescaling public responsibilities from national to subnational (and supranational) levels and during a general trend in the economy with loss of manufacturing jobs and a growth in the number of service and knowledge-based jobs. Lower levels of government, which used to serve as conveyor belts for national welfare policies, have increasingly been left alone to fight for themselves and their local territories (Brenner 2004).

Governments have developed policies that use experience economy thinking in at least three different directions.

One way is to develop flagship projects and branding (OECD 2006). The intention is to attract attention on global markets for investors and tourism in the context of globally competing regions and cities by offering unique and often themed experiences. This can be described as 'glocalisation' (Brenner 1998). It is often carried out by external actors and local states without involving the local communities. Examples reach from The Blue Planet in Copenhagen[1] to international sports tournaments like the PWA (Professional Windsurfing Association) annual World Cup held in Klitmøller, known since 2010 as Cold Hawaii.[2]

A second type of public policying is the development of experience tourism by expanding the supply of entertainment for visitors. Catalogues of potential experience offerings are developed and, contrary to many flagship projects, local providers are mostly involved in the innovation process. Theming as well as the engaging of the five senses are used as engagement techniques, and localities develop experiential tourism profiles within gastronomy, adventure, culture, wellness and other tourism offers.

A third direction of experience-based planning is related to the development of amenities more broadly. This can be seen as a strategic manipulation of image and culture (Hall and Hubbard 1997: 162). Waterfront residential areas and cultural amenities have been developed as experience offerings in big as well as small cities, such as Aalborg, Denmark. The engagement technique can be seen as immersion and active participation (as actor and spectator at the same time) in a fantastic life in the city. The focus has been to attract good taxpayers and a qualified labour force for the knowledge economy.

Experiential place development, like the ones mentioned above, have become part of urban growth strategies. They focus on enhancing the city for consumption rather than for production activities (Hall and Hubbard 1997: 162). However, this type of experience planning continues to focus on the production side. Planners as producers develop the city as experience for citizens as customers, and a certain standardization of the offer can be seen, as places often compete on the same markets with similar means (so-called me-too-ism (Waitt and Gibson 2009)). Even if experience projects may be accompanied by general improvements in infrastructure, the strategies depend on fluctuating markets and mostly have only shallow connection with local culture and local actors and citizens.

The potentials of experiential planning have not been exhausted by these three strategies however. First, it is relevant to discuss what experience(s) the city or locality should offer, and for whom. Rather than immediate economies of attention (Goldhaber 1997) planning urban experiences may include the broader intentions of welfare and quality of life and place.

Second, rather than regarding citizens (or tourists) as customers and objects of manipulation, they can be regarded as sources of knowledge for innovation. Planning would therefore benefit from access to citizens' values and knowledge. City planners would not only get a market analysis of what citizens really want, they would be able to develop place-specific projects, avoid me-too-ism and enhance urban quality. A focus on the planner–citizen relationship is therefore important.

Third, the theatre metaphor seems applicable to planning. Interestingly, Lavrinec (2013) suggests the notion of urban scenography. Her inspiration comes from a strand of thought in urban planning that sees spatial structures as producers of certain types of behaviour and emotional experience (e.g. de Certau 1984). She sees the urban scenography as a dynamic set of city elements including spatial configurations and everyday scenarios. These elements are able to encourage citizens to participate in the reorganization of the city (Lavrinec 2013: 21). Citizens interpret urban space by their routes and rhythm of walk, or by their alternative practices such as skateboarding (Lavrinec 2013: 22). In its outset the notion of urban scenography is related to the micro-practices of the citizen (Lavrinec 2013: 21). Urban scenography can be regarded as a tool in urban planning, for example in connection with revitalization. Parallels to the experience economy approach are unavoidable. If work is theatre and every business is a stage, then 'planning is theatre and every city is a stage'. This means that planning is about changing the urban scenographies by staging. Cooperation across departments around shared visions and strategies is a require-ment for successful urban staging (see also Pine and Gilmore 1999: 109; Lorent-zen 2013; Power 2009).

## Towards an urban staging system?

Planning can be seen as a social-material innovation process. From innovation studies, it is known that the road to innovation is insecure and networked. There-fore collaboration capability at different levels can be considered a prerequisite for actors (Blomqvist and Levy 2006). Even more so in urban planning, where actors and stakeholders abound and include various business as well as political interests (Healey *et al.* 2003; Healey 2007). Planning authorities therefore have to mediate between different interests. They also need to mobilize resources from different parties. In this way, planning has grown considerably more complex and market dependent since the 1980s (Brenner 2004).

Does urban staging have parallels to the territorial innovation system known from regional studies (Moulart and Seika 2003)? A system is characterized by ele-ments, structures and relationships within borders, a process as well as an output. Collaborative planning (Healey 2003) points to the fact that the planning process can be less structured and foreseeable. This means that the limits bordering the planning process are permeable, the elements and actors are changeable, and the process itself can be sequential rather than continuous. However, urban staging can be seen as a continuous although sequential process, in which actors, planners, as well as other interest groups, mobilize resources to create urban experiences. As the process needs to be orchestrated (most often by planning authorities), it is pos-sible, with these caveats, to suggest the notion of an urban staging system.

Compared to the territorial staging system described by Jeannerat (2015), it is difficult to distinguish between production factors and consumption factors. Planners stage the social-material construction of the city in which different actors take part, based on social, cultural, financial, physical, and natural resour-ces and values, but the actors play many roles at the same time and also contri-bute to innovation. Experiential engagement of the population is the immediate aim of urban staging, but this may be connected to a wider strategy of urban transformation. In the experience economy, the aim was the loyal customer. In the urban staging system the aim is the involved citizen, who cares about the city and identifies with the place. Understood this way, the aim of experiential plan-ning is – citizens' happiness.

The Canadian city of Vancouver can be seen as an example of this new reading of the experience economy in urban planning. The following section therefore investigates how the urban staging system of Vancouver can be described and understood. What are the resources, who are the stakeholders, and what are the resulting urban cityscapes and scenographies? What values have guided the urban transformation process? What has been the role of planners in the staging process? To what extent has it been possible to ground the projects in local identities? And finally, has the urban staging system been able to produce engaged citizens? The analysis will be contextualized by a brief record of the recent industrial transformation of Vancouver.

## Vancouver's journey from regional resource periphery to global metropolis

Vancouver is a young city, established in 1886 (Hutton 2010: 267), and in population size it ranks number 8 in Canada with 603,000 inhabitants.[3] It is beautifully located on the west coast at the foot of the North Shore Mountains, and bordered by the three inlets (Burrard Inlet, English Bay and False Creek). The city has been decisively formed by global flows of immigrants and foreign direct investment, mainly of Asian origin. Liberal social attitudes, lifestyles and ecological values prevail in the city as in the whole region of Northwestern USA and Southwestern British Columbia (Hutton 2011: 239; see also Garreau 1981). Vancouver's economic structure has changed from a resource-based economy up to the 1970s (forestry, mining, oil and gas) towards a service-based economy with growth in welfare as well as advanced business services (Hutton 2010: 223). In terms of services, Vancouver is Canada's principal port with a developed maritime economy (Hutton 2010: 230), and by 1950 Vancouver was a service city hosting many service industries with specialized commercial and financial services as well as retail (Hutton 2010: 230). On the other hand, the city has no history as an industrial centre of large-scale manufacturing and big corporations. Instead, the economy is characterized by small and medium-sized enterprises, and an entrepreneurial spirit, which provides the urban economy with resilience and flexibility. The growth in advanced business services (professional, scientific and technical), in advanced consumer services (information, culture and recreation), and not least in the construction industry due to the expansion of the housing sector is witness to this (Hutton 2010: 223). Over the years, the city has thus been transformed from a regional central place in the 1950s into a transnational metropolis (Hutton 2010: 222).

## The changing cityscape of Vancouver

The transformation of the city since the 1970s has involved the new use of False Creek South and the growth of corporate offices in the Central Business District. The rezoning of False Creek South was highly consequential for Vancouver by accelerating the industrial decline through privileging housing, consumption and public amenities over industrial use (Hutton 2010: 232); and instead of the obsolete areas left behind by the resource-based industries, residential communities of medium density and mixed income emerged (Hutton 2010: 226).

A milestone of urban transformation was the international exposition Expo '86. The government of British Columbia purchased False Creek North for use as the site of the Expo (Hutton 2010: 233), and railroad yards, warehouses, trucking operations and a sawmill had to close or relocate. Three levels of government joined forces to attract major investments into the area and the result was an international hotel, a convention centre, a cruise ship terminal, and even a new fixed-rail transit system (Hutton 2010: 236). The later purchase of the exposition lands by Hong Kong's most influential capitalist signaled global financial confidence in Vancouver and opened up for Hong Kong immigrants and capital to Vancouver after the transfer of sovereignty of Hong Kong from the UK to China.

The Central Area Plan of 1991 consolidated the Central Business District and favoured housing and mixed use with both public amenities and new industries (Hutton 2010: 227). New residential towers emerged. In older commercial buildings new, often small and life-style-based creative and knowledge-intensive industries emerged (Hutton 2010: 228). In addition, many businesses thrive on the artificial Granville Island which houses a colourful mix of cement factory, various light industries, arts and craft shops and a food market (Figure 12.1).

As a result, the residential population of the city core increased and a more diverse business landscape developed (Hutton 2010: 237–41). New dynamic consumption and production spaces emerged in the inner city, as, for example,

*Figure 12.1* Granville Island food market (photo © Anne Lorentzen 2014).

in Yaletown, providing it with vibrancy and diversity, and the localized rise of the cultural economy implied a recovery of the inner city's creative functions and historic diversity (Hutton 2009: 606). Since 1986 immigration has been stimulated to boost the economy by national legislation, which grants immigration status to applicants who start a company or invest financially in the province where they wish to stay (Barnes and Hutton 2009: 1256). The consequential very high inflows of immigrants, particularly from East and South East Asia, have given much of the city a multicultural character.

The 2010 Winter Olympics, held successfully in Vancouver, served as a further vehicle of urban development in the Southeast of False Creek. A Canada Line rapid transit service was inaugurated in August 2009 (Hutton 2011: 251). The new Olympic Stadium was built as a global icon and flagship, and new parts of the city south of False Creek were developed and inhabited mainly by new Asian-Pacific immigrants (Figure 12.2).

Against the dynamic of regeneration, another dynamic of dislocation can be observed (Hutton 2009: 612). Ley and Dobson (2008) show a clear east–west divide in gentrification, measured as a change of social status of the residing population over a 30-year period (Ley and Dobson 2008: 2479). Another dimension of dislocation is occupational, as the new industries emerging in Vancouver do not absorb the weaker segments of the labour market. The east–west divide is

*Figure 12.2* The Winter Olympic Stadium and new high-rise housing (photo © Anne Lorentzen 2014).

also nurtured by the stigmatization from the media of the Down Town East Side (Liu and Blomley 2013). Gentrification, on the other hand, was mostly based on massive urban housing and infrastructure projects, while cultural capital and artists, usually connected to gentrification, sought other areas with old, authentic and diverse environments in the south and east of the city (Ley 2003).

## Values guiding urban planning in Vancouver

A local election in 1972 laid the way to a new urban policy with a reform-oriented city council (Hutton 2004: 1958). In contrast to the pro-business and pro-growth values of its predecessors, who had insisted on the continuation of the old industries, the new council focused on 'quality of life', 'livable city' and 'people before property' (Hutton 2004: 1958). The rapid changes in Vancouver's cityscape are the results of a series of very big projects, and in general local policy and planning values have been highly influential in the city. The preference for mega-projects is inherited from the planning of large infrastructures for the stable economy (Barnes and Hutton 2009: 1257). Social values and urban visions have guided the use of traditional planning instruments (zoning and land-use policies, development regulations, design guidelines, public investments, fiscal mechanisms and information services) (Hutton 2004: 1954) and mobilized new ones.

Since the 1970s, post-industrial and postmodernist approaches and progressive social and environmental concerns have prevailed (Hutton 2004: 1955). Post-industrial values denote the political acceptance of industrial restructuring and the commitment to pursue alternative urban visions. Postmodern values imply the acknowledgement of diversity, pluralism, complexity and ambiguity (Hutton 2004: 1955).

This was the background for the transformation of the False Creek industrial area into a combination of residential, recreational and clean industrial uses. A further dislocation of industries, and the development of new infrastructures, followed in connection with Expo '86. Accordingly, a new economic development plan from 1985 focused on advanced services (Hutton 2004: 1962).

The Central Area Plan from 1991 celebrates diversity and pluralism in a postmodernist stance. An important goal was a lively downtown, inhabited by all people, all income and ethnic groups, and all ages. Also, the physical and functional character of the city should be differentiated. The land use plan favoured housing and public uses, while the central business district with its more monotonous offices was confined within a smaller territory (Hutton 2004: 1964). High density should reduce commuting and increase liveliness (Hutton 2004: 1965), and 20 per cent (even if this became negotiable) of the housing should be social housing (Hutton 2004: 1967).

The Livable Region Strategic Plan of 1996 for Greater Vancouver, which was based on sustainable development values, aimed at reducing dispersion and sprawl in the face of the fast-growing regional peripheries, and its focus on bicycle and pedestrian mobility (Hutton 2011: 244–5) influenced Vancouver city as well. These values have been upheld as an eco-density policy in the decades that followed (Hutton 2011: 250). Social sustainability was addressed more specifically in 2004 by the Social Issues Subcommittee in Vancouver which promoted the four values of equity, inclusion, adaptability and security, which came to permeate urban policy and planning through different areas of policy responsibility (Holden 2012: 531–2).

While these values have resulted in a lively, walkable and diverse city, they do conflict with each other. Housing has thus out-competed office space, and speculation in housing has increased the costs, because a social balance is difficult to achieve in a density paradigm (Quastel *et al.* 2012). Both more jobs and more affordable housing thus represent big challenges at present (Hutton 2011: 251).

## Governance of urban transformation in Vancouver

The governance of Vancouver emerges from continuous negotiations among a large number of organizations at sector and at neighbourhood level, city administrators and the elected officials (Brunet-Jailly 2008). The Central Area Plan from 1991 was thus developed in a dialogue with key stakeholders, among whom were the city's new elite of service workers (managers, professionals, specialists, creative workers) (Hutton 2004: 1966). Planners have a strong position, both because of the widely acknowledged quality of the city bureaucracy (Brunet-Jailly 2008: 384), and because planning decisions are in their hand. This enables both strong visions and long-term decisions (Brunet-Jailly 2008: 378).

However, neighbourhood groups have been able to challenge even the overall visions for the city, as in the 1970s when neighbourhood-based citizen groups successfully fought the plan to demolish the Strathcona neighbourhood to make way for a downtown freeway. Since then Vancouver has avoided freeways in the city (Brunet-Jailly 2008: 380) making it more liveable.

Fiscal conservatism in terms of sound public budgets and private sector participation has, since the 1970s, been combined with the mentioned progressive approach to urban development. The financial responsibility for the physical urban development of Vancouver has been in the hands of the private sector. On top of the usual planning tools, planners have been able to negotiate a trade-off between building heights and public amenities such as social housing, parks, schools and cultural facilities, the so-called social bonus policy (Brunet-Jailly 2008: 378).

Mega-events such as Expo '86 and the 2010 Winter Olympics have been used to reconstruct local policy towards market-oriented solutions and away from redistributive state-driven measures (Vanwynsberghe *et al.* 2013: 2075). However, the bids for building contracts should include social and (since 1999) sustainability concerns (Vanwynsberghe *et al.* 2013: 2078), and even in the Olympic village social housing was supposed to be included (Vanwynsberghe *et al.* 2013: 2085). Edelson (2011) even argues that the Olympics helped deliver funding to address social problems, and that preparing for the Olympics actually became an opportunity for the working group to articulate and adopt high-level inclusive goals

(Edelson 2011: 812). Equally, an organization was formed in 2002 by the province to develop an inclusive culture policy, which should 'strengthen arts, literacy, sport and healthy living, accessibility and volunteerism in communities across British Columbia leading up to, and beyond, the 2010 Olympic and Paralympic Winter Games' (Edelson 2011: 814). An example is the Culture Olympics (Sue Harvey and Burke Taylor, in interview, May 2014). As part of the urban transformation, culture policy has thus become more important in Vancouver, as can be seen in many innovations in provincial cultural administration, a high number of local cultural planners, and the highest municipal spending on culture in British Columbia (Marontate and Murray 2010: 332–4).

## Planners as stagers in Vancouver

As the expertise and values of planners have had such great importance for the transformation of Vancouver, their role in the process since the 1970s has resembled that of staging. Brunet-Jailly (2008: 386) points at 'the importance of the bureaucratic culture of Vancouver City Hall in fostering, leading and managing the very many channels of communication that connects all Vancouverites to the polity and policy of their city'. Such staging was based on policy values, and resulted in new urban cityscapes and scenographies as well as in new challenges. Conversations in May 2014 with three important actors in Vancouver's more recent planning history have provided valuable insights in the urban staging process.

### *Values and innovation*

Larry Beasley (LB) has worked for the city of Vancouver for 32 years and from 1992 to 2006 as director of planning. From the mid-1980s Larry Beasley was involved in the efforts to repopulate the town centre, which had just 37,000 residents in 1991. The vision formulated in the 'Living First Strategy' was to change the downtown area from a workplace and entertainment environment into a place where workplaces and homes came closer together. Two instruments, rezoning and quality design, were applied, and this has resulted in a population of 115,000 inhabitants in downtown today.

Larry Beasley is inspired by the notion of the experience economy, and the understanding that people in the modern world have the wealth to buy experiences. 'What people do as consumers … is much more powerful than what they do as voters. They vote every three or four years. They consume every day' (LB). And therefore:

> [i]n Vancouver we said let's understand the potential of the consumer, and let's try to reshape that potential to want to consume this kind of place, and the best way we could do that is … by creating a place that is wonderful to be in.
>
> (LB)

An in order to do this,

> I personally coined the phrase of experiential planning, because I was trying
> to say that planning to yield this kind of place is not at all the practice of
> planning that I learned in school. It is not about the systems of the city ...
> but it is about your experience in this moment and whether or not you walk
> away feeling emotionally good about that. Whether or not you had to
> struggle to live in this city or this city is a joy to you. Whether or not all
> kinds of people are in this city or it's only comfortable for a few kinds of
> people.
>
> (LB)

Therefore values and visions as well as specific preferences of citizens were
mobilized by the planning organization in a process by which, according to
Larry Beasley, more than 100,000 citizens were involved:

> telling us their preferences, what they liked ... what they were worried
> about, what they wanted to see, also their capricious ideas, not just func-
> tional ideas but like, what's in your heart.... And all those inputs came into
> the process.
>
> (LB)

The process was organized as a collective innovation process consisting of
different phases. Citizens were involved during the process of conceptualizing
the whole neighborhood, during the design of the subarea, and finally during the
design of the particular building, and 'almost without fail it [the process of interaction with the citizens] is going to find the consumer preferences' (LB).

A great deal came out of the process: 'There are thousands of those things
that we discovered by this transactional process' (LB). An example was a sceptical citizen who did not want to live above a food store due to noise issues.
Designers came up with the idea to set the apartment tower back from the street.
In this way housing is combined with retail and lively and walkable streets.
Another issue is whether high-rise towers were sufficiently attractive to people
to live in?

> A lot of consumers said to us, we'd love to come back [from the suburbs]
> and live here, but I could never live in a tower ... and I have a dog, I am
> afraid of heights.... I do not want my children to have to go down in an
> elevator to be able to play.... Then our designers said, what if you include
> row houses?... It is wonderful, it works like a charm, and it economically
> works as well.
>
> (LB)

Therefore, along the sea walk in False Creek North the first impression of
housing behind the bike and walk lanes and the parks and playgrounds is that of

low-rise housing with gardens. Behind them, the skyscrapers tower. The low-rise buildings in-between towers even help to preserve the view of the mountains in a number of view corridors.

According to Larry Beasley the experiential planning made the citizens consider whether living in the city core was more attractive than living in the green suburbs that they used to prefer. The number of inhabitants in downtown grew by more than 300 per cent between 1991 and today, and the number of children is larger than in the surrounding neighbourhoods.

### Governance and stakeholders

Senior town planner Michael Gordon (MG) has for many years been involved in area and community planning in Vancouver.

According to him citizen-based planning was introduced in the mid-1970s as the new city planner Ray Spaxman took office, as a reaction to the expert-led planning of earlier periods. An example of the planners' work with citizens is the West End Plan. The West End today appears as a colourful, low-rise and green part of the city fringed by high-rise towers.[4]

> An important moment was when we went out and we said: What do you see as the West End character? And what are the values in this community and what are the buildings you really value and what are the places you really value, and then documenting all of that. We did workshops to determine what's the character of the neighborhood, talked about the history there.... So those are the community values, and that's for the community to determine ... so I think one of the successes of the West End plan was that it was very much based on the community's values.... I think we talked to 7,000 people.
> (MG, Figure 12.3)

The diversity of Vancouver's civil society adds extra work to the interactive citizen process. 'And then there are the cultural groups, for example people of Chinese heritage ... and merchant groups.... Then you have activists ... very passionate groups of people. There are the environmental groups' (MG). Organized citizens articulate their views, but the not-so-organized can be addressed through the community centres, which, according to Michael Gordon, are good sources of information about the different members of and groupings in a community, including an overview of different types of households.

Mostly, it is the planning authority that organizes the involvement of citizens, but in some cases neighbourhood groups form themselves, especially if citizens are critical about a development proposal. 'I think it's just such a precious place to people, they just have a lot of concerns about something that might get proposed' (MG). The continuous dialogue and negotiation with citizens thus seems to motivate their participation and to nourish the identity with the place.

There are more potent players than citizen groups, namely the building community and private business organizations.

*Figure 12.3* West End, Vancouver (photo © Anne Lorentzen 2014).

'As planners, who do we spend most time with? It's architects and developers and builders, contractors. And the development community and construction community is maybe a quarter of our economy' (MG). The building community has been able to harvest considerable profits each time the city changed its zoning laws and opened up for high-rise housing. Thus, the city has been able to mobilize developers and builders each time a new planning vision reached the point of realization due to potential earnings.

> But then you have this huge other area of business, so through the business associations and groups like Board of Trade and the Downtown Vancouver Association, we can do out-reach to them, and interestingly enough those groups have a much more balanced perspective on development. And if you want to make sure the experience economy unfolds, or is not ruined by this awful development of something, those groups are certainly at the table.
>
> (MG)

Small businesses are even part of the urban experience.

> One of the things that I as a planner need to be cautious about is supporting small business and to notice that in a globalized kind of economy, where

transnational corporations get bigger and bigger, what makes places really interesting but also builds social capital is having smaller businesses.

(MG)

### The urban scenography

The visible and social characteristics of Vancouver's scenography are described by Michael Gordon and former senior planner Nathan Edelson (NE):

> The Vancouver skyline is really three lines, they're all serpentine lines, the water edge, the line of the buildings … and the mountains.
>
> (MG)

> I think, three quarters of the land is still single-family-areas, that is the pre-dominant image for most people in the city, their neighbourhood.
>
> (NE, Figure 12.4)

The planners agree, however, that a dominant principle has been the growth in high-rise development, where a distinct Vancouver style has emerged with a broader base podium, which creates street warmth and is designed to maximize the amount of light and views. The other important principle has been as much continuous access to the waterfront as possible.

*Figure 12.4* Traditional single-family houses in Vancouver (photo © Anne Lorentzen 2014).

One of our successful cultural facilities, really, are the waterfronts, access to skiing and hiking and sailing and other things.... It's not that we don't have cultural activities, arts and culture activities, we have quite a few, but to most people the easy access to nature is really important.

(NE)

### *The urban economy*

The focus on housing has, however, brought the local economy out of balance. Real estate investments have been made by international as well as domestic investors, 'and wealthier people have contributed to boosting the property values to the point that it's hard to sustain housing that's supportable to moderate income workers and their families. That's been a challenge for the city' (NE).

Apart from difficulties of getting access to the housing market, candidates from the two big universities have difficulties in finding relevant jobs in the city because of the dominance of the construction sector.

[The number of] people with university degrees that are working, making cappuccino or in tea shops is significant ... but it's part of the perception that if they want to develop their careers they have to go to places like Toronto or New York or Calgary or even the resource areas, particularly around oil development.

(NE)

An alternative creative or knowledge economy is not really thriving, even if

a lot of people who work in their homes, high tech firms, firms involved in film, entertainment, video, communication, smaller firms ... even significant projects that are supported by the universities in bio-tech, high tech, [but] Vancouver has not been able to sustain a strong footing in those areas. Once a project gets to a certain scale, the investment for continuing them tends to be depleted. So, a lot of things have started here, but they moved elsewhere.

(NE)

## The Vancouver achievement

Since the 1970s, Vancouver has transformed itself from a regional centre of resource industries into a post-industrial consumer city based on postmodern as well as inclusive values. The unique opportunity of huge brownfield redevelopments of the city centre provided ample space for innovative thinking and urban entrepreneurship. A characteristic cityscape of skyscrapers, view-corridors, and park-framed sea-walks emerged based on collaborative processes of planning. With citizens' aspirations as focal point, planners managed to stage the new urban experience in a complex process of stakeholder management, citizen mobilization and knowledge mining, and architectural innovation. The classic concept of the experience economy informed the goals and values as well as the planning processes of Vancouver. The specific urban staging system of Vancouver produced not only distinctive cityscapes, but also meaningful and diverse urban scenographies of daily life, as well as caring citizens with strong feelings of belonging. However, the liveability focus of the planners implied an unintended neglect of job creation and a circle of speculative investment in real estate, resulting in socio-spatial polarization and an unfortunate exodus of the young and educated.

## Conclusion

Emotional consumption is at the core of the experience economy, and businesses mobilize a great variety of engagement techniques in a systemic engagement of customers. In this way work is theatre and every business is a stage. Non-functional values are also increasingly found in planning, as a consequence of place competition and higher incomes of the population. Experiential development of cities has been widespread, however without proper consideration related to the citizens as customers. Therefore an alternative reading of experience-based planning is suggested, based on the idea that 'planning is theatre and every city is a stage'. Planning is about innovative staging of urban scenographies in which citizens can identify and engage themselves.

Citizen-oriented planning has been developed in Vancouver to a point where citizens' emotions and values have become the turning point. Citizens' aspirations have guided the staging of the urban scenography towards a lively, diverse, walkable, beautiful and clean city. The built and natural features have made the city a global flagship in itself. Vancouver's planners have staged the drama of urban transformation guided by progressive urban visions. Private investors and builders were important partners, but a multitude of other actors with stakes in the urban qualities also contributed. Citizens' involvement has been successfully encouraged as input to innovation and as a quality in itself.

However, Vancouver has not been sufficiently able to attract new, dynamic industries and jobs outside of construction and consumer services. If and how planners and politicians are able to revitalize an industrial economy, too, are urgent questions.

Even if Vancouver's history is unique, not least due to the Asian connections, other cities may look to Vancouver for inspiration. Comprehensive urban visions and long-term decisions are helpful in realizing integrated cityscapes and in creating identities of place. Strong value-based management of patient and untiring collaboration processes with stakeholders is conducive of financial, knowledge and cultural resources. Experiential planning need not be for the few, but can be for the many, and has at its core the engaged and trustful relationship between citizens and planners.

## Notes

1  The Blue Planet is a huge public aquarium inaugurated in 2013 and considered Denmark's best flagship project in tourism and experience economy. Source: www.denblaaplanet.dk/om-den-bla-planet/historie/ (accessed 23 September 2014).
2  Cold Hawaii has been mentioned since 2010 on the web page of PWA: www.pwaworldtour.com/index.php?id=1141 (accessed 23 September 2014).
3  http://en.wikipedia.org/wiki/List_of_the_100_largest_municipalities_in_Canada_by_population (accessed 10 September 2014).
4  A plan for the West End was approved in 2013 to increase the density of the West End along the major transit corridors. Source: www.cbc.ca/news/canada/british-columbia/west-end-community-plan-approved-in-vancouver-1.2433596 (accessed 2 October 2014).

## References

Agger, A. (2013) 'Kunden er død', *Mandag Morgen*, 28 May 2013.

Albrechts, L., Healey, P. and Kunzmann, K. (2003) 'Strategic spatial planning and regional governance in Europe', *Journal of the American Planning Association* 69(2): 113–29.

Andersson, Å.E. and Andersson, D.E. (2006) *The economics of experiences, the arts and entertainment*, Cheltenham: Edward Elgar.

Barnes, T.J. and Hutton, T.A. (2009) 'Situating the new economy: Contingencies of regeneration and dislocation in Vancouver's inner city', *Urban Studies* 46(5–6): 1247–69.

Berelowitz, L. (2005) *Dream city*, Vancouver: Douglas and McIntyre.

Blomqvist, K. and Levy, J. (2006) 'Collaboration capability – a focal concept in knowledge creation and collaborative innovation in networks', *International Journal of Management concepts and Philosophy*, 2(1): 31–48.

Bogers, M., Afuah, A. and Bastian, B. (2010) 'Users as Innovators: A review, critique, and future research directions', *Journal of Management*, 36(4): 857–75.

Brenner, N. (1998) 'Global cities, glocal states: Global city formation and state territorial restructuring in contemporary Europe', *Review of International Political Economy*, 5(1): 1–37.

Brenner, N. (2004) 'Urban governance and the production of new state spaces in western Europe 1960–2000', *Review of International Political Economy*, 11(3): 447–88.

Brunet-Jailly, E. (2008) 'Vancouver: The sustainable city', *Journal of Urban Affairs*, 30(4): 375–88.

De Certau, M. (1984) *The practice of everyday life*, London: University of California Press.

Edelson, N. (2011) 'Inclusivity as an Olympic event at the 2010 Vancouver winter games', *Urban Geography*, 32 (6): 804–22.

Friedman, J. (2008) 'The uses of planning theory: A bibliographic essay', *Journal of Planning Education and Research*, 28(2): 247–57.

Friedman, J. (2010) 'Place and place-making in cities: A global perspective', *Planning Theory and Practice*, 11(2): 149–165.

Garreau, J. (1981) *The nine nations of North America*, Boston: Houghton Mifflin.

Goldhaber, M.H. (1997) 'The attention economy and the net', *First Monday*, 2(4).

Grant, J.L. (2010) 'Experiential planning: A practitioner's account of Vancouver's success', *Journal of the American Planning Association*, 75(3): 358–70.

*Pursuing happiness in planning?* 211

Hall, T. and Hubbard, P. (1997) 'The entrepreneurial city: New urban politics, new urban geographies?', *Progress in Human Geography*, 20(2): 153–74.

Hauge, A. and Power, D. (2012) 'Quality, difference and regional advantage: The case of the winter sports industry', *European Urban and Regional Studies*, 20(4): 385–400.

Healey, P. (2003) 'Collaborative planning in perspective', *Planning Theory*, 2(2): 101–3.

Healey, P. (2007) *Urban complexity and spatial strategies: Towards a relational planning of our times*, The RTPI Library Series, Abingdon: Routledge.

Healey, P., de Magalhaes, C. Madanipour, A. and Pendlebury, J. (2003) 'Place, identity and local politics: analysing initiatives in deliberative governance', in M.A. Hajer and H. Wagenar (eds) *Deliberative Policy Analysis: Understanding Governance in the Network Society*, Cambridge: Cambridge University Press.

Holden, M. (2012) 'Urban engagement with social sustainability in Metro Vancouver', *Urban Studies*, 49(3): 527–42.

Hutton, T.A. (2004) 'Post-industrialism, post-modernism and the reproduction of Vancouver's central area: Retheorizing the 21st century city', *Urban Studies*, 41(10): 1953–82.

Hutton, T.A. (2009) 'The inner city as site of cultural production sui generis: A review essay', *Geography Compass*, 3(2): 600–29.

Hutton, T.A. (2010) *The new economy of the inner city*, Abingdon: Routledge.

Hutton, T.A. (2011) 'Thinking metropolis: From the "Livable Region" to the "Sustainable Metropolis" in Vancouver', *International Planning Studies*, 16(3): 237–55.

Jeannerat, H. (2015) 'Towards a staging system approach to territorial innovation', in A. Lorentzen, K.T. Larsen and L. Schrøder (eds) *Spatial dynamics in the experience economy*, Abingdon: Routledge.

Lavrinec, J. (2013) 'Urban scenography: Emotional and bodily experience', *Limes: Borderland Studies*, 6(1): 21–31.

Lebergott, S. (1993) *Pursuing happiness: American consumers in the twentieth century*, Princeton: Princeton University Press.

Ley, D. (2003) 'Artists, aestheticisation and the field of gentrification', *Urban Studies*, 40(12): 2527–44.

Ley, D. and Dobson, C. (2008) 'Are there limits to gentrification? The contexts of impeded gentrification in Vancouver', *Urban Studies*, 45(12): 2471–98.

Liu, S. and Blomley, N. (2013) 'Making news and making space: Framing Vancouver's Downtown Eastside', *The Canadian Geographer*, 57(2): 119–32.

Lorentzen, A. (2013) 'The experience turn of the Danish periphery', *European Urban and Regional Studies*, 20(4): 460–72.

Marontate, J. and Murray, C. (2010) 'Neoliberalism in provincial cultural policy narratives: Perspectives from two coasts', *Canadian Journal of Communication*, 35(2): 325–43.

Moulart, F. and Seika, F. (2003) 'Territorial innovation models: A critical survey', *Regional Studies*, 37(3): 289–302.

OECD Organisation for Economic Co-operation and Development (2006) *OECD Territorial Reviews: Competitive cities in the global economy*, Paris: OECD.

Pine, B.J. and Gilmore, J.H. (1998) 'Welcome to the experience economy', *Harvard Business Review* 1998 (July–August): 97–103.

Pine, B.J. and Gilmore, J.H. (1999) *The experience economy: Work is theatre and every business a stage*, Boston: Harvard Business School Press.

Pine, B.J and Gilmore, J.H. (2011) *The experience economy*, Boston: Harvard Business Press.

Power, D. (2009) 'Culture, creativity and experience in Nordic and Scandinavian cultural policy', *International Journal of Cultural Policy*, 15(4): 445–60.

212    *A. Lorentzen*

Punter, J. (2003) *The Vancouver achievement*, Vancouver: UBC Press.

Quastel, N., Moos, M. and Lynch, N. (2012) 'Sustainability-as-density and the return of the social: The case of Vancouver, British Columbia', *Urban Geography*, 33(7): 1055–84.

Toffler, A. (1970) *Future Shock*, New York: Bantam Books.

Vanwynsberghe, R., Surborg, B. and Wyly, E. (2013) 'When the games come to town: Neoliberalism, mega-events and social inclusion in the Vancouver winter Olympic games', *International Journal of Urban and Regional Research*, 37(6): 2074–93.

Waitt, G. and Gibson, C. (2009) 'Creative small cities: Rethinking the creative economy in place', *Urban Studies*, 46(5–6): 1223–46.

# 13 Engagements in place

## Bricolage networking in tourism and the experience economy

*Lars Fuglsang*

## Introduction

This chapter explores how micro-companies in a rural area can become involved in networking and the experience economy. A varied literature exists that stresses the role of networking and collaborations among companies in local areas for economic development and innovation. For example, it has been argued that innovative milieus (Camagni 1991) embedded in local network structures facilitate knowledge transfer between or within sectors (Asheim *et al.* 2011; Frenken *et al.* 2007). Or that agglomeration of firms in a regional context reduces transaction costs between them (Storper 1995). Local buzz among companies has been seen as important for global sourcing of knowledge (Bathelt *et al.* 2004). However, these studies have also been criticized for their emphasis on proximity (Crevoisier and Jeannerat 2009; Lorentzen 2007); networking today in the era of globalization may be a more globalized and geographically distributed phenomenon than previously understood; companies source knowledge globally (Lorentzen 2007). Yet, in some sectors like tourism, the engagement of companies in local systems of collaboration can be important not just for sourcing of knowledge but also for the development of local products (Fuglsang and Eide 2013). Research also shows that small companies in rural areas may be difficult to engage in large-scale cooperation and innovation.

Most of the literatures on company networks in regions have had a 'productionist' orientation (Jeannerat 2013). They tend to ignore the customers' role. Yet, for tourism companies involving themselves in the experience economy, engaging customers in an active way is central to the business. Experiences can be defined as unique events that are remembered by customers (Sundbo and Sørensen 2013). Experiences require active consumer participation (Nilsen and Dale 2013), i.e. active attention from customers. Experiences can emanate people's own activities and reflections, but these experiences can also be triggered by (economic) activities (Lorentzen and Jeannerat 2013). Experiences are combinations of the German *Erlebniss* and *Erfahrung* (Sundbo and Sørensen 2013). As *Erlebniss* experiences take place and are triggered in the present, however they also involve people's *Erfahrung*, their past experiences and learning. Some people will pay attention to more experience attributes than others due to their previous experience and learning (Andersson and Andersson 2013; Snel 2013).

Research has sought to distinguish companies whose business model is to trigger experiences as a special category of experience companies. However, classifying these companies based in, for example, NACE codes poses problems. These problems shall not be dealt with in this chapter however (see Sundbo 2009; Nilsen and Dale 2013). Rather, for the purpose of this paper it is argued that many types of companies can join forces to create experiences.

Rural companies can trigger tourist experiences in many ways, for example by organizing such activities as kayaking, bicycling or walking, and more. Tourism companies can also more specifically try to stage experiences related to place. Place is here understood, following Gieryn (2000), as a geographical location which has material/physical form and which is invested with meaning and value. Hence place is not just a physical context for companies, but it is constructed by the activities that fill it with meaning and value, including company and consumer activities. By focusing place as a locus of business activities, tourism companies contribute to invest meaning and values in the place. In this way, according to Gieryn (2000), place is different from space: space is place minus the meanings and values that are attached to it.

Attaching meaning to place can emanate from networks of companies in a local context forming value constellation in the sense of Normann and Ramirez (Normann and Ramirez 1993). A value constellation is 'interorganizational networks linking firms with different assets and competencies together in response to or in anticipation of new market opportunities' (Vanhaverbeke and Cloodt 2006: 259). Hence, companies in a tourism network within a tourism place can try to collectively develop place by creating a common web of meanings in the geographical place. However, tourism companies tend to be fragmented with different experience orientations, resources, interests and time frames.

Studies of networking and value constellations in tourism and experience sectors are rare but some studies can be found. The concept of destination has been used in varied ways to describe local tourism contexts (see, for example, Framke 2002; Pearce 2013). However, destination is perhaps a misleading concept, because tourists often explore the place rather than link up with a destination. Value networking in tourism and experiences may therefore be better described as varied economic actors' joint efforts constituting a web of meanings and values in the place. Hjalager (2000) has explored whether features of industrial districts as described in the literature on industrial districts can be found in tourism districts. She concludes that some evidence can be found. But there are also important features that discourage comparison of tourism districts and industrial districts. For example, tourism firms have a tendency of free-rider behaviour. There is a lack of stabilized collaborative structures that enhance trust and reciprocity in tourism districts (Hjalager 2000). However, literature can also be found that emphasizes the importance of collective and joint efforts (Buhalis and Cooper 1998; Hjalager 2010; Nordin 2003; Weidenfeld *et al.* 2010). These literatures tend to support the notion that tourism innovation and the staging of tourism experiences through the investment of meaning in place can be a collaborative and even collective act. Collective actions may become more important for the tourism districts in the future as new value constellations emerge, due to, among others, the increased focus on staging experiences in tourism places (Fuglsang and Eide 2013).

Yet we know little about how more dynamic and innovative network relations can evolve in tourism and experience sectors. Tourism and experience companies may be difficult to mobilize for large-scale network cooperation and innovation because they have little time and few resources for networking (Fuglsang and Eide 2013). Tourism and experience firms may have more fragmented changing relations to other companies as well as to the support structures they are surrounded by. They may be less inclined to collaborate in stabilized ways because they tend to be loosely coupled and not tightly technologically related. Alternative approaches to networking and innovation systems in services more broadly see them as loosely coupled (Sundbo and Gallouj 2000) or evolving around and from a problem and problem-solving activity that function as a focusing device (Tether and Metcalfe 2004). Small tourism companies may, however, be life-style entrepreneurs (Ateljevic and Doorne 2000) that pursue a quality of life and experiences for the owners rather than promotion of collaboration, regional development and growth. Each company has unique network relations to other companies (cf. Håkansson *et al.* 2009) but generally they tend not to add up to wider value constellations in a tourism place.

Generally we know little about how tourism and experience companies are engaged in dynamic networking and collaboration about staging experiences in a place. Tourism companies may have individualized motives and pursue unique strategies in relation to other companies. Yet they may also occasionally need to be part of more collective collaborative structures. In the following it is explored whether and how small-scale networking can be a solution to networking problems. It is suggested that 'bricolage networking' can be a model of networking in tourism and experience sectors. While participants become engaged in these networks in fragile and tenuous ways they also have the potential to stage and trigger unique experiences together related to place, hence creating spatial dynamics.

Referring to the literature on bricolage, the paper first discusses how collaboration in the experience sectors may be understood as 'bricolage networking' and how this can trigger high-level unique tourist experiences. Then drawing on the engagement theory of Laurent Thévenot (2001, 2007), the paper goes on to discuss three forms of engagement in bricolage networking. It further discusses how these three forms can be found in a revisited case study; it further discusses some of the implications for unique consumer experiences.

## Bricolage networking

The concept of bricolage comes from anthropologist Lévi-Strauss (1966). It was introduced in order to distinguish between two forms of problem-solving activity in what Lévi-Strauss called prior science (or mythical thought) and modern science and engineering. Bricolage was a metaphor for prior science. The brico-leur is a person that collects gadgets and tools over time 'on the principle that they may always come in handy' (Lévi-Strauss 1966: 18). In this way bricolage is a problem-solving activity that makes use of available resources at hand which are not designed for a specific purpose. The bricoleur is therefore also con-strained by the available resources collected over time. Bricolage does not, like science, start from 'structures which it is constantly elaborating' in the form of 'hypotheses and theories' (Lévi-Strauss 1966: 22). By contrast, the bricoleur builds structures from events. Bricolage is a model which is not limited by insti-tutional boundaries, yet it does not have the advantage of scientific method.

Lévi-Strauss's concept of bricolage has been used in research in varied ways to describe how actors can use available resources to solve problems on the spot in an incremental, unique, bottom-up way. For example, Weick (1993) demon-strates how actors can break free of an impossible situation (escaping a fire) by using resources at hand. Garud and Karnoe (2003) have shown how the Danish wind turbine industry evolved by bricolage in a stepwise manner rather than through major scientific breakthroughs. Hatton has discussed how schoolteachers work with pedagogical methods in a bricolage-like way (Hatton 1989). Fuglsang and Sørensen have discussed how home-helpers use bricolage to develop ser-vices in an effective way (Fuglsang 2010; Fuglsang and Sørensen 2011). Further, bricolage has been used to characterize certain forms of entrepreneurship where entrepreneurs create something from nothing (Baker and Nelson 2005).

The concept of bricolage has also been used to study networking. Baker *et al.* (2003) have described a phenomenon they call 'network bricolage' which is relevant for the purpose of this paper: it denotes how companies establish network relations. Rather than engaging in comprehensive strategies of resource-seeking, certain companies instead make use of resources at hand during and after their founding. Resources at hand include customers, financing, suppliers, office space, advice and employees (Baker *et al.* 2003: 265). This phenomenon is according to Baker *et al.* similar to the professionals described by Granovetter (1995), who find new jobs without searching for them (Baker *et al.* 2003: 266). Hence network bricolage translates into networking with companies that are around without searching for resources in a systematic way.

Baker *et al.* (2003) explores network bricolage from the point of view of the company. Another type of bricolage can start more from the idea of a network itself, which is then constructed by involving companies that are present in a local area. This could be called 'bricolage networking'. Participants are enrolled as members of networks because they are available in a localized place. The model of bricolage networking can be relevant in tourism and experience places, because a tourism place is a collection of tourism firms/resources that over time have been located in the area. The companies represent resources that have been 'accumulated' in the place over time with no particular destination purpose in mind. Networking constructed in this way, for example among tourism companies, can have a strong local focus on unique local products that are made available over time but can be further profiled.

## Engagement

Bricolage networking may be a model that can describe networking between tourism firms in a local area. But the literature says little about how companies can be engaged in such networks. Tourism companies in a local area are usually not interlinked in a technologically tight way. Therefore, networking in tourism is perhaps less a question of actors being tied up in common technological practices, and more a question of how companies are opening up towards, and engaging themselves in, the environment to produce meaning and value. The following draws heavily on the engagement theory proposed by Thévenot that explains three different ways in which actors can be engaged in the environment and the goods these 'regimes of engagement' produce for the participants.

Thévenot understands engagement as a relation between a human agent and the environment (Thévenot 2001, 2007) in which the agent moves between a personalized conception of the environment and a more generalized conception of the environment. For example, in a tourism network, micro-companies can participate by giving tourists access to a unique personalized environment. But they can also try to depersonalize the meaning and value by organizing their environment according to certain standardized themes and conventions thereby adapting their tourism offer more to established codes and standards. Furthermore, in some cases this can be done more explicitly with reference to the values the tourism offers are supposed to create, such as sustainable tourism.

Thévenot makes a distinction between three types of engagement: familiar engagement, engagement in plan, and engagement in justifiable action. Familiar engagement is when people relate to their environment by organizing it in a personalized way. Such a personalized environment is a bricolage of all kinds of things that have been accumulated and accommodated over time so that people become comfortable and at ease with them. The objects are not carved out in a very precise way with a specific purpose in mind, and the relation to them is almost tacit. Further, things are not organized according to explicit principles or projects but by trial-and-error processes where people incrementally learn how to organize them in a comfortable way according to personal and bodily needs. Thévenot compares this regime of engagement to 'inhabiting a home'. How we live at home is difficult to account for because everything is organized in a very personalized way.

Engagement in plan, or in regular action, is engagement in the environment according to a specific project. The plan or project represents an individual person who projects herself into the future and accomplishes an action according to this plan. This is also what Thévenot calls conventional utility, because the plan relies on certain conventions. Engagement in plan makes it possible to coordinate actions between actors that are not present at the same time (Duymedjian and Ruling 2010). Functions, roles, actions and purposes become specified. Thévenot compares this to someone who wants to rent her apartment to another person and has to reorder her home according to conventions to make it functional and recognizable for another person. Engagement in plan is a framework for 'normal' effective and intentional action.

Engagement in justifiable action is actors' attempts to critique, argue for and justify certain actions and conventions in terms of the societal/collective values they are supposed to produce. This may be triggered by a dispute, for example over a rented house. The tenant of an apartment questions whether it is in a proper state. As a consequence, the landlord needs to justify how things have been made. For example, the house that seems in bad shape can be justified in terms of efficiency, safety, market price, of patrimony (Thévenot 2001), or in terms of local conventions.

These different forms of engagement can be seen as different degrees of extension into the environment or different degrees of disengagement from what is most personalized. They are different cognitive frameworks, more or less generalized, through which people can open themselves towards the environment, coordinate action and attach certain meanings and values to it. For the purpose of this paper, it is suggested that the engagement approach can be used to explain how tourism companies and tourists in different ways are involved with bricolage networking. It is also proposed that for rural micro-companies, familiar engagement can sometimes be predominant.

First, many micro-tourism and experience companies are preoccupied with familiar engagement. They invite tourists and guests into places that have a very personalized and unique meaning and value. This can be the case of small hotels, bed and breakfasts, small rented rooms, farm shops, craftspeople and more. The environment is organized to provide comfort and ease by a personalized trial-and-error process. Tourists sometimes even expect this 'authenticity', understood as a resemblance to an idealized origin (Jeannerat 2013: 378), or local flair, to be present – rather than wanting to stay in standardized anonymous hotel rooms, for example. In some more elaborate cases, like open-door museums, or museums that deal with everyday life exhibitions, the familiar engagement with the environment can be simulated or imitated for guests and tourists, thus further stressing a search for an idealized origin.

Second, tourism companies can reorganize the environment according to conventions so that the experiential value for tourists becomes more focused, recognizable and 'planable' for the tourists and subsumed to a possible schedule that can be consulted and checked. For example, the tourist experience can be organized according to certain themes (Freire-Gibb and Lorentzen 2011) that direct tourists' expectations and plans. The experience is no longer valuated as authentic, but more as an innovation that has some elements that can be planned, compared and repeated. International standards are adapted or imitated and the varied tourist enterprises become organized under certain thematic frameworks that make them more conventional. Tourists may still experience more familiarized aspects, but it will be packed inside an event that has a more schematic appearance to tourists who can then better control experiences according to a plan.

Third, tourism experiences are subject to qualified criticism from both tourists and experts. A tourist company must contribute to making it worthwhile and legitimate for the tourist to spend valuable time at a tourist site and be able to respond to critique and complaints not only in personal face-to-face relationships but sometimes also in a semi-public sphere. Local conventions and community must be respected. The tourist and tourism experts can question in a generalized manner whether the tourism experience lives up to legitimate community expectations and conventions, and whether the tourist provider has the necessary technical, organizational and professional skills to carry out tourism and staging experiences in a sustainable way.

This model of different types of engagements of tourism firms can be applied also to bricolage networking among the tourism and experience firms (see Table 13.1). First, a network may be accommodated by participants, including tourists, so that it becomes more personalized and comfortable for the participants. People will spontaneously make contacts with certain other persons within the network and form networks in the network for comfort and ease, for example by borrowing things from each other, referring tourists to each other or word of mouth among tourists. High-level and unique tourist experiences can emerge from this.

Second, the network can become engaged in more extensive tourism projects within the tourism place. Certain concrete network activities become arranged under a project name and theme that must be executed according to a schedule and plan, and can in turn be foreseen by tourists.

By organizing activities around a theme, the network can help the single companies to create tourism experiences in a more 'state of the art' way. The network becomes a support structure for the single firm to make this 'investment in form' (Thévenot). However, network members may react against engagement in plan because it leads to a disengagement from what is the most comfortable and personalized space. Similarly, tourists may dislike the more low-level experiences that can result from this.

Further, disputes may arise in the network that require justified action, when, for example, a network member or a tourist does not find the standard of network activities acceptable, homogeneous across firms and sustainable. The network must argue that it can promote the territory and contribute to economic development of the region.

Engagement in justified action represents one step further away from the network as a personalized environment. It tends to play down the familiar network milieu in favour of a more depersonalized, codified and generalized environment. It may be more visionary and future oriented, but it requires stronger social, technical and organizational skills and may appear as more uncomfortable and outside the scope of what micro-companies can achieve.

## Method and case

In the following, I revisit a case of a network of micro-companies in tourism (Fuglsang and Eide 2013). The purpose is to investigate the notion of bricolage networking as a useful approach to understanding cooperative experience creation in a remote/rural area. The empirical focus is to examine what it takes to create a sustainable staging of tourism experiences in the rural area. Is a local

Table 13.1 The three regimes of engagement applied to staging tourism experiences through bricolage networking (adapted from Thévenot 2001)

| | Familiar engagement | Engagement in plan | Engagement in justifiable action |
|---|---|---|---|
| Which kind of experience good is engaged/staged and evaluated? | Personal and local convenience; creating a familiar network milieu with unique local experiences | Pointing out conventional experience themes carried out in a successful way by a network and its members | Creation of common goods, e.g. tourism in accordance with local conventions; sustainable tourism; regional development |
| Which reality is engaged? With what capacity? | Resources are available resources; they are personalized and used as easily available among network participants | Resources are functional instruments; organized by a network according to a plan | 'Qualified', legitimate resources used so far as it is justifiable |
| What is the format of relevant information? | Local and idiosyncratic; tacit knowledge | Codified knowledge enabling coordinated action | Codification in terms of public argument |
| Which kind of tourism agency is construed? | Tourists become involved in a personalized entourage as visitors at ease | Tourists are engaged as 'planners' who make plans from themes/ scenarios that are recognizable to most tourists | Tourists are engaged as qualified/ competent persons able to criticize what is legitimate action and behave in an appropriate way |

network of small micro-companies able to maintain the necessary activities? Is it necessary to cooperate with actors and institutions on higher institutional levels? The case study illustrates how micro-companies by small-scale bricolage networking can stage tourism experiences and invest meaning and value in place. The case study draws on a master's thesis (Petterson 2010) co-supervised by the author of this article and a previous study (Fuglsang and Eide 2013). The master's thesis is based on nine in-depths interviews, documentary studies and one observation of a network meeting. Further, in-depth interviews were conducted, by the author, in 2010 and 2013 with six core members of the network, and various documents available on the network's home page have been analysed.

The network is called Small Tourism and it was formed in 1999. In 2011 there were almost 100 members of the network and in 2013 around 70. The network is located on two islands in Southern Denmark, often referred to as Lolland-Falster, 100–150 km (driving distance) from Copenhagen. Lolland-Falster is considered a semi-peripheral area of Denmark. Unemployment rates tend to be higher than the national average, the educational level lower, health conditions worse, and income relatively low. Lolland has been categorized as a remote area and Falster as a predominantly rural area (Ministry of Food, Agriculture and Fisheries 2008). The main development problem in the area is to attract business, develop entrepreneurship and tourism. A study of entrepreneurship in this area (Fuglsang and Sørensen 2013) has shown that there are major cultural barriers in this area for entrepreneurship. Entrepreneurial activities are often initiated by outsiders, who move to the area and introduce new ideas. Outsiders must maintain a delicate balance between innovating and being part of the community (ibid.). For persons who want to establish themselves as small artists or craftspeople, Lolland-Falster may appear as an attractive area because of the relatively low prices on housing.

The case study demonstrates that a value constellation of firms was created through bricolage networking. However, clearly there are varied levels of engagement into the network and for many of the participating companies the engagement into the network activity is based on personalized relations that must be balanced against more extended and demanding forms of engagement.

## Networking in micro-tourism

The network was initiated by a businessman in 1999. He felt that there was too little focus on the many small and partly hidden tourist-related enterprises in the area. Too much attention was given to a few large tourism companies. He then asked one of his employees to drive around Lolland-Falster and look for small enterprises, asking them to come to a meeting. Thereby he identified a number of micro-companies, small eateries, ceramicists, farm shops, museums and bed and breakfasts with special identities and competencies. The meeting led to the formation of a network, and the members agreed to develop a common brochure for the whole network representing each enterprise. This brochure was placed in strategic places around Lolland-Falster by the members themselves. A further idea of the network was to provide good experiences to tourists and refer tourists to each other. Some also started to form networks in the network creating small tourism products together. A few common projects for the whole network were initiated, including yearly assemblies and exhibitions, two bicycle routes, and a common website. Some minor projects were financed by Leader+, the Danish Rural Community Development Programme and the EU's Social Fund, and the businessman was for some years able to pay a minor salary for the network coordinator and organize business courses for the companies.

### Bricolage networking

Before the network was created, the micro-enterprises were to some extent aware of each other's existence, but very little collaboration took place. In the network, the companies were not supposed to act in a fundamentally different way than before, but they decided to become more visible, coordinated, professional and extrovert. By relatively small means and available resources, they could stage tourism experiences more effectively. They attempted to create a mutually friendly atmosphere and not speak negatively of one another. Still, the network was a bricolage of different kinds of micro-companies that required almost no extra effort. Bricolage networking was for many of the companies an effective way to collaborate and become more visible because the intervention with daily activities was minimal and they could continue to do whatever they were doing. On the home page of the network this is clearly stated (December 2013):

> Small tourism is a network of engaged people on Lolland-Falster, who in one way or another with our businesses address ourselves naturally to tourists. In the network we know each other and our province, and therefore we are able to guide you and make your visit/holiday a good experience that you will remember for a long time.

However, for some of the members the network meant more work. For the network coordinator, it was difficult and challenging to convince members to become active in common network activities, the reason being that the network constituted a familiar network milieu.

### Familiar engagement

For some of the companies that participate in the network, engagement in a familiar milieu describes well how they are engaged in the network. The network is a comforting environment and they want to invite tourists into this environment. The network is used to borrow things from each other, exchange ideas for participating in exhibitions and other events. Members find friends and colleagues with whom they can share and stage experiences, and they engage tourists directly into this familiar environment. While the network has attempted to organize several large-scale common activities, such as general meetings, open-door projects and cycling routes, participation in these activities has been limited, and the work of organizing these activities has been undertaken by a few core members. Instead, networks in the network are organized, 'because we do not have a large network that functions ... we make networks in the network' (Network member 1). Familiar engagement in the case creates a kind of 'garbage can' (Cohen *et al.* 1972) model of organizing, in which the network 'is a collection of choices looking for problems, issues and feelings looking for decision situations in which they might be aired, solutions looking for issues to which they might be the answer, and decision makers looking for work' (Cohen *et al.* 1972: 1). Similarly, the familiar environment in the case is not a well-defined structure for solving problems in a rational way. Preferences are problematic, technology is unclear and characterized by trial-and-error (or bricolage), and participation is fluid (Cohen *et al.* 1972). Integrating the familiar environment into a more planned framework for tourists implies that its unique qualities as familiar network milieu would have to appear more depersonalized, codified and generalized.

### Engagement in plan

However, familiar engagement is not a sufficient characteristic of the network, because it wants to be more extrovert and open up towards tourists in a more thematic way. Members are engaged into some form of plan, reordering things and adapting to tourists' planning efforts. For one thing, the brochure has to be made according to some conventions of making a brochure, and everybody must use the same format and writing style when presenting their tourism business in the brochure, and the brochure text must be translated into English and German. The network brochure and the home page also organize the participating tourism companies to varied themes. In a similar way the home page must be made and updated in accordance with common conventions. Furthermore it is required of the companies that they pay a small membership fee every year in order for the network to finance the printing of the brochure. Thus, the companies must make some investment in form (Thévenot) and some larger-scale actions must be accomplished every year according to an agreed framework. Investment in form also concerns the behaviour and staging of tourism experiences of each of the participating companies when tourists visit them. They have agreed to give the tourists a good experience and refer them to other tourist companies in the network, thus helping the tourists around. This is not always an easy task, because members or their families are not always prepared for staging tourism experiences according to these conventions:

> It turned out that it was her husband who had opened the door [for the tourists]. He had nothing to do with her enterprise. But, if she wanted to remain a member of the network, she simply had to tell her husband that he needed to be friendly to the tourists.
>
> (Network coordinator)

It takes a lot of effort on the part of the network coordinator to be a mentor for all the different enterprises, make them adapt to a more conventional behaviour for staging experiences and regularly participate in common events.

### *Engagement in justifiable action*

In 2010 Small Tourism became registered as a formal association with a board and official statutes. This implied that it became possible to apply for relevant support from small regional and cultural funds. It also meant that the purpose and strategy of the network became somewhat more clearly formulated. Further, it became possible for members to challenge the network coordinators: 'Now the possibilities are much better to argue, hey, this is not wise what the board is doing. And you can elect some other people to administer the network' (Network coordinator). The purpose of the network is clarified in the statutes as 'promoting tourism on Lolland-Falster', and 'creating a forum where members of Small Tourism can get to know each other, share knowledge and back each other up' (Lille Turisme 2010). Thus it becomes easier to criticize the network activities not just in terms of personal interests, but also in terms of how the network is relevant for regional rural development, for creating alternative economic activities in Lolland-Falster that can add meaning and value to the place. The question is, however, whether the network really has the resources to participate at this level, because it requires engagement with local politics. Getting access to funds is time-consuming. It implies an even further detachment from the personalized and spontaneous relationships, which seem important to many of the participating companies. Several of the interviewees indicated that the administrative support from the businessman who took the initiative to the network was important and that the network coordinator and her special skills to move between the different regimes of engagement was critical for maintaining the network. Hence a combination of administrative support and the ability of the network and network coordinator to provide support for the companies' 'investment in form' can explain the ability of the network to move between personalized and generalized actions.

## Conclusion

The paper has explored how micro-companies in a rural area can become involved in networking through 'bricolage networking'. Thereby the paper aims to contribute to an understanding of how companies with limited interest in cooperation nevertheless can become engaged in the construction of place (Gieryn 2000) and in the experience economy.

Bricolage networking is a small-scale networking activity between companies at hand in a localized system. In the case study, the network was heterogeneous (the companies had different interests in the network and they produced different kinds of products), companies had little knowledge of each other before the network was constructed, and their preferences for networking were diverse and emerging. The network was neither a locally embedded structure with high levels of mutual synergy between the parties, nor a well-defined formal structure for strategic decision-making. As in a garbage can model, preferences were problematic, technologies unclear and participation fluid. Familiar engagement, creating a familiar networking milieu where companies were at ease with each other, seemed to be the predominant approach within the studied network. Several of the companies are micro-companies with little interest in large-scale network planning. Yet bricolage networking can help companies to 'invest in form', i.e. to develop small-scale plans. By supporting each other on a small scale, the companies can draw in other, more demanding and potentially more conflict-generating forms of engagement when it is needed, leading to a more generalized approach to networking and development of tourism.

A few consequences for theories about networking in tourism can be summarized.

*Consequences for theory*: The paper seeks to contribute to a theory of place by arguing that small-scale bricolage networking creating a familiar networking milieu able to spur small initiatives and small steps in an atmosphere of comfort, easiness and low conflict collaboration can infuse value and meaning into place. We know from research that networking is difficult for tourism firms, due to fragmentation and free-rider problems, but bricolage networking is a small-scale form of collaboration, which has not been investigated before, where companies are at ease with each other and with the tourists they receive. Yet bricolage networking is also a limited model that relies on a personalized use of resources. It is also dependent on some degree of formalization and plan. We need to know more about how such local network structures are able to maintain collective activities and what the limitations are. One research strategy suggested in this paper is to dig more deeply into the forms of engagement in such networks in order to understand the varied advantages and disadvantages of the familiar and personalized approach to resources and tourists as well as its limitations.

*Consequences for practice*: By low-cost, small-scale activities it is possible to create new innovative value constellations that contribute to the economy and the construction of place. This form of networking can be based in a lifestyle, hobby and familiarized approach to localized resources. Yet localized and shared resources may also give rise to disagreements and conflict among the actors. In the case studied here, it was a central person, the network coordinator, who kept the network together and saw to it that conflicts were handled for the network to remain a familiar milieu. For her, it was problematic to develop more extended forms of engagement where the network became more integrated with external support structures and regional development strategies. Bricolage networking focuses available resources that are at ease with each other, but with little attention to activating more general knowledge-based resources or external knowledge and funding. Network management in the shape of the central person becomes a crucial but difficult entrepreneurial task. The central persons of such networks must be mentors and supervisors for the enterprises and continuously encourage them to participate in collective activities. The coordinator of this network had to maintain a difficult balance between keeping the network a familiar environment and engaging the participants in more ambitious plans.

## References

Andersson, D.E. and Andersson, Å.E. (2013) 'The economic value of experience goods', in J. Sundbo and F. Sørensen (eds) *Handbook on the Experience Economy*, Cheltenham: Edward Elgar.

Asheim, B.T., Boschma, R. and Cooke, P. (2011) 'Constructing regional advantage: Platform policies based on related variety and differentiated knowledge bases'. *Regional Studies*, 45: 893–904.

Ateljevic, I. and Doorne, S. (2000) '"Staying within the Fence": Lifestyle entrepreneurship in tourism', *Journal of Sustainable Tourism*, 8: 378–92.

Baker, T. and Nelson, R.E. (2005) 'Creating something from nothing: Resource construction through entrepreneurial bricolage', *Administrative Science Quarterly*, 50: 329–66.

Baker, T., Miner, A.S. and Eesley, D.T. (2003) 'Improvising firms: Bricolage, account giving and improvisational competencies in the founding process', *Research Policy*, 32: 255–76.

Bathelt, H., Malmberg, A. and Maskell, P. (2004) 'Clusters and knowledge: local buzz, global pipelines and the process of knowledge creation', *Progress in Human Geography*, 28: 31–56.

Buhalis, D. and Cooper, C. (1998) 'Competition or co-operation? Small and medium sized tourism enterprises at the destination', in E. Laws, B. Faulkner and G. Moscardo (eds) *Embracing and Managing Change in Tourism*, London: Routledge.

Camagni, R. (1991) 'Introduction: From the local "milieu" to innovation through cooperation networks', in R. Camagni (ed.) *Innovation Networks: Spatial Perspectives*, London: Belhaven Press.

Cohen, M.D., March, J.G. and Olsen, J.P. (1972) 'Garbage can model of organizational choice', *Administrative Science Quarterly*, 17: 1–25.

Crevoisier, O. and Jeannerat, H. (2009) 'Territorial knowledge dynamics: From the proximity paradigm to multi-location milieus', *European Planning Studies*, 17: 1223–41.

Duymedjian, R. and Ruling, C.C. (2010) 'Towards a foundation of bricolage in organization and management theory', *Organization Studies*, 31: 133–51.

Framke, W. (2002) 'The destination as a concept: A discussion of the business-related perspective versus the sociocultural approach in tourism theory', *Scandinavian Journal of Hospitality and Tourism*, 2: 92–108.

Freire-Gibb, L.C. and Lorentzen, A. (2011) 'A platform for local entrepreneurship: The case of the lighting festival of Frederikshavn', *Local Economy*, 26: 157–69.

Frenken, K., van Oort, F. and Verburg, T. (2007) 'Related variety, unrelated variety and regional economic growth', *Regional Studies*, 41(5): 685–97.

Fuglsang, L. (2010) 'Bricolage and invisible innovation in public service innovation', *Journal of Innovation Economics*, 2010(5): 67–87.

Fuglsang, L. and Eide, D. (2013) 'The experience turn as "bandwagon": Understanding network formation and innovation as practice', *European Urban and Regional Studies*, 20(4): 418–35.

Fuglsang, L. and Sørensen, F. (2011) 'The balance between bricolage and innovation: Management dilemmas in sustainable public innovation', *Service Industries Journal*, 31(4): 581–95.

Fuglsang, L. and Sørensen, F. (2013) 'Entrepreneurship in the experience economy: overcoming cultural barriers', in J. Sundbo and F. Sørensen (eds) *Handbook on the Experience Economy*, Cheltenham: Edward Elgar.

Garud, R. and Karnoe, P. (2003) 'Bricolage versus breakthrough: Distributed and embedded agency in technology entrepreneurship', *Research Policy*, 32(2): 277–300.

Gieryn, T.F. (2000) 'A space for place in sociology', *Annual Review of Sociology*, 26: 463–96.

Granovetter, M. (1995) *Getting a Job*, 2nd edn, Chicago: University of Chicago Press.

Hatton, E. (1989) 'Lévi-Strauss's bricolage and theorizing teachers' work', *Anthropology & Education Quarterly*, 20(2): 74–96.

Hjalager, A.-M. (2000) 'Tourism destinations and the concept of industrial districts', *Tourism and Hospitality Research* 2: 199–213.

Hjalager, A.-M. (2010) 'A review of innovation research in tourism', *Tourism Management*, 31(1): 1–12.

Håkansson, H., Ford, D., Gadde, L.-E., Snehota, I. and Waluszewski, A. (2009) *Business in Networks*, Chichester: Wiley.

Jeannerat, H. (2013) 'Staging experience, valuing authenticity: Towards a market perspective on territorial development', *European Urban and Regional Studies*, 20(4): 370–84.

Lévi-Strauss, C. (1966) *The savage mind*, Chicago and London: The University of Chicago Press.

Lille Turisme (2010) 'Vedtægter'. Online. Available at: www.den-lille-turisme.dk/DLT-FK-medlem/2010/Vedtaegter].pdf (accessed 20 November 2014).

Lorentzen, A. (2007) 'The geography of knowledge sourcing: A case study of Polish manufacturing enterprises', *European Planning Studies*, 15(4): 467–86.

Lorentzen, A. and Jeannerat, H. (2013) 'Urban and regional studies in the experience economy: What kind of turn?' *European Urban and Regional Studies*, 20(4): 363–9.

Ministry of Food, Agriculture and Fisheries (2008) 'The Danish rural development programme 2007–2013', Copenhagen: Ministry of Food, Agriculture and Fisheries.

Nilsen, B.T. and Dale, B.E. (2013) 'Defining and categorizing experience industries', in J. Sundbo and F. Sørensen (eds) *Handbook on the Experience Economy*, Cheltenham: Edward Elgar.

Nordin, S. (2003) *Tourism clustering and innovation*, Östersund, Sweden: ETOUR.

Normann, R. and Ramirez, R. (1993) 'From value chain to value constellation – designing interactive strategy', *Harvard Business Review*, 71: 65–77.

Pearce, D.G. (2013) 'Toward an integrative conceptual framework of destinations', *Journal of Travel Research*, 53(2): 141–53.

Petterson, J. (2010) *Mikrovirksomheder og makroøkonomier: Turismens indflydelse på vækst i yderområder*, Roskilde: Roskilde University.

Snel, A. (2013) 'Experience as the DNA of a changed relationship between firms and institutions and individuals', in J. Sundbo and F. Sørensen (eds) *Handbook on the Experience Economy*, Cheltenham: Edward Elgar.

Storper, M. (1995) 'The resurgence of regional economies, ten years later: The region as a nexus of untraded interdependencies', *European Urban and Regional Studies*, 2(3): 191–221.

Sundbo, J. (2009) 'Innovation in the experience economy: A taxonomy of innovation organisations', *Service Industries Journal*, 29(4): 431–55.

Sundbo, J. and Gallouj, F. (2000) 'Innovation as a loosely coupled system in services', in J.S. Metcalfe and I. Miles (eds) *Innovation systems in the service economy, Measurement and case study analysis*, London: Kluwer.

Sundbo, J. and Sørensen, F. (2013) 'Introduction to the experience economy', in J. Sundbo and F. Sørensen (eds) *Handbook on the Experience Economy*, Cheltenham: Edward Elgar.

Tether, B.S. and Metcalfe, J.S. (2004) 'Services and systems of innovation', in F. Malerba (ed.) *Sectoral Systems of Innovation: Concepts, issues and analysis of six major sectors in Europe*, Cambridge: Cambridge University Press.

Thévenot, L. (2001) 'Pragmatic regimes governing the engagement with the world', in T.R. Schatzki, K.D. Knorr-Cetina and E.V. Savigny (eds) *The Practice Turn in Contemporary Theory*, London: Routledge.

Thévenot, L. (2007) 'The plurality of cognitive formats and engagements. Moving between the familiar and the public', *European Journal of Social Theory*, 10(3): 409–23.

Vanhaverbeke, W. and Cloodt, M. (2006) 'Open innovation in value networks', in H. Chesbrough, W. Vanhaverbeke and J. West (eds) *Open innovation: Researching a New Paradigm*, Oxford: Oxford University Press.

Weick, K.E. (1993) 'The collapse of sensemaking in organizations: The Mann Gulch disaster', *Administrative Science Quarterly*, 38(4): 628–52.

Weidenfeld, A., Williams, A.M. and Butler R.W. (2010) 'Knowledge transfer and innovation among attractions', *Annals of Tourism Research*, 37(3): 604–26.

# 14 Cultural heritage as an experiential resource in planning

*Lise Schrøder*

## Introduction

In the Danish planning context as in many Western countries the experience economy approach appeals to planners and politicians, as it opens up new possibilities and exiting ways of dealing with local development (Therkildsen *et al.* 2012). Place-bound experiential qualities, which can be exploited economically, create a direct link from the experience economy to spatial planning strategies at the city or municipal level as well as at the regional and national levels (Lorentzen 2012; Therkildsen *et al.* 2012). In that respect, cultural heritage plays a distinct role as economic as well as cultural resource (Graham *et al.* 2000). The other way around, place-bound experiences including cultural heritage seem to possess an interesting potential, when it comes to creating awareness and facilitating collaboration among stakeholders in the field of spatial planning (Jensen 2009; Delman and Nielsen 2009; Delman 2011; Landry 2008). For instance, Landry (2008: 119) emphasizes the role of local identity and distinctiveness as a means of cooperation for the common good, as it creates 'a bond between people with different institutional interests'. In that regard physical cultural heritage can be understood in terms of a 'tangible trace of collective memory', as expressed by Kerr (2000: 71). Kerr refers to the specific role of public monuments, but he points out that 'the fabric of the city itself represents a visible aide-mémoire'. As argued by Graham *et al.* (2000: 169) 'the heritage of the conserved built environment, like culture more widely, is called upon to play a number of different roles in neighbourhood regeneration'. From that point of departure, this chapter focuses on how cultural heritage as part of the urban matter can function as an experiential resource in spatial planning.

The national survey performed by the Danish Cultural Heritage Agency and the Realdania Foundation in 2004–5, emphasized the role of material cultural heritage as an experiential quality valued by citizens as well as enterprises (Kulturarvsstyrelsen and Realdania 2005). This survey initiated the nationwide Cultural Heritage Municipality programme, launched by the Danish Cultural Heritage Agency in 2005 (Kulturarvsstyrelsen and Realdania 2007). In order to facilitate the proper management of cultural heritage in Danish municipalities, the main goal of this programme was to promote and mobilize cultural heritage in urban as well as rural areas as a resource for spatial planning. A specific purpose of the programme was thus to facilitate local political awareness towards basic use-values as well as value-adding experience-oriented qualities of cultural heritage buildings, sites and environments. Furthermore, the programme intended to demonstrate the potential of cultural heritage as a source for place construction and creation of spatial narratives and identities as part of the Danish municipality reform in 2006–7 (Kulturarvsstyrelsen and Realdania 2007; Pluss 2011).

The specific aim of the following analysis is to investigate how the tangible cultural heritage in the built environment can function as an experiential resource in municipal planning processes. To that purpose, the chapter includes a design exercise in order to establish a conceptual framework capable of categorizing different roles of cultural heritage in spatial planning projects.

The empirical object of study will be the process related to the local Cultural Heritage Municipality Project in the municipality of Aalborg, which was one among four municipalities chosen to be 'cultural heritage municipalities' in the first of two periods (respectively 2006–8 and 2008–10) of the Danish cultural heritage municipality programme (Kulturarvsstyrelsen and Realdania 2008; Pluss 2011). The case study is based on experiences from active participation of the author in the collaborative planning process primarily during the period from 2006 to 2008 and again from 2010 to 2011.

The cultural heritage project of Aalborg Municipality provides a nuanced example of how the perspectives of the experience economy have contributed to create positive awareness among stakeholders and a creative collaborative attitude among cultural heritage professionals. The case study is introduced in part 2 of the chapter.

Methodologically, the experience economy concept establishes a platform for the analysis of holistic experience-oriented innovation processes in local development (Lorentzen 2013). The theoretical approach to the case analysis will be the conceptualization of territorial staging systems as described by Jeannerat (2015) in this volume. In part 3 this model will be transformed into the context of planning in order to establish a conceptual and analytical framework, as a means of identifying elements of the planning process as well as their dynamic relationships.

In part 4, the empirical findings will be presented and analysed within the conceptual framework. The analysis will include the cultural heritage project period 2006–8 and the following collaboration until 2011, when the local plan for one of the industrial heritage sites of the project, Østre Havn, was introduced to the public. Finally, there will be a brief summing up, a conclusion and some further perspectives.

## Exploring values of industrial heritage in the municipality of Aalborg

The following analysis is based on empirical findings from the municipality of Aalborg in the northern part of Denmark (Figure 14.1). As a result of the Danish

*Figure 14.1* Aalborg Municipality consists of the former municipalities of Aalborg, Hals, Nibe and Sejlflod, and is located in the northern part of Denmark (map © Lise Schrøder 2014).

municipal reform in 2007 the former municipalities of Aalborg, Hals, Nibe and Sejlflod were merged into the new municipality of Aalborg. Aalborg Municipality thereby became the second largest in Denmark due to its size of 1,152 square kilometres and the third largest referring to its population of approximately 200,000. More than half of the citizens live in the city of Aalborg, which makes it the fourth largest in Denmark.

Aalborg was a major player in the Danish industrial landscape until the decline of the industrial era during the last part of the twentieth century. In 1974, a university, which has played a central role in the transition towards a more knowledge-based economy of the region, was established in Aalborg. The city has also been very active in the EU movement on sustainable cities and towns, and is facilitator of the UN Agenda 21 on sustainability. Aalborg has thus given its name to the 'Aalborg Charter' from 1994 (European Sustainable Cities and Towns Campaign 1994) and the following 'Aalborg Commitments' from 2004 (European Sustainable Cities and Towns Campaign 2004). Among other issues on sustainability these commitments emphasize the municipal responsibility concerning cultural heritage. Another is public participation as a central element of the governance processes at the municipal level. On this background, this chapter is motivated by the overall hypothesis that important potentials are connected to cultural heritage as a means of communication and collaboration in the planning process.

## Cultural heritage as a planning resource in Aalborg Municipality

As a result of the Danish municipal reform in 2007 the former counties were eliminated as administrative entities and the number of municipalities was reduced from 271 to 98. Among other things, the municipalities were granted new responsibilities as authority managers of the cultural heritage of the built environment. Therefore, the Danish Agency on Cultural Heritage launched the 'cultural heritage municipality project' in order to enhance the inter-municipality capacity in this respect. The central aim of this programme was to increase awareness among public and private stakeholders towards the local cultural heritage. On this background the goal of the programme was to promote the understanding of cultural heritage as resource in overall municipal strategies, spatial planning processes, and local development projects (Kulturarvsstyrelsen and Realdania 2007; Pluss 2011). The projects received much attention from the merging municipalities all over the country due to its focus on cultural heritage as a means of communicating local identity. Half of the Danish municipalities applied, and the new municipality of Aalborg as well as three other new municipalities (Haderslev, Hals, Hjørring) were selected to implement the four cultural heritage municipality projects starting in 2006. The projects were then integrated in the municipal planning strategies of 2007, thus forming the basis for the municipal plans of 2009.

A main goal of the cultural heritage municipality project in Aalborg was to create a common understanding, which referred to a shared identity based on stories of the local industrial heritage and its foundation in the natural resources of the whole area, and not just of the city of Aalborg (Jensen *et al.* 2006). The project was managed by the Historical Museum of Northern Jutland in close collaboration with municipal spatial planners as well as historians and cultural heritage archivists from the four merging municipalities. Researchers from Aalborg University also participated in the project. The aim of the project was threefold: (1) At the operational level, the aim was to develop a methodology for the ongoing management of the cultural heritage of the built environment. As a co-product, important cultural heritage elements and environments had to be identified; (2) From an internal organizational point of view, a separate goal of the project was to facilitate collaboration across the newly established municipal organization. The primary purpose was to contribute to establishing a consensus concerning the municipal planning strategy 2007 across the new municipal organization, thus enabling the merging of the four separate municipal plans from 2005 into the joint municipal plan for 2009 (Aalborg Kommune 2009); (3) Finally, in accordance with the intentions of the national cultural heritage agency, the project was focused on how to create awareness among enterprises, citizens and politicians of the local industrial cultural heritage as a resource for branding, experience economy and public involvement in the planning processes. In that regard, the project had a specific focus on the interaction between cultural heritage and the progressive use of new kinds of information and communication technology (Jensen *et al.* 2006).

During the first phase of the cultural heritage project the municipality of Aalborg in 2006 sold one of its most characteristic industrial heritage sites 'Østre Havn' to a local developer, A. Enggaard. The cultural heritage project initiated a planning process, which focused on the industrial heritage of the area. The collaborative process in focus in this chapter continued until the municipality's launching of the local plan in 2011. The process integrated the two objectives: mapping and prioritizing the values of the area, as well as conducting experiments with new ways of involving the stakeholders.

In the following section the background for the physical transformation of the industrial heritage of Østre Havn will be presented in further detail.

### *Creating awareness on Østre Havn*

Østre Havn or Eastern Harbour was established in 1901–03 as a central part of the infrastructure facilitating the rapidly growing industrial production sites of the city of Aalborg. The central element of this harbour area is a huge granite basin, which, from the beginning of the twentieth century, has been surrounded by rail tracks, silos and storehouses primarily for foodstuff production and trade. The area was, at the time of the sale in 2006, characterized by imposing concrete silo complexes, which stem from the peak of the Danish industrial era in the 1960s and 1970s (Figure 14.2). A variety of huge chimneys and spectacular aggregates for production, storage and transportation completed the industrial look.

Neighbouring Østre Havn, an important shipyard, was in operation between 1912 and 1988. For many years it was Aalborg's most important employer and producer. Nevertheless, by 2006, only a single workshop building had survived, which reflects the lack of interest in preserving the industrial heritage, a prevalent characteristic of this period. Similarly, the immediate intention of the new owner of Østre Havn was to demolish the buildings and physical remains from the industrial production period and replace them with modern multistorey houses for dwellings and city functions.

However, the increased awareness of cultural heritage as a resource in planning, which in part was created by the cultural heritage municipality initiative, made the municipality slow down the transformation process. Instead, resources were allocated from the local cultural heritage project in order to carry out a proper mapping and prioritization of the functional, architectural and historical values of the area. This was followed by different attempts to create attention and engagement among the stakeholders.

In 2007 one of the former storage buildings neighbouring the harbour basin functioned as spectacular scenery for a public workshop, where the initial ideas

*Figure 14.2* View towards the skyline (photo © Lise Schrøder 2007).

for the transformation of the area were debated (Gehl Architects 2012). In collaboration with the new owner, the municipality arranged the event, where five esteemed Danish architectural firms presented their visions for the future of the area. Afterwards, approximately 100 citizens, students and planning professionals worked together in small groups in order to generate new ideas for further debate. One of the visible results was the 'Platform4' initiative (named after the number of the storage building), aiming at exploring how temporary use of the areas could contribute to the transformation process (Metopos By- og Landskabsdesign and Aalborg Kommune 2009). The initiative took place from 2008 to 2012, where A. Enggaard allowed the group of creative grassroots behind Platform4 to use some of the buildings and the wharf area around the harbour basin for free (Figure 14.3).

As part of the cultural heritage project, surveys of the architectural and historical values of the industrial environment were conducted. These functioned as a platform for establishing a shared understanding among professional parties as well as a starting point for communicating the potential values of the area to other stakeholders. The analysis of the area's spatial qualities emphasized how the iconic skyline of silos and chimneys functioned as a condensed image of the industrial character and scale of the area. Mappings and archive studies focusing on the functional elements from the industrial era illustrated how the railway-based transportation system from the beginning of the nineteenth century had given shape to the characteristic curved arrangement of the buildings and silo

*Figure 14.3* Looking from the pier towards 'Platform4' located at the wharf along the harbour basin (photo © Lise Schrøder 2011).

complexes. Photos and other archive material contributed to the categorization and prioritization of the value of the buildings due to their historical roles in the area. Catalogues based on photographic documentation were produced to illustrate the characteristic industrial look and the use of robust materials such as granite, concrete and iron.

Unfortunately, a technical survey revealed that most of the characteristic silos were polluted due to their use for storing cereal seed grain preserved with toxic chemicals. As a result, most of the buildings had no future in the new plan for the area, despite their architectural and historical qualities. In order to document the daily life at the production sites for the future before the buildings were demolished, supplementary funding was received from the Cultural Heritage Agency in 2010. This made it possible to perform further fieldwork before the buildings vanished forever, and to interview former workers before those visible local memories were erased.

In order to draw attention to the local municipal plan for the area, it was decided to communicate the results of the documentation project in an exhibition, which could function as a kick-off for the mandatory public hearing period. An interdisciplinary team, with participants from the municipality, the historical museum, the city archive and the university, planned the exhibition during 2011, which resulted in an on-site physical exhibition combined with supplementary mobile-based digital mediation.

## Framing cultural heritage within the scenery of planning

Landry points out how cultural heritage 'connects us to our histories, our collective memories' and 'anchors our sense of being and can provide a source of insight to help us face the future' (Landry 2008: 6–7). In this regard, Landry sees cultural heritage in the form of buildings, artefacts, skills, values and social rituals of the past as central resources in local development. In his 'toolkit for urban innovators', this also relates to user involvement and the facilitation of innovation processes, which he expresses in terms of 'learning through empowerment' (Landry 2008: 113).

Graham *et al.* (2000) argue how the cultural heritage of the built environment plays a central role in planning as physical manifestations of the cultural backgrounds and historical developments of our living environments. They point out how 'heritage elements can provide a stage or background for other profit-seeking enterprises' in local revitalization schemes (Graham *et al.* 2000: 170–1). They focus on how heritage can contribute to city qualities by bringing people into the streets and thereby contribute to liveliness, which in itself is spectacular, and which makes visitors act as both performers and audience.

This aspect of performers and audiences co-producing spectacular experiences on a stage, defined by aesthetic, historical and physical place qualities in the cityscape, provides a link to the concepts of the experience economy. The idea of cultural heritage as cultural memory has a direct link to the notions of adding value by creating memorable experiences (Pine and Gilmore 1998).

Considering the planning perspective in the local construction of places, the experiences from Vancouver presented by Lorentzen (2015) in this volume, illustrate a similar approach. Lorentzen refers to Pine and Gilmore (1999) when she argues that the practice of planning like 'work' can be theatre, and the city can replace the 'business' as stage, in their renowned metaphor.

Pine and Gilmore (2013) emphasize that even if they talk about work being theatre in the experience economy (Pine and Gilmore 2013: 28), it is important to focus on not just the realm of 'entertainment', but also to be aware of the realms of 'educational', 'escapist' and 'aesthetic' experiences (Pine and Gilmore 2013: 32). The role of cultural heritage sites as a means of staging experiences is well known, as is also illustrated in this volume by the classical example of how value is added to coffee because of its spatial relations to a famous cultural heritage site in Venice (Jeannerat 2015; Guex and Crevoisier 2015). Likewise, Graham *et al.* (2000) emphasize the role of cultural heritage as an economic and cultural capital, which functions as a multifaceted experiential commodity as well as a resource in the context of local development.

The territorial staging system conceptualized by Jeannerat and Crevoisier (2010) and introduced in this volume (Jeannerat 2015), may be useful as an analytical framework for this research. The staging system may conceptualize how cultural heritage can be mobilized as an experiential resource for collaboration in planning. As described by Jeannerat (2015), the concept of territorial staging systems is based on the idea of stakeholders interacting in a process of stage setting and experiential engagement. This interaction functions as a symbiotic value creation process.

To perform spatial planning and to make plans can be compared to the production aspect in the territorial staging system model, while the consumption aspect can be compared to citizens and other stakeholders taking part in the planning process. Thus, the conceptual framework of the territorial staging system as described by Jeannerat (2015) can be translated into the planning context (Figure 14.4). The production factors and resources such as knowledge, culture and production tools influencing the stage setting will then be the plethora of knowledge, culture and planning tools available in the planning processes. Similarly, the consumers will be replaced by stakeholders, who are engaged on the planning stage and add value to the process by drawing on resources such as knowledge, culture and social capital.

An approach to distinguish the different parts played by cultural heritage in this kind of creative transformation process could be the conceptualization of how urban space is created as presented by Healey (2007: 204–5), who has translated Lefebvre's spatial triad (1991: 38–40). Referring to Lefebvre, space is produced in terms of being 'perceived', 'conceived' or 'lived' interacting in a continuous process, which will be exemplified in the context of cultural heritage below.

At the perceptual level, space can be understood as a 'spatial practice', which Healey translates into 'routine material engagement and experience of being in and moving around urban areas'. Cultural heritage as the scenery for daily-life functions could be an example – for instance when citizens enjoy living in areas with historical qualities (Graham *et al.* 2000: 170–1; Kulturarvsstyrelsen and Realdania 2005).

At the conceptual level space can be understood as a 'representation of space', which as expressed by Healey can be termed as 'intellectual conceptions of urban areas, produced for analytical and administrative purposes' Healey (2007: 204). Considering the role of cultural heritage, the professional conceptualization of 'genius loci' (spirit of place) as a fundamental parameter in the creation of place identity could be an example (Norberg-Schulz 1975).

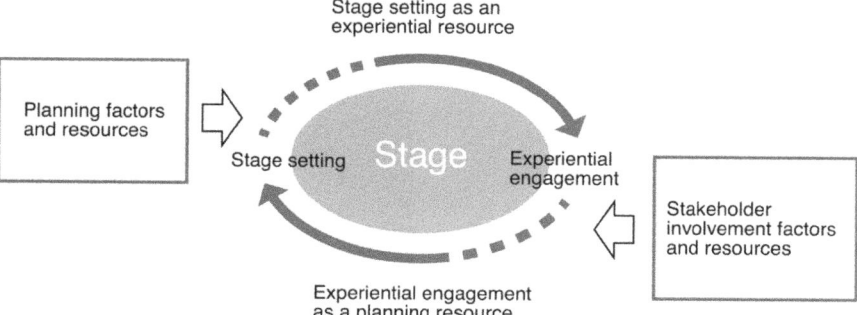

*Figure 14.4* The territorial staging model translated into the concept of a spatial planning staging model (adapted from Jeannerat 2015).

The idea of lived space can be understood as 'representational spaces', which, according to Healey, can be interpreted as 'cultural expressions of place qualities and spatial meanings' Healey (2007: 204). Healey refers to Liggett (1995), when she links representational spaces to 'meanings within a cultural memory'.

Though, Healey (2007: 205) emphasizes the importance of not using too rigid systemic concepts, she stresses the importance of distinguishing the intellectual conceptions of the planning professionals from the local knowledge, which is based on the material experience as well as the cultural imageries. In this process cultural heritage resources related to the perceived space as well as the lived space might contribute to experiential engagement involving passive as well as active participation of the stakeholders. In that respect, both aspects will function as a planning resource, which can contribute to the intellectual constructs of the planning process. It could be understood as a distinction, which reflects the difference between passive and active participation, as formulated by Pine and Gilmore (1998), and the idea of 'inging' things in order to transform goods into memorable events by adding an active dimension (Pine and Gilmore 2011: 22). Furthermore, it could be seen as a parallel to progression on 'the ladder of participation' illustrating the degree of citizen participation, as conceptualized by Arnstein (1969). On the other hand, intellectual conceptions such as guided tours to the area or workshops can function as experiential resources setting the stage for further experiential engagement in the planning process. Figure 14.5 illustrates this understanding.

As described above, the understanding of planning processes can be related to the creation of spaces and places based on human contributions in the form of routine material engagement, intellectual conception and cultural expression. These three cognitive dimensions can also be related to the conceptualization of cultural heritage as a means of collaboration, which can be expressed in terms of the staging system metaphor as: the stage, the staging system, and the staging process.

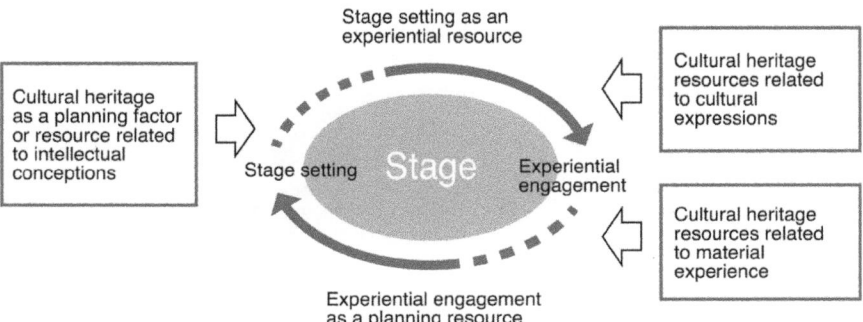

*Figure 14.5* The concept of a spatial planning staging system incorporating cultural heritage assets contributing to creation of spaces based on material experience, intellectual conceptions and cultural expressions (referring to Healey 2007).

The first perspective puts focus on cultural heritage in the built environment as a 'stage', which facilitates material engagement in itself. In this context, the 'stage' can be identified as a physical arena for interaction in local development. Hence, the focus is on how cultural heritage contributes to the transformation of the specific urban matter and the planning processes relating to it.

The second perspective is grounded in the conception of a 'system', where the systemic approach facilitates the analysis of interconnected entities, their relations and representations. In this optic the 'staging system' can be understood as an immaterial vehicle for collaboration among actors in municipal planning processes. Thus, this perspective contributes to examine how cultural heritage projects can function as a communication platform mediating different understandings and thereby facilitating collaboration among citizens and professionals.

The third perspective puts focus on the results of organizational processes in the form of cultural expressions. Thereby the 'staging process' can refer to the development of an organizational culture changing the ways of doing planning, which could be expressed in terms of an organizational capacity building apparatus concerning municipal planning matters.

## Cultural heritage and experimental engagement in planning

Above, three aspects of staging (the stage, the system, the process) were used to distinguish the role of cultural heritage as a means of collaboration in different respects. Referring to that optic, cultural heritage objects and sites can function as a physical arena. Cultural heritage projects can function as a platform for collaboration. And cultural heritage can be part of organizational capacity building efforts. In order to analyse the role and value of cultural heritage as a resource in planning, each of these perspectives will be related to the conceptual understanding of space as being constructed by means of material engagement, intellectual conception as well as cultural expression.

### *Østre Havn as a physical arena for interaction in local development*

For decades, Østre Havn, being a working industrial site, was closed to the public, and only the former workers could be considered to have a 'routine material engagement and experience of being in and moving around' this area, to use the expression by Healey (2007: 204). This means that in terms of spatial practice the space had to be reinvented almost from scratch. Not least, the Platform4 initiative attracted people to the area. The Platform4 site functioned as a laboratory, where artistic and entrepreneurial grassroots worked together with researchers from the university and students from creative educations. During the four-year period, different kinds of artistic and explorative activities, a café, a temporary sail-in-cinema in the harbour basin, music events and art performances contributed to create attention and invited people to experience and use the area. Thus, the spectacular industrial remains functioned as settings for a new era of daily spatial practice, where citizens jogging, walking the dog or climbing

240   *L. Schrøder*

the massive walls of the silos were given the chance to sense the industrial atmosphere characterized by its scale, authentic materials and functional appearance.

Regarding the conceptual aspect of the model in Figure 14.5, the value of cultural heritage as part of the urban matter is understood in terms of 'intellectual conceptions of urban areas, produced for analytical and administrative purposes' Healey (2007: 204). All kinds of representations of space played a central role during the planning process. They functioned as a means for cultural heritage professionals and planners to communicate the functional, architectural and historical values in the area. Among the visions for the future of the area was the central square, which was named the 'Star Square' after the star-shaped structure formed by the railway (Figure 14.6). The metaphor of the 'Star Square' was one of the central elements in branding this new place. But also different kinds of physical and virtual spaces, which mediated cultural heritage values, were important elements in setting the stage for the presentation of the future plan for the area.

As the third dimension in the conceptual framework, space can be understood as 'cultural expressions of place qualities and spatial meanings' Healey (2007: 204). The physical manifestations in the area, such as art, production sites and various events created by 'Platform4', are examples of such cultural expressions. Another kind of cultural expression is the staging of the 'Platform4' initiative, together with the various kinds of professional conceptualizations produced by architects and city planners as part of the physical and digital storytelling on Østre Havn.

Even if most of the buildings were going to be replaced by new ones, the structure and scale of the area were going to be preserved. By means of huge

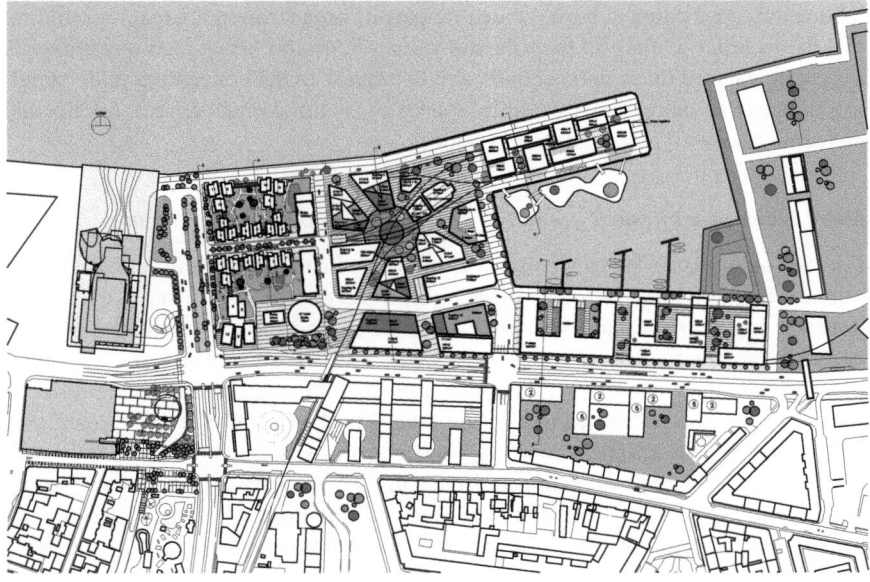

*Figure 14.6* The local plan for Østre Havn 2012 (source: permission to use map granted by Aalborg Municipality).

posters mounted directly on the silos and storage buildings, visitors were invited to experience aspects of the former, the present and the future character of the area. The digital layer added an extra virtual dimension to that experience, making it possible to tell stories of the past augmented by authentic set pieces. Sounds of trains and pictures of hardworking people popping up on the smartphone along the route contributed to bring the past to life. Likewise, digital technology made it possible to take the visitor on a digitally guided tour, where the new plan for the area functioned as a map on the smartphone, and where pictures of the planned buildings were displayed along the route.

The physical and virtual exhibitions are good examples of how cultural heritage can add authenticity and experiential values to the presentation of the plan on-site (Figure 14.7). Visitors interviewed during the hearing period confirmed that the exhibition had not only been informative, but also exciting due to the location.

### The cultural heritage project as an immaterial vehicle for collaboration

Focusing on the relational aspects, the staging system could also be understood as an immaterial vehicle for collaboration in municipal planning processes. In the following, this optic will be used to focus on how cultural heritage can contribute to

*Figure 14.7* The city mayor and the chief architect from the planning department introducing the local plan for Østre Havn on location (photo © Pernille Wamberg Broch 2011).

and strengthen relations among stakeholders. Doing mappings of the physical environment at Østre Havn can be understood as a kind of routine material engagement, which contributes to experiential engagement in the collaborative planning process.

Considering cultural heritage as a resource related to professional conceptions and representations of space at this systemic level, including the participation of professionals from different stakeholders in different joint activities, had a great impact as a means of creating shared imageries. An example is the study trip to Emscher Park in the Ruhr District in 2007, where the entire cultural heritage project team, including archivists, historians from the museum, municipal planners, municipal strategists, and developers, participated. Also, local events were arranged as part of the project paved the ground for a common understanding, for instance arranging a digital game as part of a public historical event at one of the former cement plant sites (Jensen 2009) as well as a boat trip introducing the public to some of the main industrial heritage objects (Figure 14.8).

*Figure 14.8* Citizens, planners, and cultural heritage professionals experiencing the cultural heritage from the waterfront (photo © Lise Schrøder 2007).

The result of the study trip to Emscher Park was a shared understanding of the potentials of reusing large-scale industrial heritage sites for experiential purposes. The increased awareness of the value of the cultural heritage environment lead to implementation of cultural heritage elements in the Municipal Strategy for 2007 (Aalborg Kommune 2007).

### *Cultural heritage as a means of organizational capacity building*

The third perspective of the analysis concerns the role of cultural heritage as part of organizational capacity building efforts. Following this optic, the shared experiences based on visiting and perceiving industrial heritage objects and sites at Østre Havn can be understood in terms of perception and material engagement. Also, the quite material on-site collaboration tasks, such as collecting artefacts or testing the smartphone game on-site, can be considered as a kind of spatial practice. Regarding the collaboration process in the cultural heritage project, it was obvious that this shared spatial practice based on material experiences has functioned as a backbone for further experiential engagement among the cultural heritage professionals.

The collaboration resulted in 'intellectual conceptions of urban areas, produced for analytical and administrative purposes' Healey (2007: 204). These were translated into new tools, which can be activated in a creative collaborative process setting. Working together to create content for the smartphone game at the former cement plant was one of the first steps in a process of working together in new ways, for instance performing creative experiments with interactive information and communication technologies in order to attract citizens to be involved in the planning process.

## Cultural heritage as an experimental planning resource

In the section above, experiences from the cultural heritage project and the following planning process at Østre Havn have been described in order to identify how cultural heritage can be an experiential resource in planning. In the following, the analysis will be summed up and presented in overview. See Table 14.1.

As a first aspect, the role of the industrial heritage site itself was in focus as the material scenery for the transformation of the urban matter. Cultural heritage objects and sites can function as a physical arena, where 'spatial practices' based on material engagement can function as a resource, when activated in the planning process. At Østre Havn, for instance, experiences from the former workers as well as the new inhabitants at Platform4 functioned and were actively mobilized as a planning resource, by acting as set pieces in the scenery of the public hearing process.

Second, the collaboration process among stakeholders in the cultural heritage municipal project was examined. Cultural heritage projects can function as a platform for collaboration, which, understood in terms of the staging system, puts focus on the interaction among professional stakeholders in the working processes of the project. Referring to the staging system by Jeannerat (2015), the production factors and resources of the 'spatial planning staging system' include cultural heritage assets in the form of knowledge, culture as well as production tools represented in professional conceptualizations. These conceptualizations are based on knowledge and material engagement from managing the cultural heritage objects and sites, and contributed to the setting of a stage for further experiential engagement. During the cultural heritage project, the new, professionally generated, physical and virtual spaces facilitated communication and discussion of the cultural heritage values of the environment. And, as a result, these shared experiences, imageries and understandings contributed to setting a stage, making it possible to implement industrial cultural heritage issues in the municipal plans.

The third perspective of the analysis was the role of cultural heritage as part of organizational capacity building efforts. The experiential engagement in the project tasks functioned then as a resource for inventing new exploratory approaches as a planning tool among the cultural heritage professionals. The implementation of these new collaborative practices amongst cultural heritage professionals in the municipality is in itself a cultural expression.

The matrix in Table 14.1 is organized in order to distinguish the values of cultural heritage (listed above) on two dimensions: as an experiential resource by referring to three aspects of space (material experience, intellectual conception, cultural expression) and as three perspectives of staging (stage, system, process).

## Conclusions and perspectives

As illustrated by the analysis cultural heritage can function as an experiential resource and contribute to the planning process at different levels and in various ways. Cultural heritage as part of the urban matter can be characterized as having specific spatial characteristics and place-bound qualities, which can be experienced, communicated and mediated by various means.

The methodological approach was based on a translation of the conceptualization of the territorial staging system, as formulated by Jeannerat and Crevoisier (2010), where the idea of a 'spatial planning staging system' was referring to the semiotic approaches as formulated by Lefebvre (2002) and Healey (2007). Due to this conceptual framework it has been possible to distinguish roles and qualities of cultural heritage as an experiential resource in planning in two dimensions (Table 14.1). One dimension refers to the conceptualization of cultural heritage as a means of collaboration, which can be expressed in terms of the staging system metaphor as: the stage, the staging system, and the staging process. Another dimension refers to the role of cultural heritage as a means of the creation of spaces and places in terms of material experience, intellectual conception and cultural expression.

As emphasized by Graham *et al.* (2000) the roles and values of cultural heritage as part of the built environment are multifaceted. And in itself cultural

Table 14.1 Cultural heritage as an experiential resource referring to three dimensions of space (Healey 2007) and three dimensions of staging (stage, system, process)

| | Cultural heritage resources related to material experience | Cultural heritage as a planning factor or resource related to intellectual conception | Cultural heritage resources related to cultural expression |
|---|---|---|---|
| The stage as a *physical arena* for interaction in local development | Knowledge and engagement in the local space and the material place-bound cultural heritage objects and sites in it | Mapping and prioritizing qualities of industrial cultural heritage objects and sites | Creation of physical and virtual spaces for the experience of the cultural heritage values of the built environment |
| The staging system as an *immaterial vehicle* for collaboration in municipal planning processes | Knowledge and engagement in the process of managing the cultural heritage objects and sites as part of the cultural heritage project | Physical and virtual spaces facilitating the communication and discussion of cultural heritage values of the environment | Shared understandings making it possible to implement industrial cultural heritage issues in municipal plans |
| The staging process as an *organizational capacity building apparatus* concerning municipal planning matters | Knowledge and engagement in dealing with the various values of the cultural heritage objects and sites | New tools for managing the cultural heritage as a resource in planning | Implementing new ways of collaboration among cultural heritage professionals in the municipality |

heritage plays a major role as a highly valued commodity in the experience economy. Within the context of spatial planning the results of this research show how these two perspectives emerge in the context of collaborative attempts within the field of spatial planning. Still, spatial planning is a complex task, as Healey emphasizes, and too simple concepts have to be avoided. On the other hand the holistic concepts of the experience economy seems to be one of the paths towards the understanding of those complexes and ongoing transformations of areas and planners.

# References

Aalborg Kommune (2007) 'Planstrategi 2007: Planstrategi for Aalborg Kommune', Aalborg: Aalborg Kommune.

Aalborg Kommune (2009) 'Kommuneplan 2009: Hovedstrukturen kort', Aalborg: Aalborg Kommune.

Arnstein, S.R. (1969) 'A ladder of citizen participation', *Journal of the American Institute of Planners*, 35(4): 216–24.

Delman, T.F. (2011) 'Den igangværende by', unpublished PhD thesis, Aarhus School of Architecture, Aarhus.

Delman, T.F. and Nielsen, R. (2009) 'The AELIA-model: Involving users in urban development', in proceedings from U-Drive:IT, Conference for User-Driven Innovation from ICT to other Fields, Aalborg.

European Sustainable Cities and Towns Campaign (1994) 'Charter of European Cities and Towns Towards Sustainability', European Sustainable Cities and Towns Campaign. Online. Available at: www.sustainablecities.eu/fileadmin/content/JOIN/Aalborg_Charter_english_1_.pdf (accessed 28 October 2014).

European Sustainable Cities and Towns Campaign (2004) 'Aalborg+10 – Inspiring Futures, European Sustainable Cities and Towns Campaign'. Online. Available at: www.sustainablecities.eu/fileadmin/content/Aalborg_Test/finaldraftaalborgcommitments.pdf (accessed 28 October 2014).

Fisker, J.K. (2015) 'Municipalities as experiential stagers in the new economy: Emerging practices in Frederikshavn, North Denmark', in A. Lorentzen, K.T. Larsen and L. Schrøder (eds) *Spatial dynamics in the experience economy*, Abingdon: Routledge.

Gehl Architects (eds) (2012) *Den samarbejdende by*, Aalborg Kommune (Denmark) and Lillestroem Kommune (Norway). Online. Available at: www.e-pages.dk/aalborgkommune/564/ (accessed 28 October 2014).

Graham, B., Ashworth, G.J, Tunbridge, J.E. (2000) *The geography of heritage*, London: Hodder.

Guex, D. and Crevoisier, O. (2015) 'A comprehensive socio-economic model of the experience economy: The territorial stage', in A. Lorentzen, K.T. Larsen and L. Schrøder (eds) *Spatial dynamics in the experience economy*, Abingdon: Routledge.

Healey, P. (2007) *Urban complexity and spatial strategies: Towards a relational planning of our times*, The RTPI Library Series, Abingdon: Routledge.

Jeannerat, H. (2015) 'Towards a staging system approach to territorial innovation', in A. Lorentzen, K.T. Larsen and L. Schrøder (eds) *Spatial dynamics in the experience economy*, Abingdon: Routledge.

Jeannerat, H. and Crevoisier, O. (2010) 'Experiential turn and territorial staging system: What new research challenges?', paper presented at Regional Studies Association

Workshop on the experience turn in local development and planning, Aalborg University, Aalborg, September 2010.

Jensen, J.F. (2009) 'Communicating cultural heritage through games and experience-based products: A case of experience design', in proceedings 27th EuroCHRIE Annual Conference 2009, HAAGA-HELIA University of Applied Sciences, Helsinki, Finland.

Jensen, J.F., Bender, H., Birket-Smidt, T., Nielsen, J.P., Nørbach, L.C., Schrøder, L., Kjærgaard, K., Nielsen, H.G., Christiansen, E.S., Henningsen, B.V., Jensen, B., Nielsen, K.R. and Jakobsen, H. (2006) 'Industrikultur – kulturarv', Kulturarvskommuneprojektet i Aalborg, Aalborg: Aalborg Kommune and Aalborg historiske Museum.

Kerr, J. (2000) 'The uncompleted monument: London, war, and the architecture of remembrance', in I. Borden, J. Kerr, J. Rendell, with A. Pivaro (eds) *The Unknown City: Contesting Architecture and Social Space*, Cambridge, MA: MIT Press.

Kulturarvsstyrelsen and Realdania (2005) *Kulturarv – en værdifuld ressource for kommunernes udvikling: En analyse af danskernes holdninger til kulturarven*, Copenhagen: Kulturarvsstyrelsen.

Kulturarvsstyrelsen and Realdania (2007) *Kulturarv – en ressource: Anbefalinger fra fire kulturarvskommuner*, Copenhagen: Kulturarvsstyrelsen.

Kulturarvsstyrelsen and Realdania (2008) *Kulturarven et aktiv*, Copenhagen: Kulturarvsstyrelsen.

Landry, C. (2008) *The creative city: A Toolkit for urban innovators*, London: Earthscan.

Lefebvre, H. (1991) *The production of space*, Oxford: Blackwell.

Lefebvre, H. (2002) *Critique of everyday life: Foundations for a sociology of the everyday*, London: Verso.

Liggett, H. (1995) 'City sights/sites of memories and dreams', in H. Liggett and D. Perry (eds) *Spatial practices*, London: Sage.

Lorentzen, A. (2012) 'Cities in the experience economy', in A. Lorentzen and C.J. Hansen (eds) *The city in the experience economy: Role and transformation*, London: Routledge.

Lorentzen, A. (2013) 'Post-industrial growth: Experience, culture or creative economies?', in J. Sundbo and F. Sørensen *Handbook of the experience economy*, London: Edward Elgar.

Lorentzen, A. (2015) 'Pursuing happiness in planning? The experience economy as planning approach', in A. Lorentzen, K.T. Larsen and L. Schrøder (eds) *Spatial dynamics in the experience economy*, Abingdon: Routledge.

Metopos By- og Landskabsdesign and Aalborg Kommune (2009) *Mental byomdannelse: Midlertidig anvendelse som kick starter for en omdannelsesproces*, Copenhagen: Indenrigs- og Socialministeriet.

Norberg-Schulz, C. (1975) *Meaning in Western Architecture*, London: Studio Vista.

Pine, B.J. and Gilmore, J.H. (1998) 'Welcome to the experience economy', *Harvard Business Review*, 76(4): 97–105.

Pine, B.J. and Gilmore, J.H. (1999) *The experience economy: Work is theatre and every business a stage*, Boston: Harvard Business School Press.

Pine, B.J. and Gilmore, J.H. (2013) 'Experience economy: Past, present and future', in J. Sundbo, and F. Sørensen (eds) *Handbook of the Experience Economy*, Cheltenham: Edward Elgar.

Pluss (2011) *Kulturarvskommuneprojektet*, Copenhagen: Kulturarvsstyrelsen.

Therkildsen, H.P., Hansen, C.J. and Lorentzen, A. (2012) 'The experience economy and the transformation of urban government and planning', in A. Lorentzen and C.J. Hansen (eds) *The city in the experience economy: Role and transformation*, London: Routledge.

# Index

Page numbers in *italics* denote tables, those in **bold** denote figures.

For Product Safety Concerns and Information please contact our EU
representative GPSR@taylorandfrancis.com
Taylor & Francis Verlag GmbH, Kaufingerstraße 24, 80331 München, Germany